Amazingly Easy

Easy

Puppet

Plays

42 New Scripts
for One-Person
Puppetry

American Library Association

Chicago and London

1997

Dee Anderson

The paper used in this publication meets the minimum requirements of American National Standard for Information Sciences—Permanence of Paper for Printed Library Materials, ANSI Z39.48–1992. ⊗

Project editor: Joan A. Grygel

Cover designer: Evelyn Horovicz

Text designer: Dianne M. Rooney

Composed in Helvetica and Frutiger by Graphic Composition, Inc. using a Miles 33 system.

Printed on 50-pound Arbor, a pH-neutral stock, and bound in 10-point C1S cover stock by Edwards Brothers.

Anderson, Dee.
    Amazingly easy puppet plays : 42 new scripts for one-person puppetry / by Dee Anderson.
      p.   cm.
    Includes bibliographical references and index.
    ISBN 0-8389-0697-4
    1. Puppet plays, American. 2. Puppet theater. I. Title.
PN1980.A63   1996
812′.54—dc20   96-32752

Printed in the United States of America.

01   5 4 3 2

*To Mabe Wassell,
because I can never thank her
enough for her interest in this
book and her cheerful and
invaluable help with word
processing.*

*I don't know how I would have
managed without her!*

CONTENTS

▼▲▼▲▼▲▼▲▼

ACKNOWLEDGMENTS

▼▲▼▲▼▲▼▲▼▲▼▲▼▲▼▲▼▲▼

The ideas and scripts in *Amazingly Easy Puppet Plays* developed over a lifetime of playing with puppets, reading, and talking with others. Although it isn't possible to name everyone who has somehow enriched my work or this book, the following people deserve a special thank you: Joan Allee, Jewel Anderson, John Boone, Dee Boydstun, David Collins, Janet DeDecker, Susan Granet, Larry McLain, Kathy Manthey, Delores Neff, Kendra Hodgson Newton, and Mabe Wassell.

In addition, I'd like to thank the staff of the Moline (Illinois) Public Library, the English teachers who taught me how to write, the people who have watched my puppet skits (especially the ones who tell me afterward how much they like them), the teachers who allow me to share stories with their students, and everyone who has ever encouraged me to write a book.

Finally, I'd like to express appreciation to ALA Editions and the American Library Association.

INTRODUCTION

▼▲▼▲▼▲▼▲▼▲▼▲▼

Perhaps you've seen and enjoyed puppet shows in the past but never tried giving any yourself because you thought you lacked the necessary time, talent, knowledge, and equipment. Perhaps other books you've read on puppetry scared you off because they made the whole business sound terribly difficult, demanding, and time-consuming. Puppetry doesn't have to be hard.

I sincerely hope this book will give you confidence that you can successfully share puppet skits with children and the enthusiasm to try it. You'll learn a simple and accessible style of puppetry that has worked for me over the past sixteen years and might work for you as well. Simple and accessible, these scripts require no prior knowledge or experience with puppetry. They don't demand from you a great deal of preparation time or technical skill. You won't need a stage, curtain, lights, sound system, or even a large collection of puppets. You can perform one third of all the skits using any two puppets. (See figure 1.) Appendix A lists the puppets alphabetically as well as the skits featuring them. Suggestions for puppet substitutions are given following the list of characters for many skits. If you don't already own two puppets, you can easily make some out of old socks, gloves, or mittens by following the directions in appendix B. You won't need a lot of fancy props, either—many of the skits require no props at all. You can give the skits that call for props by using items you already have (I imagine you have a book or two lying around!) or

FIGURE 1.   Skits That Require Minimum Materials

Skits for Which You Can Use Any Puppets

Little Blue Riding Hood

Play It Safe, Jiggs!

A Christmas Story for Jiggs

Take Me Out to the Ball Game

The Valentine Party

Jiggs Plays a Trick

It Isn't Fair!

The Mysterious Visitors

The Amazing Jiggs

Only Two Hops

Something Good to Eat

Any Book in the World

Tell-ephone Me a Story

Look It Up

Don't Monkey Around with Library Books

Skits That Require No Props

Little Blue Riding Hood

Play It Safe, Jiggs!

A Monkey for Lunch

The Urge to Scratch

A Ghost in the House

by making them out of cardboard boxes and other cheap, readily accessible materials. Suggestions for making some of the props follow the list of props for many skits.

The table of contents lists skits within each section in order of their difficulty. The ones using only two puppets and no props appear at the beginning of each category. Those calling for the greatest number of characters or props come at the end of each section.

You may wonder how children can enjoy bare-bones puppetry after watching the slick technical wizardry of television programs. I've wondered myself, but they do. After sharing thousands of skits with thousands of children ages eighteen months to twelve years, I've heard many say, "I like your puppets!" Even fourth, fifth, and sixth graders enjoy them. When I was starting out, I walked into a fourth grade class I'd heard was really tough. One boy spotted the characters and said mockingly, "Oh, a puppet show!" I wanted to turn right around and leave the room, but I had to brazen it out. I performed "Detective Jiggs Takes the Case" and heard later that the teacher had told her colleague she'd never seen the class so attentive all year. (This happened in May!) After another class visit, a fifth grade teacher told me, "When I saw you bring out those puppets, I thought, 'Uh-oh.' But the kids really liked them."

Even adults have told me they like the skits. As I was leaving her room one day, a teacher told me how much she and her colleagues had enjoyed "How the Bear Lost Its Tail." "Here we are, these fifty-year-olds, laughing at the fox." A grandmother even told me she considered attending preschool storytimes by herself after her grandson started kindergarten.

People have enjoyed this simple method of puppetry, so I am now sharing some of my skits and ideas in this book. I offer these skits and ideas as suggestions to inspire your own creativity, not as dictates you must slavishly obey. Of course, you may want to act out the skits exactly as they're written, but I must confess that the next time I present one, I'll probably deviate from the script a bit. (I doubt if I've ever performed any skit exactly word-for-word and action-for-action the same way twice.)

I'll present a skit as many as eighty-four times in one month, and the scripts evolve through the many repetitions. During a performance, a good line of dialogue or idea for a bit of business might suddenly pop into my head and go on to become a permanent part of the skit. You might experience your own flashes of inspiration as you perform, or you might prefer revising the material before you start to suit your own taste, personality, or sense of what would work best for your audience. Feel free to record your alterations in the second column of each script. In fact, some suggestions for adaptations of dialogue or characters' actions already appear there.

Because many programs serving children operate with a small staff and budget, this book offers only simple ideas one person can carry out without spending much time or money. If you have the time, talent, personnel, inclination, and funds to be fancier, however, feel free to elaborate on these suggestions in any way you desire. If you prefer working with a partner, two people instead of just one could perform these skits.

To help you inspire children to read, a short bibliography of related titles follows most skits. You might want to read or recommend some of them before or after the skit or display them for checking out after the program. I have listed only titles in print at the time I prepared this manuscript. However, many other stories would work with these skits as well, so browse through your library's collection.

In fact, you can read any of your favorite stories with any of the skits. Programs planned around a single topic can be fun and serve a purpose, but storytimes do not need to follow a theme. Although I once based all my story programs on themes, I gave this up eleven years ago. I found I was reading some stories I didn't much like so I could keep with the themes, and I was skipping wonderful books that didn't tie in with the chosen topics. Besides, some of the themed storytimes lacked variety because the books I read were too similar to each other. If you share good stories with enthusiasm and expression, children will like them even if they're about totally different things. I've never heard a child complain, "You didn't have a theme!"

▼▲▼▲▼▲▼▲▼▲▼▲▼

PART ONE

For
the
New
Puppeteer

1 Getting Started in Puppetry

▼△▼△▼△▼△▼△▼△▼△▼△▼△▼

Even though the skits in this book are simple, presenting them will require more preparation time than reading a book aloud. If you have trouble accomplishing everything you need to do now, you may wonder if puppetry is worth squeezing the extra time and effort into your already overcrowded schedule. Before you decide one way or another, however, please read this chapter describing some of the benefits of puppetry and ways to get the puppets you need. (If you want to try puppetry but need permission from a supervisor or funding from a sponsor, this chapter may help you plead your case successfully.)

Good Reasons to Present Puppet Skits

The top ten reasons for using puppets with children are

1. Children like puppets!
2. Children like puppets!
3. Children like puppets!
4. Children like puppets!
5. Children like puppets!
6. Children like puppets!
7. Children like puppets!
8. Children like puppets!
9. Children like puppets!
10. Children like puppets!

Perhaps you think it's frivolous to use puppets just because children like them so much, but it's not. Because children like puppets, they will pay attention to your skits and enjoy them. Therefore, you can make good things happen when you act out stories with puppets.

With puppetry you can achieve the following outcomes:

You can nurture children's enthusiasm for reading.
As they enjoy your skits, they'll come to associate books and reading with fun and good times. Children need these pleasurable encounters

with literature if they're to develop positive attitudes about the world of print and grow up to be lifelong readers. Youngsters who never experience good feelings about books may learn to decode, but they'll probably never read unless they absolutely have to.

You can hold your audience's attention during storytimes. I've noticed children who looked disinterested when I read or told stories move in closer and pay more attention once puppets took over the program. (I've also noticed teachers put down their paperwork to watch puppets!)

You can teach more effectively with puppet skits than with regular lessons. Some of the skits in this book, e.g., "Do Not Disturb" and "Look It Up," came about because I had received requests to educate children on certain subjects. Although they are didactic, children will still find them more entertaining than straight lectures and will probably remember their messages longer.

You can inspire children to try producing their own shows. By doing so they will be exercising their imaginations and creativity as well as their language and problem-solving skills. Because many children today spend much of their time participating in structured activities, watching television, and engaging in video games, they often need some type of encouragement to play imaginatively. Your skits can provide that. One mother told me her son played with puppets more after seeing me perform at school.

You can relieve people's stress and brighten their days. Many comments I've heard testify to this, so I'd like to share two of my favorites with you. A fourth grader once visited me at the library several days after seeing me share a puppet version of Leo Lionni's *Alexander and the Wind-Up Mouse* at his school. He said, "That was so funny when the mouse stuck his head in the garbage can and called, 'Willy?' Sometimes you just need a break." A mother once told me she planned to attend storytime with her children that day and watch "The Wizard's Sneeze," because "I could use some cheering up."

You can help children develop positive attitudes about libraries and librarians. Many negative portrayals of librarians exist in the media. Take the classic movie *It's a Wonderful Life,* for example. Clarence acted as if Mary's choice of profession was far worse than Harry's drowning, Uncle Billy's insanity, and the deaths of hundreds of sailors! When children see your puppet skits, however, they'll realize libraries can be places to have fun, and librarians can be enjoyable people to know.

You can make your library and yourself special and offer people something enjoyable they won't experience at many other places. Although I could be wrong, I would guess the majority of libraries don't include a puppet skit in every weekly storytime. A colleague once told me, "Puppet shows are too much work. I don't have time for that." Although elaborate productions do demand extensive preparation, the skits in this book do not. Thus, you can delight your audiences with puppet skits every week—or at least once a month.

You can boost your self-esteem. The looks of enjoyment on young faces, the sound of childish laughter, and such enthusiastic comments as "I like your puppets!" will give you immense gratification.

You can have fun! Releasing your inner child by playing with soft, cuddly toys and making people laugh will put more joy in your life.

The First Steps

If you now want to give puppet skits but still worry about not having enough time, try listing all the duties you now perform and evaluating each one critically. Isn't there some task a coworker or volunteer could take over? Isn't there some job you could eliminate completely? For example, do you really need to make name tags for storytime? Children will benefit more from seeing a puppet skit than from wearing a name tag, no matter how cute and elaborate it is. Besides, you will use those tags you labored over only once, but after you've learned a puppet skit, you can perform it over and over again for the rest of your life.

If you're feeling self-conscious and uncertain about your ability to work with puppets, join the club! I felt that way for quite some time. Over the years, however, I've reached the point where I usually feel pretty comfortable presenting skits in front of most people. (I confess, however, I still feel self-conscious about using puppets to introduce books, recite poems, ask riddles, or converse directly with the audience.)

My work as a solo puppeteer began very modestly because I knew only two skits. One was "A Monkey for Lunch," and the other was based on a Little Golden Book called *Cookie Monster and the Cookie Tree* by David Korr. The preschoolers at the day-care center where I worked liked both stories and requested performances of them almost every day. When I became a children's librarian, I continued sharing "A Monkey for Lunch." (At one point, all the local schoolchildren had probably seen it at least twice!) Over time, however, I gradually added other skits to my repertoire.

You, too, can ease into puppetry with one or two skits. You might want to start simply with a skit featuring only two characters and no props. "Little Blue Riding Hood" works well for beginners because you can use any two puppets you already have. Besides, it's easy to learn; you could even improvise new dialogue as you go along. Other simple skits include "Only Two Hops," "A Monkey for Lunch," and "How the Bear Lost Its Tail." Since you'll probably repeat this maiden effort many times, choose a story that really appeals to you.

At first you might feel most comfortable performing only for preschoolers. Chances are, their laughter and delighted cries of "Do it again!" will give you the incentive and confidence to perform more puppet skits.

When you're just starting out, you may muff a few lines, knock over or drop a prop, face a restless audience, or feel your performance just isn't up to par. After a skit that didn't go off as well as you would have liked, you may feel discouraged and wonder whether you should be attempting puppetry. You might even consider quitting. Don't give up in despair, however! I've goofed in all these ways—and more. (I once knocked over a whole stage!) I still make little mistakes at times, but people enjoy my skits anyway. They'll like yours, too. Fortunately, the great appeal of puppets compensates for shortcomings in their operators. Besides, people might not notice what you consider to be mistakes. After all, they don't have a copy of the script in front of them they way you do!

So keep on sharing skits. When you perform regularly, you'll improve your puppetry skills, and everything will get easier for you. In addition, you'll develop more self-confidence and have more fun while you work.

Getting Puppets without Spending a Fortune

You won't need to amass a large and expensive assortment of puppets to perform the skits in this book. The scripts call for twenty-seven different puppets, but you could perform them with fewer by making substitutions.

If you already have puppets, look at the figure in the introduction to find skits that can star any two puppets. Then look in appendix A to see which skits feature each of your little actors. (Don't write a puppet off, however, just because the cast of characters doesn't list it. It can always play a role in the skits that use any puppets. It might also be able to fill in for some of the players in other stories.)

Key Features

Puppets suitable for one-person performances come in two varieties: those with movable mouths and those with movable arms. Although you can perform every skit in this book with either kind, the monkey, elephant, alien, and people puppets will best act out their roles if their arms move. On the other hand, the crocodile, Honey Bear, and the wolf in "The Three Little Pigs" will play their parts most effectively if their mouths move. You might want to keep this in mind when choosing puppets. For the most part, the roles in these skits call for standard characters (e.g., bears, rabbits, pigs, and people), so any puppets you acquire for these skits can also act out many other published scripts, picture books, and fairy tales.

If you don't currently have any puppets or want to expand your collection, try asking people to donate those with which their children no longer play. Advertise your request through posters, notes that go home, in-house newsletters, or the news media. If you receive duplicates, put extra ones out for children to play with on their own.

Homemade Puppets

If skits you want to perform call for puppets you don't have, you might be able to make the necessary characters quickly and inexpensively. You can create an instant puppet, for example, merely by splitting open the back seam of a stuffed animal and removing some of the filling from its head, arms, and back. You can also turn old socks, gloves, and mittens into stars for your stories or fashion a cast of characters out of felt. (See the directions in appendix B.)

If you like to sew, knit, or crochet, you can make fancy puppets. Look for patterns in craft magazines, fabric stores, and the books listed in appendix D. Perhaps you know of other sources or prefer to make your own. If necessary, you might want to adjust patterns to make the puppets slide on and off your hand easily.

Recruiting Volunteers

If you lack the time, inclination, or expertise to make puppets, you might try recruiting volunteers to create a repertory company. Advertise for people who enjoy crafts through the media as well as in the newsletters of the library, churches, needlework clubs, and senior citizen groups. Ask home economics teachers to announce your request to their students. Contact a clearinghouse that matches people wanting to help with organizations needing their services, if your area has one.

Supply your volunteers with patterns and all necessary materials. To avoid spending a fortune on supplies, ask people who sew or do crafts to give you their leftover material, yarn, buttons, and trim or scout for these items at thrift shops or yard sales. If you're buying new material, look for fabric that won't stretch or ravel. Durable, colorfast, washable materials will help your puppets look good and last longer.

Puppet Suppliers

If you prefer commercially manufactured puppets over handmade creations, you can purchase them locally or through catalogs. To save money, try visiting garage sales and your community's thrift shops first. You might be able to find puppets you can use in good condition. (I've run across two that still had the store tags attached!) You can look for new puppets in novelty, toy, school supply, and department stores (check the children's section) as well as in children's specialty shops and card and

gift shops (including those in hospitals and museums). You can also shop for puppets through mail-order catalogs. Appendix E lists a few such suppliers. Before you order, however, you might want to check on the company's return policy. Find out if you can send a puppet back if it doesn't fit your hand well or doesn't quite meet your expectations.

Puppets are expensive, but you can build a collection without breaking your organization's budget by using some of the following suggestions.

Library Donation Programs

At some libraries, families donate books on their children's birthdays. You could adapt this idea to suggest that people give you puppets.

First, decide how you will operate such a program. Will you order puppets in advance and keep each one in the back room or on display until someone chooses to buy it for the library? Will you ask patrons to select puppets circled in a catalog or pictured on a poster? (If so, tell the family how far in advance to order so the donation arrives before the birthday.) Will you post or distribute a notice listing the types of puppets you want (e.g., bear, monkey, dog) and let families shop on their own? Or will you accept any puppet a child brings in?

Once you've worked out details, publicize this idea through articles in your newsletter and the media. You could also make posters, flyers, or bookmarks decorated with party hats, wrapped packages, birthday cakes, streamers, or balloons.

To show appreciation for contributions, give each birthday child a thank-you note or certificate signed by the children's librarian. List donors' names in your library newsletter and on a poster displayed in the children's department. You might also take a picture of each child holding his or her puppet and posing with a staff member who isn't camera shy. Display this photo in the library or give a copy to the family. (Perhaps your local newspaper would photograph all contributors every month, three months, or six months, depending on how many people participate in this program.)

You could also try soliciting funds to purchase puppets. Appeal to the Friends (if your library has such a group), civic organizations such as the Lions and Junior Woman's Club, and businesses that cater to families such as banks and toy stores.

2 Bringing Puppets to Life

▼△▼△▼△▼△▼△▼△▼△▼△▼

To be at their best, puppets need to move. That doesn't mean you should just jiggle them aimlessly, however, or constantly wave their arms around. It means moving your fingers, wrists, and arms to make your characters perform actions appropriate to the situations. For example, you can make puppets laugh at something funny, nod their heads to agree with someone, and pant after exerting themselves. If you're just starting out and have no idea of what to do with a puppet, this chapter can give you some ideas for manipulating and talking for your characters effectively.

Trying on Your Cast

Obviously, you begin by putting the puppet on. If the puppet has a movable mouth, slide your fingers into the upper jaw and your thumb into the lower jaw. If it has movable arms, try inserting your index finger into the head and your thumb and middle finger into the arms while folding your remaining fingers into your palm. If this doesn't feel quite right, experiment with the other positions

shown in figure 2 until you find one that allows you to manipulate your puppet comfortably and easily.

Try every puppet on each hand to see if it fits one better than the other. Although the scripts suggest which hand to use for each character, feel free to use your opposite hand if that works better for you. The puppet I use to play Jiggs feels better on my right hand, but the opposite might be true for you. I perform "The Wizard's Sneeze" with the animals on my right hand because I can change puppets more easily that way. If you're left-handed, you might prefer the opposite arrangement. (If you switch a puppet to your other hand, however, remember to reverse the stage directions as well. You may want to note this in the right column of the script. That will allow you to operate right-hand puppets at the right side of the stage and vice versa.)

When putting your puppets on, insert your fingers all the way up into their heads to avoid the appearance of broken necks. Holding both your wrists and arms straight will give your puppets good posture. Bending your wrists will make them

FIGURE 2.   Finger Positions inside Hand Puppets

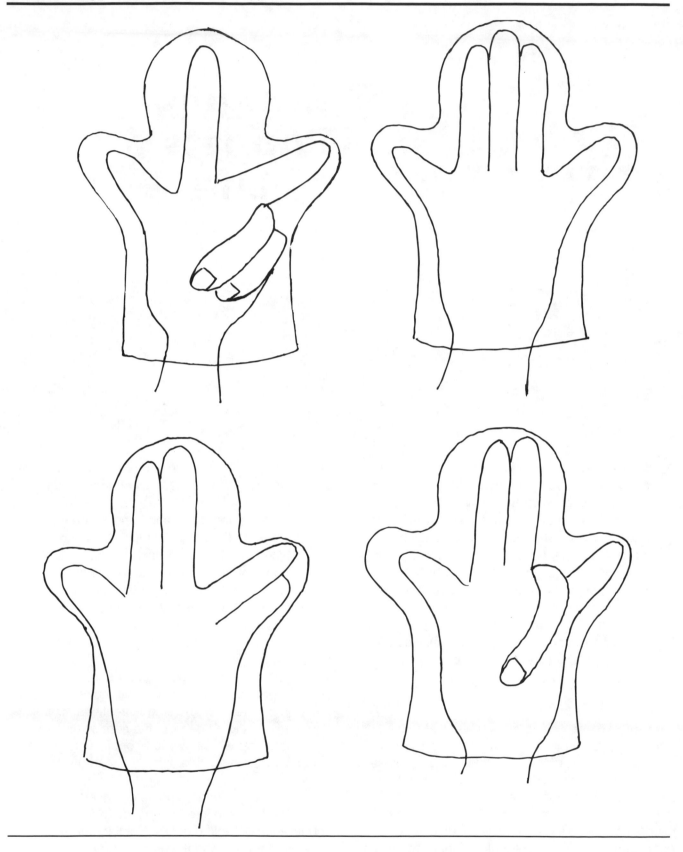

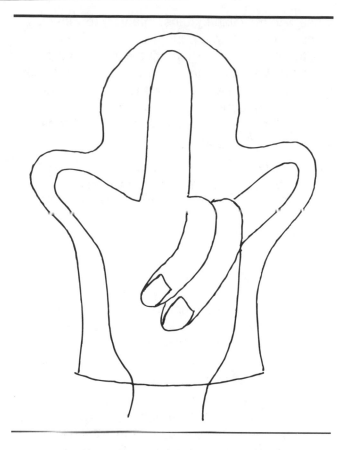

droop while tilting your arms will cause them to lean.

Put on the first two characters listed before beginning every story except "Something Good to Eat" and arrange the others in the order in which you'll need them. (Put right-hand puppets on your right side and vice versa.) Sometimes only one puppet appears on stage at the opening, but having its partner on your other hand will allow it to enter without delay at the appropriate time. Directions in bold-faced type will tell you when to take off and put on the other puppets. Usually, it's best to slide a new puppet on as soon as you take an old one off. That allows you to be ready to introduce the new character on time. You can keep the story moving along by having the puppet that is onstage talk while you're changing characters.

Body Language for Puppets

Once you're wearing the puppets, they're ready to make an entrance. When acting with a stage, puppets usually enter (and exit) from the sides. When performing in the open, they can come out from behind your back or at your side and leave the same way. In "Wanted: A Whiz of a Wiz" and "The Wizard's Sneeze," however, the animals just pop up and down from below to create the illusion of magic, as does the wizard in "The Golden Touch."

As characters enter, exit, and cross the stage, they show their profiles to the children. (If you must make one puppet cross in front of another, hold the stationary one back slightly to give its moving partner room to pass.) When characters address the audience, however, they face it directly. When talking together, puppets look toward each other with their bodies angled to give the audience a three-quarters view of them.

During the conversation, move only the puppet who is talking. Make the other stand at attention while looking toward the speaker. If the puppet's mouth moves, open it at the beginning of each speech and close it completely at the end. While it's talking, open and close your hand at a comfortable speed instead of just flapping the puppet's mouth. When the character isn't speaking, keep its mouth firmly closed. Bending your wrist down will allow your audience to see the puppet's eyes instead of the bottom of its lower jaw.

If the puppet's mouth doesn't open, it can gently nod its head or move its body back and forth slightly as it talks. It can also make appropriate gestures. It can shake its head during negative comments (e.g., "I'm not so sure about that") and nod while making affirmative statements (e.g., "I'll be there").

A puppet with movable arms can show expression in many ways. For example, it can clap its hands when expressing an affinity (e.g., "I'd love to"). It can pat its stomach to indicate hunger and rub it while murmuring "Mmmmm." (A puppet with a movable mouth can smack its lips when discussing something delicious.) To seem more lifelike, a puppet can jerk an arm downward before muttering "Rats!" but raise it when crying "I know." When a puppet says "I," it can point to itself; when it says "you," it can point to its partner. It can beckon when inviting someone to come closer and wave when bidding someone hello or good-bye. To congratulate, compliment, or comfort, a puppet can pat its partner on the back or put an arm around it. Puppets can shake hands to indicate "It's a deal!" and clap them to express happiness, excitement, or approval. When feeling sad, a puppet can hang its head or cry.

Gestures such as these help children understand the puppets' thoughts and feelings in the absence of changing facial expressions. They also enliven your skits by adding action and humor. Stage directions in the scripts suggest actions your puppets can perform, and the next section describes ways to carry them out. If you prefer conveying the stories' feelings, thoughts, and actions by other means, feel free to do so.

Regardless of the action, remember to exaggerate your movements. Because puppets are small, audiences can see broad gestures better. Exaggerated movements also add humor to your skits. Children laugh when characters throw props offstage in disgust, jump up and down with excitement, or scream and leap away from something scary.

At first, you may be concentrating so hard on the lines, you neglect to perform the actions. Gesturing will come more naturally to you, however, as you continue to give puppet skits. Even if you forget a few actions at times, don't worry about it. Children won't be checking your performance against a copy of the script and will never know you left out something you'd planned to do.

If you're using a stage (see chapter 3), manipulate the puppets in a way that keeps their hems (or feet, if they have them) at the same level as the shelf for props (unless, of course, they are flying, hopping, or jumping around). This allows the audience to see the entire puppet while giving the impression it is standing on solid ground. If your arms get tired, however, your puppets might gradually sink until only their heads show above this window. You're more likely to avoid this problem if you use a stage that allows you to work the puppets in front of your face instead of over your head. If you need to rest your arms, try performing skits in which only one character is on stage at times. "Detective Jiggs Takes the Case," "How the Bear Lost Its Tail," "The Golden Touch," "Peter Rabbit," "Help! Help! Help!" and "Something Good to Eat" all allow you to give one arm a rest while you present them.

Suggestions on Carrying Out Stage Directions

The following list of stage directions provides appropriate actions for movable arm puppets and for those with movable mouths. In a very few instances (e.g., when a puppet is to clasp hands to mouth), there are no alternative actions for a puppet without movable arms. However, such puppets can usually be made to show most actions. Note, however, that puppets with movable mouths carry props in their mouths but must put them down prior to delivering dialogue.

Address audience: Hold the puppet so it faces the audience directly. You might also want to extend your arm out toward the children. At appropriate times, you might make a puppet with movable arms place one hand confidingly next to its mouth.

Admonish: Turn the puppet so it faces its partner. If it has movable arms, have the puppet extend one arm toward its partner while you jerk your wrist forward and backward. If it has a movable mouth, bend your elbow and move your whole arm forward and backward to make the puppet bob its head toward its partner.

Argue: Arguing puppets (such as the monkey and the elephant in "Who's Really Better?" and Brer Rabbit and Little Cricket in "Only Two Hops") stand close to each other, with the speaker leaning forward and the listener leaning back. Increase the angles at which they tilt as the argument progresses until the listener is almost horizontal and the speaker is on top.

Beckon: Bring your thumb in toward your palm to make a puppet with movable arms invite someone to come over. A puppet with a movable mouth can beckon with a jerk of its head. (Jerk your wrist away from the puppet's partner.)

Bend: Bend your wrist forward. Make puppets bend over to pick up props or sometimes to pretend to smell something or eat.

Blow: To accomplish this with a puppet with a movable mouth, bend your elbow. Then open and close the puppet's mouth while you move your wrist and lower arm forward and backward, forward and backward. You might want to shake your wrist a little when you're holding the puppet's mouth open. For a puppet with movable arms, spread its arms out and bring them back together each time you move your wrist and arm forward and backward.

Bounce: Move your whole arm up and down as you also move it from side to side. Bounce puppets around to show they're excited or happy. You might also have puppets tilt their bodies from side to side or clap as they bounce.

Bow: Bend your wrist down. If your puppet has movable arms, bring one arm in toward your palm during the bow. If you like, make several bows, having the puppet face a different part of the audience each time.

Call: Have the puppet face the appropriate direction as you shout its lines. If the puppet's arms move, you might want to bring its hands up to either side of its mouth.

Clap: Move your finger and thumb in the puppet's arms together and then apart, together and then apart, together and then apart. Make a movable mouth puppet jump up and down. If appropriate, shout "Hooray" or "Bravo," depending on the situation. Clap to show approval, delight, or excitement.

Clear Throat: Bend your wrist up and down slightly while you make a loud noise as if you're clearing your own throat. If the puppet has a movable mouth, keep its jaws tightly shut. If the puppet has movable arms, make it put one hand in front of its mouth.

Climb: Turn the puppet sideways to the audience so it faces whatever it will climb. While holding the puppet right next to this object, raise your arm to push the puppet up. If the puppet has movable arms, move your thumb and finger toward each other and then away to create the illusion that the character is pulling itself up. For a puppet with a movable mouth, you might want to move the puppet up from behind the object and just poke its head over the top of it.

Collapse: Quickly lower your whole arm so the puppet flops onto the stage or into your lap. It can fall either forward or backward (depending on what seems appropriate to the situation) with its arms, if it has any, spread-eagled.

Comfort: Make one puppet comfort another by having it pat the other's arm, rub its back, or put an arm around its shoulders. Have a puppet with a movable mouth lean its head against its partner.

Congratulate: Show a puppet with movable arms congratulating another by having it pat or slap the other on the back. The puppet could also grasp one of its partner's hands in both of its

own while you move your wrist up and down vigorously to create a hearty handshake. Make a puppet without movable arms gently bump its body against its partner several times.

Cough: Bend your wrist up and down while you cough. As you do this, hold open the jaws of a puppet with a movable mouth. For a puppet with movable arms, put one arm up to its mouth while it coughs.

Cringe: To make a puppet cringe, lower its head and turn it away from the audience. A puppet with movable arms can hold its head in its hands. Shake your wrist a little.

Cry: With a puppet with movable arms, bend your fingers to make it lower its head and rub its eyes while you make a crying noise. If the puppet is supposed to be very sad, you might want to bend your wrist as well to make it hang its head even lower. For a puppet with a movable mouth, bend your wrist to make the puppet lower its head and turn away from the audience.

Cup hands to mouth: Bend the puppet's head forward a little as you put its hands on either side of its mouth. Ignore this direction for puppets without movable arms.

Dance: Move your whole arm to make the puppet bounce back and forth across the stage. You can also bend your wrist back and forth to tilt the puppet's body from side to side all the while.

Dust: A puppet with movable arms can be made to grasp the dust cloth (which can be just a handkerchief) between its hands. A puppet with a movable mouth can hold the cloth in its mouth. Both types should vigorously move the cloth around the sides of the stage. If you're performing in the open, dust nearby objects and even yourself. Start with your feet, and work up to your shoulders, face, and the top of your head. Hum or sing as the puppet dusts.

Eat: A puppet whose arms move can hold the food up to its mouth. Wiggle your finger(s) inside the head to make it bob up and down a little as you make loud munching noises. Inside the puppet with a movable mouth, open and close your hand over the food to create the illusion of chewing while you make appropriate eating sounds. With both types of puppets, drop the food down below the stage after eating. (If you're performing in the open, the puppet can drop the food into a box or tote bag next to your chair. Before you begin, ask the children, "Can a puppet really eat?" When they answer in the negative, say something like, "That's right, so it will really have to drop the food into the bag [or box] instead of swallowing it. Please do me a favor and forget about the food once it's in the bag [or box]. Don't try to peek in and see it, because we don't need it anymore.")

Enter: Have the puppets come in from either the left or the right side of the stage, depending on the direction called for in the script. Stage left refers to *your* left and vice versa. If you're performing in the open, bring the puppets out from behind your back or at your side. When entering, present puppets' profiles to the audience. They can appear to walk, hop, run, or skip, depending on what's appropriate to the situation.

Exit: Move puppets to leave the scene at either the left or right side of the stage, depending on the directions. Stage left refers to *your* left and vice versa. If you're performing in the open, you can move the puppets behind your back or off to your side. When leaving, present puppets' profiles to the audience. They can appear to walk, run, skip, hop, or stomp, depending on what's appropriate to the situation.

Faint: Move the puppet in small circles before having it collapse onto the stage or into your lap. If you're performing in the open, you could also drop your arm straight down by your side.

Fly: Spread the puppet's arms as far apart as you can. Raise your own arm high and swing it back and forth.

Gag: For a puppet with a movable mouth, bend your wrist down to lower the puppet's head and move your fingers away from your thumb to open its mouth. Bend your elbow and move your whole arm down and up and down and up while you make a gagging sound. For a puppet with movable arms, hold its hands up to its mouth while you bend your wrist down and up and make a gagging sound. Gag after exclamation of "Yuck!"

Groan: For a puppet with a movable mouth, bend your wrist to lower the puppet's head. Then shake its head back and forth while you groan loudly. For a puppet with movable arms, bend your finger(s) to lower its head. Have the puppet hold its head in its hands as you twist your wrist back and forth and groan loudly. (A puppet groans to show exasperation. For example, the waiter or waitress might groan in "Cow Eats Out." Miggs might groan often in the skits where Jiggs mixes everything up.)

Hit: Hold the striking puppet slightly behind its partner with one of its arms out. Quickly twist your wrist to bring the puppet's extended arm into contact with its partner's body. Make a movable mouth puppet butt its partner with its forehead.

Hoe: Have the puppet hold the handle of the hoe (which can be a cardboard cutout) in its mouth or in both hands so the blade touches the stage (or your lap). Move your whole arm backward, so the puppet drags the hoe across the stage for about three to four inches. Then lift your arm slightly, move it forward, and bring the hoe back down on the stage near where it was before. Repeat this action a number of times.

Hop: Turn the puppet sideways to the audience. While holding it upright, raise and lower your arm to make the puppet jump up and down. As you lift it up, move it forward as well.

Hug another puppet: Move the puppet close to its partner and have it wrap both arms around it. During a very hearty hug, twist both of your wrists back and forth. A puppet with a movable mouth could kiss its partner to show gratitude or affection (see description following).

Hug self: Quickly bring both the puppet's hands to its chest and twist your wrist from side to side. This action suits statements such as "I'd love it!" A puppet might also hug itself while shivering from the cold. Ignore this direction for puppets without movable arms.

Jump back: Lift the puppet up and then bring it down on either the left or right side of the stage, depending on which hand is wearing it. A left-hand puppet will come down on the left side and vice versa. Jumping back slightly can indicate surprise. Jumping back a long way shows fear.

Kiss: Move the puppet next to its partner and make its mouth touch the other character's cheek. If the puppet is supposed to be very grateful or affectionate, repeat the kiss several times all over its partner's face while you make loud kissing sounds. For example, the raccoon can be very demonstrative in "Do Not Disturb."

Laugh: For a puppet with a movable mouth, hold its mouth open as you bend your wrist up and down. For a puppet with movable arms, lower the puppet's head slightly and hold its hands up to its mouth as you bob your wrist up and down. You could also hold one of the character's hands to its mouth and the other on its stomach. If a puppet is supposed to be really amused, have it roll around on the stage or in your lap as it laughs.

Lean: Bending your wrist down slightly makes the puppet lean forward. Bending it slightly back makes the puppet lean backward. To show surprise, have a puppet lean backward with its arms spread out. Have it lean forward to confide (in its partner or the audience) or to shout angrily at other puppets. Have puppets lean back and forth when they are supposed to be arguing or engaging in a tug-of-war.

Lick: Bend your wrist down to put the puppet's mouth near the object it will lick. Push your hand forward several times to move the mouth of a puppet with movable arms across the object. Hold open the mouth of a puppet with a movable mouth and jerk your wrist forward several times to brush your thumb across the object.

Lie down: Bend your wrist to the side to gently lower the puppet to the stage floor or into your lap.

Listen: For a puppet with movable arms, wiggle your finger(s) to cock its head toward the sound. You might also want to hold one of the puppet's hands up to its ear that's next to the noise. For a puppet with a movable mouth, tilt your whole wrist to cock its head in the appropriate direction.

Look around: If the puppet is going to stay in place, twist your wrist from side to side. You might also want to bend your finger(s) to make the puppet look down as well. (A puppet whose arms move might hold a hand up next to its eye.) If the puppet is supposed to look all around the stage, move your whole arm around the opening in your theater as you twist your wrist from side to side. You can even have the puppet look under the shelf for props and off beyond the sides of the stage. If you're performing in the open, you can have it peek behind your back, under your chair, behind children in the audience, etc.

Look down: For a puppet with movable arms, bend your finger(s) inside the head. You might also want to make the puppet hold up one of its hands next to its eye. For a puppet with a movable mouth, bend your whole wrist to make the puppet look down. You might also want to twist your wrist to make the puppet appear to look around.

Nod: For a puppet with movable arms, wiggle your finger(s) to bob its head up and down. For a puppet with a movable mouth, bend your whole wrist up and down. In general, make a puppet nod when it is supposed to be agreeing with someone and making any affirmative statement (e.g., "I think I will, too"). The more heartily the puppet agrees or means the statement, the more vigorously you should make it nod.

Pant: Make the puppet collapse onto the stage or into your lap. For a puppet with movable arms, bend your finger(s) up and down to move its head toward its chest and then back to the floor or your lap. Repeat this action several times. For a puppet with a movable mouth, you will have to bend your whole wrist to move the puppet's head up and down. Huff and puff to make the appropriate sound effects.

Pat stomach: Make a puppet with movable arms pat its stomach with either arm when it talks about being hungry. For a puppet with a movable mouth, make it smack its lips in this situation.

Pick up: Bend your wrist forward to make a puppet lean over and grasp props between both of its hands or in its mouth. (You can make puppets pick up flat props, like cutouts, more easily if you arrange them ahead of time so that parts of them overlap the stage. Cutting your props out of thick cardboard will also make them easier to grasp.)

Point: For a puppet with a movable mouth, indicate objects or directions with a jerk of the puppet's head, a gesture accomplished by jerking your wrist toward the appropriate object or direction.

For a puppet with movable arms, make it hold one of its arms near its body and extend its other arm toward the character or object being talked about. Have a puppet point to its partner when saying "you," especially if it is talking emphatically. Make a puppet point offstage to indicate a general direction.

Point to self: Have a puppet with movable arms hold one arm away from its body while bringing the other one in toward its chest. Have a movable mouth puppet toss its head to one side. Make these gestures when saying "I," especially when the script calls for boasting or speaking emphatically.

Pounce: Hold the puppet sideways to the audience with its arms spread apart or its mouth held open. Make an arc with your arm as you push the puppet up in the air several inches, thrust it forward, and bring it down so it grabs its target with both hands or jaws.

Pretend to plant: Hold the puppet's hands together while you bend your wrist down to make the hands touch the stage or your lap. Repeat this action several times while moving your arm to the left or right, whichever direction seems appropriate. If the puppet doesn't have movable arms, make it perform these actions with its mouth.

Pretend to pull weeds: Hold the puppet's hands together and bend your wrist to make the hands touch the stage or your lap. Then jerk your wrist to one side so it looks as if the puppet is pulling up weeds and throwing them away. If the puppet lacks movable arms, make it perform these actions with its mouth.

Pretend to push: Hold the puppet sideways to the audience with either its hands or forehead touching the object it will push. Move your hand forward just a little to make the puppet seem to push against the object. Make huffing, puffing, and grunting noises to indicate how hard the puppet is straining.

Pretend to throw: While thrusting your arm out the way you would when throwing a small ball overhand, bring one of the puppet's arms in toward its chest or open its mouth.

Pretend to water: Move the puppet so it picks up a watering can (which can be a cardboard cutout) and tips it so the spout points to the floor of the

stage or your lap. Then move your whole arm back and forth to make the puppet seem to be watering the crops.

Pull up: Bend your wrist inside the pulling puppet to make it grasp its partner's hands. Then bend that wrist back while bending the other wrist forward. If the partner lacks movable arms, the pulling puppet can grab the other puppet's ear.

Push: Turn the pushing puppet sideways to the audience and extend both its hands until they touch its partner's body. If one puppet is supposed to be pushing its partner offstage, move both your arms either to the left or the right, depending on the stage directions. If the pushing puppet doesn't have movable arms, use its whole body to butt its partner (or an object) out of the way.

Put things down: Bend your wrist to make the puppet lay the object on the stage shelf (or whatever you're using) or in your lap.

Read: Bend your finger(s) inside the head of a puppet with movable arms to make it look down at a book in your lap or on the stage. Bend your wrist to accomplish this for a puppet with a movable mouth. Move the puppet's head from left to right across the page a few times to simulate reading. Move the head from the top to the bottom of the page as well. If the book is propped up, move the puppet so it seems to look intently into the open pages. Once again move its head from left to right and from top to bottom several times to simulate reading.

Roll onstage: Lay the puppet on its back on the shelf of the stage or in your lap and twist your wrist to make it roll from side to side. Make a puppet whose arms move hold its hands on its stomach or up to its mouth. This action suits hearty laughter.

Roll over: Lay the puppet on its back on the shelf of the stage or in your lap. Flip your hand over so the puppet lands on its face.

Rub chin: Move one of the puppet's arms against its chin. You might have to bend your finger(s) to lower its head a little. This indicates the puppet is pondering something. Cock the head of a movable mouth puppet.

Rub hands: Move your thumb and the tip(s) of your finger(s) inside the puppet's other arm against each other. Make a movable mouth puppet laugh nastily. This can indicate that a puppet is contemplating mischief.

Rub nose: Move one or both of the puppet's arms against its nose. (You might have to bend your fingers to lower its head a little.) If the puppet has a movable mouth, curl your fingers into your palm to wrinkle its nose. Make puppets carry out this action after they fall on their faces.

Rub stomach: Move your thumb against your palm to make a puppet with movable arms rub its stomach when talking about food and after eating. Make a puppet with a movable mouth smack its lips in these situations.

Run: Turn the puppet sideways to the audience. Tilt your arm and wrist forward a little. Then bounce your whole arm up and down very fast to make the puppet move forward quickly. Keeping the bounces small will distinguish running from hopping.

Scratch: Move one of the puppet's arms vigorously against the part of its body that itches. If the puppet is supposed to scratch its face or ears, you might have to lower its head a little by bending your finger(s). Make a movable mouth puppet rub against something.

Scream: For a puppet with movable arms, hold one or both of its hands up to its mouth or spread its arms as far apart as possible. For a puppet with a movable mouth, just hold its mouth open. Perform these actions while you scream. You might make a character also jump away from whatever is frightening it.

Shake: Twist your wrist back and forth very fast to make the puppet tremble with fear. You might also stammer or talk with a quaver in your voice to express a puppet's fear.

Shake hands: Bend your wrist up and down while you make a puppet grasp one of its partner's hands in both of its own. The faster you bob your wrist, the heartier the handshake. Shake hands to seal a bargain ("It's a deal") or congratulate ("That was sensational, Happy"). A movable mouth puppet might just nod emphatically in these situations.

Shake head: Both types of puppets can shake their heads when you twist your wrist back and forth. In general, make a puppet shake its head when disagreeing with something and while making negative statements (e.g., "No, you can't"). If the puppet is supposed to feel strongly about something, twist your wrist vigorously.

Shiver: Twist your wrist while saying "Brrrrr!" Make a puppet with movable hands hug itself while it shivers.

Show anger: You could make a puppet with movable arms admonish its partner. A puppet with a movable mouth can express rage when you curl its mouth up by making a fist inside it. Turn away both types of puppets from their partners or make them stomp as they enter and exit.

Show disgust: Twist your wrist for both types of puppets. For puppet with movable arms, jerk an arm toward the puppet's stomach as you twist your wrist. This gesture can accompany all exclamations of "Rats!"

Show dismay: The gesture that conveys disgust can also express dismay.

Show excitement: Move your whole arm to make the puppet bounce about. You might want to twist your wrist to tilt its body first to one side and then to the other as it bounces. During these actions, make a puppet with movable arms clap its hands.

Show fear: Make a fearful character jump back while you scream. For a puppet whose arms move, either spread them out or hold one or both hands up to its mouth while jumping. If you want a frightened character to shake, twist your wrist.

Show happiness: The action that conveys excitement also expresses happiness.

Show horror: For a puppet whose arms move, quickly bring its hands up to its face. For a puppet with a movable mouth, simply open its mouth. These actions precede exclamations of "Uh-oh!"

Show sadness: Bend your finger(s) forward to lower the puppet's head. Slowly twist your wrist to make the character's body sway back and forth gently. Speak the line(s) in a sad tone of voice. You might also sniff loudly as you have the puppet pretend to wipe a tear from its eye. If it's supposed to be very unhappy, move the puppet as if it were crying.

Show surprise: Bend your arm back from the elbow to make the puppet lean back. If it's supposed to be very surprised, make the puppet jump back. For a puppet with movable arms, spread its arms as far apart as possible while making it lean or jump.

Sigh: Slowly raise and then lower both types of puppets while you sigh. During this action, open wide the mouth of a movable mouth puppet and then close it. Have a puppet with movable arms gradually spread them wide and then bring them together.

Skip: Turn the puppet sideways to the audience and hold it upright. Swing your arm toward the audience and then away from it as you move the puppet forward. You might also hum a little.

Sleep: Bend your wrist to lay the puppet onstage or in your lap. Make the puppet lie on its side so the audience can't see its open eyes. If you like, you can snore or say "Zzzzz."

Smack lips: When a puppet with a movable mouth is supposed to be thinking about food or to have just eaten, bend your fingers a little as you move your thumb up to your fingertips. Then straighten your fingers out as you move your thumb back as far as you can. Repeat this action several times. For a puppet with movable arms, substitute rubbing its stomach for smacking its lips.

Snap: For a puppet with a movable mouth, open the jaws very wide. Then thrust the puppet out toward the audience as you quickly snap its jaws shut. For a puppet with movable arms, spread the arms as far apart as you can. As you thrust it out toward the audience, quickly bring its arms together as if it's grabbing something.

Sneeze: Bob your wrist up and down on each syllable of "Ah, ah, ah, ah-choo!" For a puppet with movable arms, hold one or both of its hands up to its mouth as well.

Sniff: Bend your wrist until the puppet's nose is close to what it pretends to be smelling. Inhale loudly as you raise the puppet's head away from the sniffed object.

Stagger: Turn the puppet sideways to the audience. Use your whole arm to jerk the puppet toward the audience and then away from it with large movements.

Stand up: When a puppet is lying down, your elbow will be bent (if you're working the characters in front of your face). Raise your arm to make the puppet stand straight. If you're working with your arms above your head, you need only bend your wrist to hold the puppet erect.

Stomp: Hold the puppet upright with its profile to the audience. Jerk your whole arm up and down as you make the puppet enter or exit in a huff.

Stretch: For a puppet with movable arms, spread its arms as far apart as possible. You might also want to extend your arm out toward the audience while twisting your wrist slightly. For a puppet with a movable mouth, simulate yawning by holding its mouth open wide as you extend your arm and twist your wrist.

Swim: Hold the puppet so it lies sideways to the audience with its face down. Undulate your whole arm forward as you bend your wrist gently up and down. For a puppet with movable arms, try approximating a breaststroke by spreading its arms apart and then bringing them together out in front of the puppet. Hold its head up slightly.

Tackle: Using your whole arm, move the tackling puppet up and over. As soon as it grabs its opponent with both hands, bend your other arm back to make the opponent lie flat on its back on the stage or in your lap with the tackler on top of it.

Think: Twist your wrist slightly to make a puppet with a movable mouth cock its head from side to side as you murmur, "Hmmmmm. Hmmmmm. Hmmmmm." You might also try moving your thumb forward and backward against your fingers. For a puppet with movable arms, cock its head to one side while making it rub its chin, cheek, or ear. You might also want to twist your wrist from side to side as you murmur, "Hmmmmm. Hmmmmm. Hmmmmm." When the puppet is supposed to have reached a conclusion, straighten it up, raise one of its arms, and exclaim, "I know."

Tickle: Have the tickler rub one or both of its hands against its partner's body. You could also move your whole wrist to run the tickler's hands back and forth across the other puppet's body. You might giggle for the one being tickled and roll that puppet around on the stage or in your lap.

Tilt head: Tilt your wrist first to one side and then to the other. For a puppet with movable arms, you might also hold one hand up against the side of its head. This action is appropriate for giving a puppet a thoughtful look or for studying something carefully.

Tiptoe: Hold the puppet sideways to the audience and tilt your arm forward. As you move the character toward its destination, slowly lean your hand first toward the audience and then away from it. This action is appropriate when a character is supposed to be quiet or sneaky.

Turn: Twist your wrist to make the puppet turn.

Wake up: Make your puppet stand up, yawn, and stretch.

Walk: Hold the puppet erect with its profile to the audience. Use your whole arm to move it up and down slightly as you also move it forward.

Wave hands: Wiggle either of a puppet's arms several times. Use this action whenever puppets are bidding each other hello or goodbye. Make the puppet wave both of its arms wildly if it is supposed to be excited or agitated. Just make puppets with movable mouths nod at each other.

Wave object: Have the puppet hold the object in its mouth or both hands while you twist your wrist back and forth. In addition, you might want to move your whole arm back and forth.

Wipe brow: Lower the head of a puppet with movable arms and move one of its hands across its forehead. This action follows hard work or a close call and accompanies exclamations of "Whew!" Jerk the head of a movable mouth puppet to one side in these situations.

Wipe eye: Lower the puppet's head. You might want to sniff loudly while doing so. Make a puppet with movable arms rub one of its hands under its eye. This action can accompany expressions of sorrow. In "Brer Fox's (Not So) Great Idea," Brer Rabbit dabs at Brer Wolf's eyes with a handkerchief.

Wrinkle nose: For movable mouth puppets, curl your fingers into your palm. Substitute a rubbing-nose action for movable arm puppets.

Write: Using its mouth or hands, have the puppet hold a pencil (or crayon) with the point touching a sheet of paper. Move your wrist to scribble a little.

Yawn: For a puppet with a movable mouth, open its mouth as wide as you can. For a puppet with movable arms, bend your finger(s) to lower its head slightly and pat its mouth several times with your thumb. In both cases, yawn loudly. You might also want to extend your arm out toward the audience and twist your wrist back and forth a little. Use this action whenever puppets are supposed to wake up or be bored.

How to Talk for Your Puppets

The basic principles for reading aloud also apply to speaking lines of dialogue. Because you probably already read and tell stories to children, you are ready to talk for puppets as well.

During your skits, speak loudly and clearly enough to allow everyone in the audience to hear and understand you. If you're working behind a stage, you might need to speak up more than usual because that barrier can muffle your voice. Don't talk too fast or let your voice drop at the end of sentences.

Speak with expression. Put the same type of feeling into each line that the character would. For example, make Monkey's lines in "Who's Really Better?" sound appropriately mocking by imitating the way children tease each other on the playground. Depending on the situation, your tone of voice can convey happiness, triumph, excitement, gratefulness, anger, indignation, sadness, or remorse. It can also indicate a puppet is up to something. Speak very slyly when the fox says "trust me" in "How the Bear Lost Its Tail" and when the crocodile invites the monkey to "climb on my back" in "A Monkey for Lunch." Words that receive special stress are written in all capital letters and boldfaced type. For example, "I do **NOT** want to leave."

If you like, you can talk the way you normally do. Creating a different voice for every character isn't necessary because the audience will know who's speaking by the way you operate the puppets. Only the character who is talking moves. The other stands still and looks toward its partner as if listening attentively.

However, because different voices enhance the skits, you might want to attempt a few changes of voice unless you feel terribly self-conscious. You can start out very simply by talking the way you normally do for one character and pitching that everyday voice a little higher or lower for another. You can also try speaking through your nose or imitating someone else. (My sister used to talk like W. C. Fields for some characters.)

Fool around with different voices, but don't use ones that make you cough or feel a strain. When experimenting, consider the type of character who's speaking. For example, you might want to give a deep, growly voice to a bear or monster and a robotlike monotone to the aliens. You might want to sound rather goofy when you speak for Jiggs.

During your skits, you might sometimes lapse into your regular voice or speak one puppet's lines in another character's voice. If this happens to you (as it does to me), quickly switch to the appropriate voice and continue as if nothing were amiss. The children may not notice the mistake. Even if they do, they'll still enjoy the skit. Besides, seeing you correct your error without losing your cool can show children how to handle their own mistakes when they make them.

If you want distinct voices for each character but don't feel comfortable or competent enough to create them yourself, ask colleagues, family members, or relatives to help you record the dialogue on a tape to play during performances. Assign parts on the basis of who can best portray each character. (For more information on taping, see the next chapter.)

3 Staging the Skits

▼▲▼▲▼▲▼▲▼▲▼▲▼▲▼▲▼▲▼

You've assembled your cast of puppets. They all fit, and you can make them move and talk. Now it's showtime. What do you need? In keeping with the spirit of this book, not much. The scripts include notes on the props you'll need. Whether or not to use a stage is your choice because children will enjoy the skits either way. The most important thing to do is to organize your materials in advance. This chapter will give you the basics on preparing for showtime.

Creating Props with Household Items

Some of the skits in this book do not require any props at all. (See figure 1.) Others use a few. Chances are, you already have many of the items called for; others will be easy to get.

If you like, you can buy props. Try looking for them in toy stores, craft shops, and thrift stores. To save money, however, you may prefer making your own. Notes following the list of props will give you ideas for doing so. Because many people who work with children have limited budgets but unlimited demands on their time, this book offers only simple, inexpensive suggestions. If you (or another staff member or volunteer) have the time, talent, or funds to be fancier, however, feel free to go all out.

When making props, try looking at familiar objects with new eyes. You can convert boxes of various sizes into stoves, tables, and containers for laundry detergent. Pill bottles can turn into vases and jugs of honey and milk. A handkerchief can serve as a tablecloth, sheet, or dust cloth. A Popsicle stick can be the handle for a broom or a magic wand. A small pillow can be a bed, as can a baby blanket folded into a small rectangle.

You can also draw items on cardboard, color them with crayons or markers, and cut them out. (Avoid using paint, because it might flake or bend the prop.) Pictures cut out of colored paper, magazines, catalogs, newspapers, etc. will also work. Glue them to thick cardboard (like the kind used in boxes for shipping books) for sturdiness and ease in handling. You might even want to cut two identical shapes out of cardboard and glue them together to make your props easier for the puppets to pick up.

It's all right if your props look homemade because that will encourage children to make their own creations out of household objects. When I told a friend I sometimes thought I should be fancier, she urged me to continue with simple methods. She remembers feeling bad as a child when her projects did not look at all like the elaborate samples adults had created.

If a cardboard cutout, like a tree, needs to stand on its own, tape it to something like a metal bookend, wooden block, or small box. (The size of the box will depend on the size of your prop.)

Props that stand their own need something on which to rest. If you're using a regular puppet theater, you can use the shelf in front. If you're performing in the open, you can either sit behind a table or desk or pull over anything with a flat, level surface. (I've used toy ironing boards, piano benches, record stands, metal carts, the seats of chairs, student desks, and anything else that was available.) If a prop doesn't need to stand up, you might be able to just lay it in your lap. (The book the personnel director reads in "Storybook Characters Look for Work" and the bed in "Brer Fox's [Not So] Great Idea" fall into this category.)

Props do not need to be in proportion to the puppet's size. Oversize props actually work better because they're easier for the audience to see and the puppets to handle.

For skits requiring the use of books, you can always use the real things, of course. If you want to ensure that particular titles will always be available for performing certain skits, however, you might want to make your own replicas. To make a simple book, fold a sheet of construction paper or posterboard in half and write a title and author's name on it. If you want to get fancier, photocopy the jacket of an actual book and glue it on the cover of your prop. You could also make new jackets to cover books you are discarding from your collection. As with the paper books, you can merely print a title and author's name on the new jacket or attach a photocopy of an actual book cover to it. You can store these fake books with your other props and have them available whenever you want them.

Ready for Wear and Tear

Choose unbreakable items because puppets have butterfingers and might drop them or knock them over. When these accidents happen, don't panic. If you're performing in the open, just bend over, pick up whatever you dropped, and carry on. If you're working behind a stage, have the puppet exclaim, "Whoops! Will somebody please get that for me?" Several children will probably happily retrieve your prop for you, and the show can go on. You are less likely to drop props or knock them over if you're performing in front of your audience or sitting behind a stage that allows you to work the puppets in front of your face. Holding the characters over your head makes handling objects more awkward because you can't see what you're doing.

Unbreakable props are a must in skits calling for characters to throw them offstage. When performing from behind a stage, you can make the puppet toss the object behind the stage. When you're sharing them directly in front of your audience, make the puppet throw the prop off to one side. Before beginning the skit, ask children to please do you a favor and leave things where they land until after the story because the puppets won't need them anymore. Unless you make this request, children will interrupt your skit by trying to return the props to you.

Pack Your Bags

Before performing a skit, check the list of required props and puppets at the beginning of the script to make sure you have everything you need. (I have neglected to do this at times and have had to do some fast thinking to work around the absence of an actor or prop.) To minimize the likelihood of this ever happening again, I now store puppets and props that appear in the same skit with each other whenever possible.

You may prefer to set up a different method for storing your materials, but I encourage you to organize your collection in a way that allows you to retrieve your characters and props easily and quickly whenever you want them. You'll be more likely to present skits if gathering the necessary materials isn't a big chore. One way to do this is to store everything you need for each skit in a plastic grocery bag with the handles tied loosely together.

Label the bags and keep them inside a large storage container or cupboard with those you use most often on the top or in the front. If you use a certain prop only with a particular puppet, store those two things together.

Consider keeping a separate box for items you don't know what to do with now but think might come in handy later. Things like artificial fruit, miniature flags, and toy cameras might be just what you need someday, and you'll be glad you have them right at your fingertips.

You can make props easier to handle if you arrange them carefully before beginning the skit. Set them on the stage (table, or whatever you're using) so that the parts the puppets will grab overlap the edge. It also helps to put all props within easy reach. This means laying them out on the appropriate side in the order in which you'll need them. Props for your right hand puppets go on your right side (and vice versa) with those you'll need first closest to you.

If possible, arrange the props before your audience arrives. Directions for necessary preparations precede the dialogue for skits. If you must get ready in front of children (which will happen if you visit schools and move from classroom to classroom), you can introduce the skit while getting settled. If you are about to perform "Brer Fox's (Not So) Great Idea," for example, you might say something like "Brer Fox and Brer Wolf are going to try catching Brer Rabbit again. Do you think they can? If you like this skit, you might want to borrow a book about Brer Rabbit next time you visit the library." (Mentioning a skit's connection to books helps children associate reading with fun and might motivate them to read.)

All the World's a Stage . . . Do You Need One?

Because you've probably watched professional puppet productions involving stages, you may think you need to use a theater, too. You can present the skits in this book with a stage if you like, but you don't have to; you could perform them directly in front of your audience. Children enjoy both styles of puppetry, although each presents certain advantages and disadvantages for the puppeteer, as described in the following sections. Before deciding how you'll present skits, consider your feelings, preferences, and circumstances and try both ways to see which suits you better.

Advantages of Using a Stage

It's traditional.

It provides a shelf where puppets can rest props during the skit.

It allows you to tape your script in front of you, so you can read your lines instead of learning them all.

It might help you feel less self-conscious because it hides you from the audience.

It might help you concentrate on your puppetry because it cuts you off from distractions.

It keeps the audience from seeing you change puppets.

Disadvantages of Using a Stage

It restricts your freedom of movement because you must work within the confines of the theater's opening.

It might muffle your voice, so you'll have to speak up more loudly and enunciate more clearly.

If it requires you to hold your hands above your head, your arms can get tired and your puppets may sink below the level of the stage until only their heads show. You will probably also find handling props more awkward with this type of stage.

It may block the view of some members of the audience, depending on where they are sitting. (Try to avoid seating people in those blind spots.)

It prevents you from supervising children's behavior. (Perhaps a responsible adult could take charge while you're working behind the stage. Before starting the skit, ask the children to stay seated and not come up to try and touch the puppets.)

It doesn't allow you to see the expressions of interest and enjoyment on the children's faces, so you might feel as if you're just talking to yourself.

It takes time and effort to set up and dismantle if you are performing in different locations. (If you want to take a theater on outreach programs, keep that in mind when considering stages. Some theaters are more portable than others. A good traveling stage is easy to carry and assemble but sturdy enough not to collapse during your performance.)

Advantages of Performing without a Stage

You have more freedom of movement. If you like, you can even walk around the room.

Your arms won't get as tired as they would if you used a stage because you won't have to hold them up as high.

You can handle props more easily because you can see what you're doing.

The children may be able to hear you better because nothing stands between you and them.

The audience can see the puppets from everywhere in the room because no stage blocks their view.

You can perform anywhere at any time because you don't have to carry around a stage and spend time setting it up and dismantling it.

If you like, you can sneak peeks at the children from time to time and enjoy their expressions of pleasure and interest.

Disadvantages of Performing without a Stage

You don't have a shelf on which to set your props. (You can, however, sit behind a desk or table or set any available object with a flat surface—piano bench, chair, or stool—next to you. Some props can just lie in your lap.)

It's better to know your lines than have the audience see you reading them. (If you must perform a skit without much preparation time, however, you can sit behind a table or desk and refer to the script spread out in front of you from time to time. Besides, you never have to memorize any script word for word; you can always paraphrase the dialogue in your own words.)

Sometimes children close to you reach out to touch the puppets, making it hard for you to maneuver. (Before you begin, ask the children to

please do you a favor and stay right where they are. Explain that if they come too close or try to touch the puppets, you can't do the story.)

You might feel self-conscious. (Keep in mind that people will look at the puppets, not you. If you like, you can hold the characters up in front of your face and focus all your attention on them. Ignore the audience completely.)

The audience can see you changing puppets. (This doesn't seem to bother them. If it bothers you, try keeping the characters in a box or tote bag until you need them. Reach your hand down inside it to switch puppets.)

Try Both Presentations!

You don't have to choose either method exclusively. You might like to perform some of the simpler skits, e.g., "A Monkey for Lunch," "How the Bear Lost Its Tail," and those featuring Miggs and Jiggs, in the open. On the other hand, you might prefer using a theater for stories involving quick changes of puppets, such as "The Wizard's Sneeze" and "Wanted: A Whiz of a Wiz." Perhaps you'll work behind a stage when one is available but out in the open when one is not. For example, your library may have a stage that you will use for presenting skits during in-house programs. For storytimes at other places, however, you might prefer performing directly in front of your audience. (This is the way I've always operated.)

If you decide to perform directly in front of your audience, don't worry that your obvious presence and lack of ventriloquy skills will make the puppets seem less real. People watch the characters and ignore the puppeteer. I concluded one storytime by manipulating a cat puppet while saying, "Please stay where you are until I give you a letter. Then you can go." As the puppet and I distributed papers in the back, a girl up front told her friend, "Let's go. The cat said we could."

You also don't need to worry that the lack of a stage will diminish the dramatic impact of your skit. Children can get caught up in a story even when the puppeteer sits directly in front of them. One day I performed "Brer Fox's (Not So) Great Idea" in front of a class of primary students. When Brer Rabbit mentioned going to his enemy's house, a boy cried out, "No! Don't do it! You'll get killed!"

Building Your Theater

If you want a theater, you can either buy one or build your own. Commercial stages are very expensive, so you might prefer constructing one. If you lack the necessary expertise, you can either recruit a volunteer or ask the high school shop teacher to allow woodworking students to build a theater for you.

There are many different kinds of stages. You can find designs for various types in puppetry books or request plans from Puppeteers of America. You might want to look at the theaters of other libraries and puppeteers. Go behind each one to see what it would feel like to work with it.

While considering plans, keep in mind your needs. Do you require something you can travel

FIGURE 3. Simple Stage: Back View

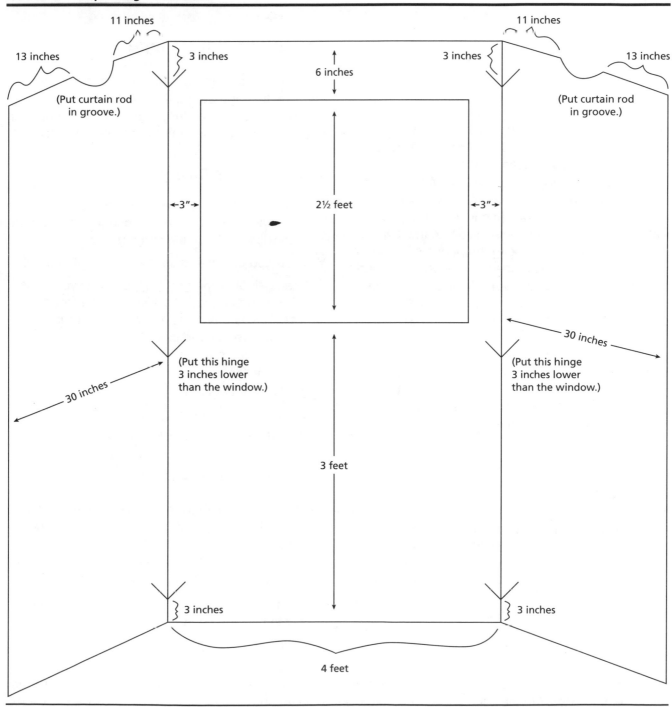

FIGURE 3. (*continued*)   **Shelf for Stage**

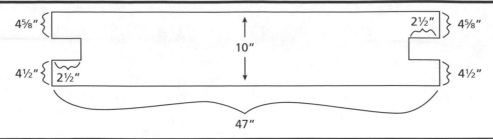

Measurements based on Silvis, Illinois, Public Library puppet stage.

with conveniently? Do you want something big enough to allow a number of children to perform behind it during puppet workshops? What will allow you to work comfortably and easily?

(By the way, a stage can also serve as a fish pond, fortune-telling booth, or information kiosk at a carnival, mall, or community fair. Your imagination might dream up other uses for it as well.)

Figure 3 shows the dimensions for the type of stage that has allowed me to work most comfortably and easily. You might find it will suit you as well. When performing behind it, you can sit on a bench or chair while working the puppets in front of your face. A backdrop made out of a semitransparent material (such as burlap) will allow you to see what you're doing. (Suspend this curtain about eleven inches behind the stage opening, so you won't tangle puppets in it as you have them enter and exit.) A shelf provides a place for your props during the skit. The sturdiness of the plywood ensures you won't knock it over if you lean your wrists against it. It will fold up flat, so you can store it if necessary or transport it during outreach programs.

Placing the Stage

Once you have a theater, you will need to choose a location for it. Look around the space where you hold storytimes. Where can you put the stage to provide maximum visibility and avoid traffic areas? (You don't want the distraction of people walking in and out right next to your theater.) When you have your stage in place, go behind it and hold up some puppets. Ask someone else to move around the room and check for visibility. If the person can't see the puppets from some places, move the theater or avoid seating people in the blind spots.

To Tape or Not to Tape

Many puppeteers record their shows in advance and play the tape during their performances. Others speak the lines as they manipulate the puppets. Each method has advantages and disadvantages.

Advantages of Taping

You can record over and over again until you are satisfied with your performance. Each presentation will then have the same quality.

You can add music and special effects, if desired.

You can ask other people to record with you, thus giving each puppet a distinctly different voice. (Ask family members, colleagues, or friends who can read expressively and well. Assign parts on the basis of whose voice best fits each character.)

You won't need to learn all the lines.

You won't have to talk when a cold makes your throat sore and your voice croaky.

Disadvantages of Taping

You can't be flexible. You must perform at the pace of the tape, which does not allow extra time for laughs or the retrieval of fallen props.

You cannot shorten the skit if your audience is restless or you're running out of time.

You can't draw out sequences that provoke laughter to milk their humor.

You can't ad lib or allow audience participation.

You are not as mobile because you have to carry around more equipment and take more time setting up.

If your recorder plugs in, you'll need to set up near an electrical outlet.

You may fall prey to technical malfunctions. Tape players sometimes jam. Batteries run down. Tapes may break or wear out.

You may weary of hearing the same tape over and over again. (Your mind might even start wandering during the show.)

Advantages of Performing Live

You give children the immediacy and intimacy of live theater, an experience they may not often get otherwise.

You can respond to the reactions of your audience. If the children are laughing, you can milk the humor by repeating those actions that have elicited the giggles. If the children are fidgety or time is running out, you can shorten the skit. If necessary, you can have a puppet ask the audience to settle down. If you like, you can even allow audience participation.

You can ad lib. Changing the lines can keep them fresher and more natural, enable you to respond to the audience, improve the skit, and make performing more fun for you.

You won't have to worry about technical difficulties.

You can perform anywhere at any time because you don't have to carry around lots of equipment or search for an electrical outlet.

If a prop falls off the stage, you can stop talking and retrieve it or somehow work this glitch into the show.

Some Disadvantages of Performing Live

You need to work more at learning the lines, especially if you're performing in the open. (If you're using a stage, you can tape a copy of the script inside it.) You never need to memorize any script word for word, however. You can always paraphrase the dialogue in your own words.

You must speak for all the characters yourself.

You can't have special music and sound effects.

You might muff a few lines or be a little "off" sometimes, so each performance will not have the same quality.

If you have a cold or sore throat, your voice may sound croaky.

Try Both

If you don't already have a preference, you might want to try both taping and performing live before deciding which way you want to present puppet skits. Perhaps you'd like to use different methods at different times, depending on the circumstances. You might, for example, tape some skits for elaborate presentations during special events at the library but perform live for regular weekly storytimes or outreach programs.

Working with Recorded Scripts

If you record your skit, leave time for changing puppets and handling props, if necessary. You might want to manipulate the puppets while you make the tape, so you'll know how much time these things will take. (If you like, you could even record a little music to play during scene changes.)

After making the tape, play it back right away to make sure you can hear and understand all of it. Better yet, let someone who hasn't read the script listen to it and judge its clarity. If necessary, redo parts that aren't clearly audible and intelligible.

Before your audience arrives, play the tape while you move around the space where you'll be performing. If necessary, adjust the volume until you can hear it wherever you sit.

You can minimize the possibility of mechanical failures if you buy high-quality cassettes and equipment. It also helps to keep a second tape and backup recorder handy when you're going to present skits. You might even consider making a work tape to practice with and reserving your good copy for performances only. If all else fails, keep a copy of your script nearby or know your lines. Then you can perform live if necessary.

If you're using a cassette player outside the library, think about bringing along your own extension cord and adapter in case you need them. If this isn't possible, however, request that they be available for the performance. Battery-operated equipment will eliminate this problem as well as the need to set up in a less-than-ideal location, simply because it's near an electrical outlet. Batteries run down, however, so bring along spares or be prepared to perform live, if necessary.

Have Puppets, Will Travel: Storytimes in Schools and Day-Care Centers

For the past ten and a half years, I've been performing these skits in schools and day-care centers. If you don't already "take your show on the road," I strongly encourage you to do so because outreach programs provide many benefits.

Many children will benefit from your outreach program. You will share the delights of literature with those children whose parents never read to them or bring them to the library. Because these youngsters may never have had positive experiences with the world of print at home, they need to encounter the joys of books elsewhere if they're to become lifelong readers. Teachers have told me that my programs provide many students with their only exposure to storytelling and puppetry.

Through your outreach program you help promote your library because you can conclude each storytime with an invitation to visit. You can briefly describe some books related to the stories you just shared (perhaps some of the titles listed after each skit), mention some exciting new books the library just received, or talk about upcoming programs at your building. If you see that the class is reading a certain book together, you can recommend other books your library has by that author or titles that are related to it. (For example, students who are reading *Charlotte's Web* might enjoy E. B. White's other novels as well as *Babe: The Gallant Pig* by Dick King-Smith.) If you notice from room displays that the class is learning about a certain subject, you can talk about some books your library has on that topic.

Children are more interested in going to the library after seeing a program at school. One day, for example, a boy came in right after school to borrow the new Goosebumps books I'd told his class about. His mother said that when she'd picked him up at school, he jumped into the car, crying, "Quick! Take me to the library, so I can check out the new Goosebumps books!" His excitement about going to the library pleased her. At a day-care center one day, I ran into a mother who told me, "We made sure we got a card at your library, because my daughter likes it so much when you read here."

Outreach programs make your library more visible in the community and create great goodwill. The visits I made to schools resulted in several newspaper photos, mention in school newsletters, and the greatest advertising of all: word of mouth. Judging by the number of positive comments I've heard, many people highly regard these outreach programs. One mother said she voted for the library's referendum because she didn't want budget cuts to stop the service.

Such programs make you more approachable. When children and teachers visit your library and see a familiar face, they'll probably feel more comfortable about asking for help. One teacher said she asked me for book recommendations instead of visiting the library close to her house because "I kind of know you."

Outreach programs acquaint you with new books and ideas. Browsing through the classroom collections of teachers has introduced me to a number of books I really like and would not have known about otherwise. Seeing students' artwork on display has given me ideas for crafts children can make at library programs.

These storytimes are a very cost-effective form of programming. Once you've learned your stories, you can present the same ones over and over again to a large number of children with no extra preparation time.

If you'd like to start visiting schools, decide on the times when the library could spare your presence. If necessary, ask your director for permission to leave the building. Next, contact the schools. An informal but effective way to do this is to talk with teachers who come to your library. If they take you up on you offer to read to their students, ask them to see if any of their colleagues would also like a storytime. One teacher in each building can set up a schedule for you to follow when you visit there.

If your library serves many schools, you may have to limit your storytimes by reading only to children in one or two grades. If your community is small, however, you could read to children of all ages. Teachers will often agree to combine their classes with those of colleagues, so you can share stories with many students at one time.

PART TWO

Skits Featuring Miggs and Jiggs

A Note about the Miggs and Jiggs Skits

▼▲▼▲▼▲▼▲▼▲▼▲▼▲▼▲▼

Any two puppets, animal or human, can play Miggs and Jiggs. Simple puppets made out of socks or mittens would work for these characters. Either character can have movable arms or a movable mouth because stage directions include both types. These puppets can play other roles in other skits as well. For example, a bear could portray Miggs in addition to the many other parts that call for bears. If you already do puppet skits with a comedy team of your own, you could perform these stories with the characters your audience already knows and likes.

I chose the names Miggs and Jiggs because they rhyme, lack gender association, and probably won't match up with the name of anyone in the audience. If you don't like these names, however, feel free to change them.

I realize these skits violate a fundamental principle of puppetry: Most of them have no plot and feature more talk than action. You can make the skits livelier if you speak the lines with plenty of expression. You might want to make Miggs sound exasperated and groan frequently. Giving Jiggs a goofy voice will add to the fun as well. When talking for this puppet, I sound as if I had a cold.

For some reason, however, Miggs and Jiggs have been very popular with children and teachers—so popular that I've had to keep finding new material for them.

Jiggs is always listed as a right-hand puppet because my character for this part fits better on my right hand. If the opposite arrangement works better for you, work Jiggs on your left hand and Miggs on your right. In that case, however, be sure to reverse all stage directions.

Books with Wordplays

Gwynne, Fred. *A Chocolate Moose for Dinner.* Simon & Schuster, 1988.

———. *The King Who Rained.* Simon & Schuster, 1988.

———. *A Little Pigeon-Toad.* Simon & Schuster, 1988.

———. *The Sixteen-Hand Horse.* Simon & Schuster, 1987.

Parish, Peggy. Amelia Bedelia series.

Wiseman, Bernard. Morris and Boris series.

Books about Silly Characters

Allard, Harry. The Stupids series. Houghton.

Cole, Joanna. *Big Goof & Little Goof.* Scholastic, 1989.

———. The Clown-Arounds series. Parents.

Denim, Sue. The Dumb Bunnies series. Scholastic.

Schwartz, Alvin, retel. *There Is a Carrot in My Ear and Other Noodle Tales.* HarperCollins, 1982.

Spirn, Michele Sobol. *The Know-Nothings.* Harper-Collins, 1995.

Little Blue Riding Hood
A Fractured Fairy Tale

Characters: Jiggs (right hand)
Miggs (left hand)

Jiggs: *(looks down and to the right)* Once upon a time . . .

Miggs: *(enters stage left, crosses stage as Jiggs talks, and taps Jiggs on shoulder)* Are you talking to yourself?

Jiggs: *(turns to face Miggs)* Oh no. I'm telling the ants a story.

Miggs: May I listen, too?

Jiggs: Sure. I hope you like "Little Blue Riding Hood."

Miggs: Don't you mean "Little Red Riding Hood"?

Jiggs: I suppose so. Once upon a time there was a girl named Little Green Riding Hood.

Miggs: Red.

Jiggs: Yes, I've read the story. Now don't interrupt.

Miggs: That's not what I meant. You called her Little Green Riding Hood, but her name is really Little Red Riding Hood.

Jiggs: Picky, picky, picky. What's the difference? I like green better than red anyway.

Miggs: So do I. But you should tell the story the way it really is.

Jiggs: Oh, all right. Have it your way. One day Little *(shouts in Miggs's face)* **RED** Riding Hood went to school with a bushel of apples for her teacher.

Miggs: No! No! No!

Jiggs: What's the problem? I called her Little Red Riding Hood.

Miggs: But you got everything else wrong. She was supposed to go to her grandmother's house with a basket of cakes.

Jiggs: Oh, all right. Little *(shouts in Miggs's face)* **RED** Riding Hood went to her *(shouts in Miggs's face)* **GRANDMOTHER'S** house. *(skips to stage right and back to Miggs while singing)* "A tisket, a tasket, a green and yellow basket. La la la la la la la la la la la la la." And she met a giraffe.

Miggs: She met a what?

Jiggs: A giraffe. You know. One of those funny-looking animals with the looooong necks.

Note: Raise your arm to lift Jiggs up.

Miggs: I know what a giraffe is, all right. But that's not what Little Red Riding Hood met.

Jiggs: Of course, it wasn't. I remember now. It was a rhinoceros.

Miggs: No.

Jiggs: That's right. It was really a hippopotamus. *(laughs)* Silly me. I get rhinos and hippos mixed up, because I keep forgetting that hippos are the ones with the horns on their noses.

Miggs: You **ARE** mixed up. Little Red Riding Hood didn't meet a rhino or a hippo.

Jiggs: Then it must have been a porcupine.

Miggs: No.

Jiggs: Good. Because she might have hurt herself on the quills. *(bends over, stretches arm out as if touching porcupine, and then jumps back, waving arm as if in pain)* Ouch! I bet she met a skunk.

Alternative Action: If using a movable mouth puppet, have Jiggs just jump around.

Miggs: No.

Jiggs: Good. Because skunks stink. P.U.! *(holds nose with one hand and waves the other one)*

Alternative Action: If Jiggs is a mouth puppet, curl your fingers into your palm to wrinkle its nose.

Miggs: Jiggs, Little Red Riding Hood met a wolf.

Jiggs: Oh yeah. And the wolf said to Little Purple Riding Hood,

Miggs: Little **RED** Riding Hood.

Jiggs: Yeah, yeah, yeah. The wolf said, "How now, brown cow?"

Miggs: No, he didn't.

Jiggs: That **IS** kind of a silly thing to say, isn't it? I'll bet he said, "How much wood could a woodchuck chuck if a woodchuck could chuck wood?"

Miggs: No.

Jiggs: Then he probably said, "Peter Piper picked a peck of pickled peppers. If Peter Piper picked a peck of pickled peppers, how many pickled peppers did Peter Piper pick?"

Note: Say this very fast, so you stumble over the words.

Miggs: He didn't say that either.

Jiggs: Good. Because that twists your tongue all up.

Miggs: The wolf said, "What do you have in your basket, little girl?"

Note: If Jiggs is a movable mouth puppet, curl your fingers into your palm and rub them against your thumb.

Jiggs: So he did. And after the wolf said whatever you said the wolf said, Little Orange Riding Hood . . .

Miggs: Little **RED** Riding Hood.

Jiggs: Yeah, yeah, yeah. Little *(shouts in Miggs's face)* **RED** Riding Hood said, "I have skunk cabbage in my basket."

Miggs: She did not! She said, "I have cakes in my basket."

Jiggs: Yeah, that is what she had, isn't it? So then the dragon . . .

Miggs: What dragon? It was a wolf.

Jiggs: Right. And the wolf burst into song. "Happy birthday . . ."

Miggs: The wolf didn't sing "Happy Birthday."

Jiggs: But you said Little Rainbow Riding Hood . . .

Miggs: Little **RED** Riding Hood.

Jiggs: Yeah. You said Little What's-Her-Color had all those birthday cakes in her basket.

Miggs: They weren't birthday cakes. They were plain, ordinary, everyday cakes.

Jiggs: Then what did the dinosaur sing?

Miggs: It wasn't a dinosaur. It was a wolf, and it didn't sing anything. You're so mixed up, you'd better let me tell a story.

Jiggs: O.K. What story are you going to tell?

Miggs: The one about the brother and sister who got lost in the woods. You know, Hansel and Gretchen. . . . No, I'll tell the story about the beautiful girl who lived in the forest with a bunch of little men. You know, Snow White and the Seventeen Elves. . . . No, I'll tell my favorite story of all, the one where the boy trades his cow for some magic beans. You know, Jack and the Beanpole.

Jiggs: *(addresses audience)* I don't think I'm the only one who's mixed up, do you? *(turns to Miggs)* Let's borrow a book of fairy tales from the library. We can read it and get our stories straight.

Miggs: That's a good idea.

Jiggs: *(addresses audience)* Maybe you'd like to get a fairy tale at the library, too. If you're lucky, you can find the story about the clever cat named "Puss in Slippers."

Miggs: You mean, "Puss in Sneakers."

Jiggs: Oh, that's right. *(addresses audience)* Look for "Puss in Sneakers" on your next visit to the library. Good-bye. *(Miggs and Jiggs exit stage right.)*

Note: Bend your elbow and move your whole arm to swing Jiggs back and forth while singing.

Versions of "Little Red Riding Hood"

Araujo, Frank P. *Nekane, the Lamina & the Bear: A Tale of the Basque Pyrenees.* Rayve Prod., 1993.

Bornstein, Harry, and Karen L. Saulnier. *Little Red Riding Hood: Told in Signed English.* Gallaudet Univ. Pr., 1990.

Emberley, Michael. *Ruby.* Little, Brown, 1990.

Ernst, Lisa Campbell. *Little Red Riding Hood.* Simon & Schuster, 1995.

Harper, Wilhelmina. *The Gunniwolf.* Dutton, 1970.

Rowland, Della. *Little Red Riding Hood & The Wolf's Tale.* Carol Publ. Group, 1991.

Vozar, David. *Yo, Hungry Wolf! A Nursery Rap.* Doubleday, 1993.

Young, Ed. *Lon Po Po.* Putnam, 1989.

Twists on Familiar Stories

Briggs, Raymond. *Jim and the Beanstalk.* Putnam, 1989.

Granowsky, Alvin. *Bears Should Share!* Raintree Steck-Vaughn, 1996. ("The Three Bears" from Goldilocks's point of view)

———. *Brainy Bird Saves the Day!* Raintree Steck-Vaughn, 1996. ("Henny Penny" with a happy ending)

———. *Friends at the End.* Raintree Steck-Vaughn, 1996. ("The Tortoise and the Hare" from the hare's point of view)

———. *Giants Have Feelings, Too.* Raintree Steck-Vaughn, 1996. ("Jack and the Beanstalk" from the giant's point of view)

———. *Help Yourself, Little Red Hen.* Raintree Steck-Vaughn, 1996. ("The Little Red Hen" from her friend's point of view)

———. *Just a Friendly Old Troll.* Raintree Steck-Vaughn, 1996. ("The Three Billy Goats Gruff" from the troll's point of view)

Jackson, Ellen. *Cinder Edna.* Lothrop, 1994.

Little, Jean, and Maggie De Vries. *Once Upon a Golden Apple.* Puffin, 1994.

Mann, Pamela. *The Frog Princess?* Gareth Stevens, 1995.

Minters, Frances. *Cinder-Elly.* Viking, 1994.

Myers, Bernice. *Sidney Rella and the Glass Sneaker.* Simon & Schuster, 1985.

Petach, Heidi. *Goldilocks and the Three Hares.* Putnam, 1995.

Scieszka, Jon. *The Stinky Cheese Man and Other Fairly Stupid Tales.* Viking, 1992.

———. *The Frog Prince Continued.* Viking, 1991.

Tolhurst, Marilyn. *Somebody and the Three Blairs.* Orchard, 1991.

See also books listed for the skit "The Three Little Pigs."

Play It Safe, Jiggs!

Characters: Jiggs (right hand)
Miggs (left hand)

(Jiggs stands center stage, shaking.)

Miggs: *(enters stage left)* What's the matter, Jiggs?

Jiggs: A big car almost ran me down!

Miggs: No wonder you're shaking. That's scary.

Jiggs: I'll say. I was crossing the street when I heard, "EEEEEEEE!" I whirled around, and there was a big car right on top of me!

Miggs: Didn't you notice the car before you crossed the street?

Jiggs: How could I? I was looking straight ahead *(looks straight out at the audience)*, and the car was off to the side. *(jerks head toward one side)*

Miggs: Jiggs, you're supposed to look both ways *(looks around)* before crossing the street. If there's a traffic signal, wait for the light to turn green.

Jiggs: That reminds me of a riddle. Why did the traffic light turn red?

Miggs: To let people know when to stop.

Jiggs: Well, yeah, but this is a riddle, so it has a silly answer.

Miggs: What's the silly answer?

Jiggs: You'd blush, too, if you had to change in the middle of the street.

Miggs: That's a pretty funny riddle, Jiggs, but safety is a serious subject. I think we'd better discuss all kinds of safety to make sure you don't get hurt. Do you know what to do in case of a fire?

Jiggs: Yes. You stop, drop, and roll around in it. *(rolls around)*

Miggs: No, Jiggs. You don't roll around in a fire!

Jiggs: Yes, you do. A firefighter came to our school and told us, "Stop, drop, and roll." I remember distinctly.

Miggs: The firefighter probably **DID** tell you to stop, drop, and roll, but that's only in case your clothes catch on fire. If that ever happens, you stop, drop to the ground *(drops)*, and roll back and forth *(rolls)* to smother the flames. But if you see a fire anywhere else, get away from it. *(Move Miggs away from Jiggs.)* Don't wallow around in it.

Jiggs: I don't have to worry about my clothes catching on fire, because I don't wear any clothes.

Miggs: You may not have to worry about your clothes catching on fire, but your house could catch on fire. if that ever happens, get out right away. *(Move Miggs away from Jiggs.)*

Jiggs: I will. As soon as I save my gum wrapper collection.

Miggs: No, Jiggs, don't stop for your gum wrapper collection.

Jiggs: I have to! Because I've saved wrappers all my life, I have the world's greatest collection.

Miggs: That may be, Jiggs, but you shouldn't stop to save your gum wrapper collection or anything else.

Jiggs: You're saying that because you're jealous. You don't have a good gum wrapper collection, so you don't want me to have one either.

Miggs: I'm saying that because your life and safety are more important than anything else.

Jiggs: Oh, all right. I **WILL** leave right away. But I sure hope a fire never breaks out at my house, because I'd hate for anything to happen to my gum wrapper collection.

Miggs: There **ARE** some things you can do to prevent fires from starting.

Jiggs: Like what?

Miggs: Don't plug too many appliances into one electrical outlet. If you see a frayed electrical cord, ask your parents to replace it. Don't put things that burn easily—like paper and rags—next to hot places such as stoves and furnaces. And never, ever play with matches.

Jiggs: Rats! Playing with matches is my favorite game.

Miggs: *(shows horror)* **YOU** play with matches?

Jiggs: Sure, all the time. So do you when you visit me.

Miggs: I've never played with matches in my life!

Jiggs: Sure you have. Don't you remember all the times we put the cards facedown on the table and then turned them up two at a time, trying to find the pairs that match?

Note: I use an animal to play Jiggs. If you use a human puppet, delete the lines about not wearing any clothes.
Alternative Dialogue: If there's ever a fire in your house, don't wallow around in it. Get out right away.

Note: When presenting to preschoolers, delete all but last sentence about matches in this piece of dialogue.

Miggs: Oh, Jiggs, it's all right to match up pairs of cards that look alike. Just don't play with the kind of matches people use to start fires.

Jiggs: *(scornfully)* I wouldn't play the match game with **THOSE.**

Miggs: Good!

Jiggs: Yeah, that would be really boring. All those matches look alike, so it wouldn't be any challenge at all to pair them up.

Miggs: Well, now that you know about fire safety, let's discuss stranger danger. Would you speak to a stranger, Jiggs?

Jiggs: No way! If I ever see a mean, scary, strange-looking person, I'll zip my lip. *(closes mouth tightly or puts hand to mouth)*

Miggs: Good, but strangers aren't always mean and scary-looking. Sometimes they look very nice, wear nice clothes, and act really friendly. But even if people act nice and friendly, it's better not to talk to them if you don't know them.

Jiggs: Well, shut my mouth. *(closes mouth tightly or puts hand to mouth)*

Miggs: Would you take candy from a stranger, Jiggs?

Jiggs: That depends. Are we talking about candy bars or salt-water taffy?

Miggs: It doesn't matter what kind of candy we're talking about.

Jiggs: It most certainly does! Candy bars are yummy, so I'd take those. Mmmmm. But saltwater taffy is yucky *(gags)*, so I wouldn't take that.

Miggs: It doesn't matter whether you like the candy or not. Never take food or any other present from a stranger.

Jiggs: Well, shut my mouth again. *(closes mouth tightly or puts hand to mouth)*

Miggs: Don't take rides from strangers either, Jiggs. Never get in a car with someone you don't know.

Jiggs: Not even if I'm so tired, I'm about to drop? *(collapses)*

Miggs: Not even then. *(pulls Jiggs up)* But if you're getting into a car with your family or friends, what's the first thing you should do?

Jiggs: Sit down.

Miggs: Of course. After that, though, you need to fasten your seat belt.

Jiggs: Remember? I don't wear any clothes, so I don't need a belt.

Miggs: I'm not talking about the kind of belt that keeps your pants up. I'm talking about the belts in the car.

Jiggs: Do cars wear pants?

Alternative Dialogue: I don't need a belt. My pants stay up all by themselves. (or) I always wear dresses, so I don't need a belt.

Miggs: No!

Jiggs: Then why do they need belts?

Miggs: Seat belts in cars are not to keep the car's pants from falling down. They're to keep passengers safe while they're riding in the car.

Jiggs: That reminds me of another riddle. What did one ghost say to the other ghost when they got in the car?

Miggs: I don't know.

Jiggs: "Fasten your sheet belt." Get it? Sheet belt, seat belt?

Miggs: Yes, Jiggs, I get it. Now make sure **YOU** get it. Whenever you're riding in a car, wear your sheet *(claps hand to mouth)*—I mean, seat belt.

Jiggs: I will.

Miggs: Good! Now let's pretend that you're home alone. What would you say if someone called and asked to speak to your parents?

Jiggs: I'd say, "I'm sorry, but Mom and Dad aren't here right now. May I please take a message?"

Miggs: No, don't say that.

Jiggs: Why not? I was very polite. Mom and Dad always tell me to be polite on the phone.

Miggs: Yes, you were polite, and that's good. But you let the caller know you were home alone, and you don't want to do that.

Jiggs: Well, I can't say my parents are home, because that would be a lie. Mom and Dad have told me never to lie.

Miggs: You don't have to lie. Just say, "My parents can't come to the phone right now. May I please take a message?"

Jiggs: Oh, that's what I say when Mom's in the bathroom! I used to say, "Mom's in the bathroom." But she got really embarrassed, so she asked me to tell people she couldn't come to the phone.

Miggs: Now you can say it if she's not home, too.

Jiggs: O.K.

Miggs: If you were home alone and someone tried to break in, what would you do?

Jiggs: I'd be so scared, I'd cry. *(cries)*

Miggs: It **WOULD** be scary, but you'd need to get help. You'd have to call 911.

Jiggs: Like this? *(jumps around, shouting)* "911, 911, 911." *(looks at Miggs)* I think it would be easier to just yell, *(yells)* "Help! Help! Help!"

Note: When presenting this to preschoolers, shorten the skit by omitting the dialogue about being home alone and bicycle safety. Pick up again at asterisk.

Miggs: You don't shout out the numbers, Jiggs. You dial them on the phone. When somebody answers, you tell them your name, your address, and what your problem is. They'll send someone to help you.

Jiggs: That's good to know.

Miggs: It's always good to know how to be safe, so let's talk a little bit about bike safety.

Jiggs: I don't need to know about bike safety.

Miggs: Sure you do! Everybody needs to know how to be safe on a bike, so listen to these tips. Wear a helmet. Ride along the curb in the same direction as traffic. If you're riding with another person, ride single file. Obey all traffic laws.

Jiggs: I don't need to know that, because I don't have a bike.

Miggs: Well, remember the rules anyway, in case you ever do get one.

Jiggs: O.K. Say, do you know why elephants don't have bicycles?

Miggs: Why?

Jiggs: They don't have a thumb to ring the bell!

Miggs: Please don't get started on elephant jokes. We're trying to talk about safety.

Jiggs: I'm tired of talking about safety. I want to go to the library and get some good books.

Miggs: All right. Go ahead. Reading is good for you and lots of fun, too. Maybe you could look for a book about safety while you're there.

Jiggs: I'd rather look for a riddle book.

Miggs: You could get a riddle book **AND** a safety book.

Jiggs: O.K. I'll see you later. *(turns to leave)*

Miggs: Wait, Jiggs.

Jiggs: *(turns back to Miggs)* Yes?

Miggs: Be sure to look both ways *(looks around)* before you cross the street in front of the library.

Jiggs: I will. *(addresses audience)* I hope **YOU'LL** look both ways before you cross the street, too. Good-bye. *(exits stage left)*

*

Books about Safety

Brown, Marc T., and Stephen Krensky. *Dinosaurs, Beware! A Safety Guide.* Little, Brown, 1982.

Rathman, Peggy. *Officer Buckle and Gloria.* Putnam, 1995.

A Christmas Story for Jiggs
Clement Moore's Classic Poem

Characters: Miggs (left hand)
Jiggs (right hand)

Prop: copy of *The Night Before Christmas*

Note: Because it's hard for puppets to turn pages, you might want to photocopy a version of the poem that is contained on one or two pages. If you are performing behind a stage, tape this copy to the wall in front of you. If you are working directly in front of your audience, insert the photocopy inside an actual copy of the book or a dummy book made by folding over a sheet of posterboard. You might want to cross out those lines Miggs doesn't read and put asterisks after the words that serve as cues for Jiggs's speeches. For your convenience, the script includes the beginnings and ends of the passages Miggs pretends to read.

Preparation: Open book flat on stage or in your lap and have Miggs read it.

Jiggs: *(enters stage right, singing raucously)* "Santa Claus is coming to town."

Miggs: Please be quieter, Jiggs. I'm trying to read.

Jiggs: How can you be so calm? *(shows excitement)* It's only _____ more days until Christmas!

Note: Fill in appropriate number.

Miggs: If you could settle down a little, I think you'd like this story, too. It's all about Santa Claus.

Jiggs: *(shows excitement)* Oh, boy! Santa Claus! Would you read it to me, please?

Miggs: Yes, if you'll stop jumping around. *(reads)* "'Twas the . . . a mouse."

Jiggs: Why weren't they stirring their hot chocolate? If you don't keep mixing your cocoa, you get yucky sludge at the bottom of your mug. *(gags)*

Miggs: They weren't drinking hot chocolate. They were sleeping.

Jiggs: I'd rather drink hot chocolate than sleep.

Miggs: But if you don't go to sleep, Santa can't come.

Jiggs: Oh, that's right.

Miggs: *(reads)* "The stockings . . . through their heads."

Jiggs: Let's boogie! *(dances)*

Miggs: *(pulls him back by book)* Stop, Jiggs. I can't read when you're hopping around.

Jiggs: Oh, sorry. Guess I got a little carried away.

Miggs: *(reads)* "And mamma . . . the matter."

Jiggs: I bet I know what happened. I bet raccoons knocked over their garbage cans.

Miggs: No, Jiggs. Raccoons did **NOT** knock over the garbage cans.

Jiggs: Then it must have been some dogs. **P.U.!** *(holds nose with one hand and waves other one around)* What a mess!

Miggs: Jiggs, nobody knocked over any garbage cans.

Jiggs: Then what made all the noise?

Miggs: I'll tell you, if **YOU** stop making noise!

Jiggs: Ooooo! *(claps hands over mouth or closes mouth tightly)*

Miggs: *(reads)* "Away to . . . the sash."

Jiggs: No wonder you threw up. You should have known you'd get sick if you ate a scarf.

Miggs: I **DIDN'T** eat a scarf. This sash is part of the window. I was just telling you that I opened the window.

Jiggs: Why didn't you just say, "I opened the window"?

Miggs: Because that doesn't rhyme. It isn't poetic.

Jiggs: *(sarcastically)* Well, la di da! Ex**CUSE** me!

Miggs: *(reads)* "When what . . . be St. Nick."

Jiggs: Rats! I thought it was going to be Santa Claus. You said this story was about Santa Claus.

Miggs: It **IS** Santa Claus.

Jiggs: Make up your mind. **NOW** you're telling me it's Santa Claus, but first you said it was somebody named St. Nick.

Miggs: St. Nick **IS** Santa Claus.

Jiggs: Huh?

Miggs: He has **TWO** names, Jiggs. *(holds out one arm)* Some people call him St. Nick, and *(holds out other arm)* some people call him Santa Claus.

Jiggs: That's confusing. I'm glad I have only one name. Everybody calls me just plain Jiggs.

Alternative Action: If Jiggs is a movable mouth puppet, wrinkle its nose.

Alternative Action: If Miggs is a movable mouth puppet, cock its head to one side and the other.

Miggs: I could think of some other names to call you, but I'm too polite.

Jiggs: Ooooo!

Miggs: *(reads)* "So up to . . . St. Nicholas too."

Jiggs: St. Nicholas makes three names. Does he have trouble knowing who he is?

Miggs: Not as much trouble as I have keeping you quiet.

(Jiggs claps hands to mouth or closes mouth tightly.)

Miggs: *(reads)* "And then in a . . . each little hoof."

Jiggs: *(looks up and calls)* Careful up there. Don't fall off!

Miggs: *(reads while performing appropriate actions)* "As I drew . . . with a bound."

Jiggs: What a crummy present! Who wants a bound for Christmas?

Miggs: A bound isn't something Santa is giving away. It's a way of saying Santa Claus jumped down the chimney.

Jiggs: Then why didn't you just say, "Santa jumped down the chimney"?

Miggs: Because that doesn't rhyme.

Jiggs: Oh, that's right. It's not *(mockingly)* poetic.

Miggs: Jiggs, be quiet and let me read. *(reads)* "He was dressed . . . ashes and soot."

Jiggs: I'll bet his mommy got mad at him for getting dirty.

Miggs: I'M getting mad at you for interrupting.

(Jiggs claps hands over mouth or closes mouth tightly.)

Miggs: *(reads)* "A bundle . . . his pack."

Jiggs: *(incredulously)* Santa Claus was riding his bicycle around the Christmas tree?

Miggs: No!

Jiggs: But you said he was pedaling.

Miggs: I SAID, "He looked like a peddler." A peddler is someone who carries around what he sells.

Jiggs: Oh.

Miggs: *(reads)* "The stump of . . . a wreath."

Jiggs: Doesn't Santa know smoking is bad for him?

Miggs: I don't know.

Jiggs: I'd better tell him. I don't want Santa getting sick.

Miggs: Neither do I. But tell him after the story. *(reads)* "He had a . . . full of jelly."

Jiggs: Kind of like you, huh, Miggs?

Miggs: *(warningly)* Jiggs!

Jiggs: You have to admit, you have a little paunch. *(pokes Miggs in stomach)*

Miggs: *(warningly)* Jiggs!

Jiggs: I know. I know. Be quiet. *(claps hands over mouth or closes mouth tightly)*

Miggs: *(reads)* "He was chubby . . . in spite of myself."

Jiggs: And that made your little "bowl of jelly" shake, huh, Miggs? *(pokes Miggs in stomach)*

Miggs: *(warningly)* Jiggs!

(Jiggs claps hands over mouth or closes mouth tightly.)

Miggs: *(reads)* "He spoke not a word," *(turns to Jiggs and says reproachfully)* unlike **SOME** people I know, *(reads)* "but went straight . . . with a jerk."

Jiggs: I thought you said you were too polite to call people names.

Miggs: I am.

Jiggs: Then why did you call Santa a jerk?

Miggs: I **DIDN'T** call Santa a jerk. I said he "turned with a jerk."

Jiggs: I beg your pardon. I thought you said **LIKE** a jerk. Go on.

Miggs: *(reads)* "And laying . . . chimney he rose."

Jiggs: *(looks up)* How'd he **DO** that?

Miggs: *(comes back down)* Santa is magic.

Jiggs: Wow!

Miggs: *(reads)* "He sprang . . . thistle." *(Move Miggs up and over away from Jiggs. Then bring Miggs back to the book.)* "But I heard . . . a good night."

Jiggs: *(looks at Miggs. Miggs looks at Jiggs.)* Well? Well?

Miggs: Well, what?

Jiggs: What happens next?

Miggs: Nothing, Jiggs. That was the end of the story.

Jiggs: Then read it again. I liked it.

Miggs: *(closes book)* No, Jiggs. I don't think I could stand to go through that again.

Note: Raise your arm to lift Miggs up.

Jiggs: Then I'll get my own copy at the library. Before I go, though there's something we ought to do.

Miggs: What's that?

Jiggs: *(points)* See all those people out there?

Miggs: *(looks out at each child individually)* Yes.

Jiggs: Don't you think they look like a nice group?

Miggs: Yes. They were good listeners, too.

Jiggs: Then let's wish them what Santa said in the story.

Miggs: Good idea. Ready, set, go!

Miggs, Jiggs: Happy Christmas!

Note: Extend both your arms out toward the audience and operate both puppets while talking.

Christmas Picture Books

Breathed, Berkeley. *A Wish for Wings That Work: An Opus Christmas Story.* Little, Brown, 1991.

Brett, Jan. *Christmas Trolls.* Putnam, 1993.

————. *Wild Christmas Reindeer.* Putnam, 1990.

Croll, Carolyn. *The Little Snowgirl.* Putnam, 1989.

Cuyler, Margery. *The Christmas Snowman.* Arcade, 1992.

De Paola, Tomie. *Merry Christmas, Strega Nona.* Harcourt, 1986.

Howe, James. *The Fright Before Christmas.* Morrow, 1988.

Moore, Clement. *The Night Before Christmas.* (any version)

Parish, Peggy. *Merry Christmas, Amelia Bedelia.* Greenwillow, 1986.

Price, Moe. *Reindeer Christmas.* Harcourt, 1993.

Seuss, Dr. *How the Grinch Stole Christmas.* Random, 1957.

Take Me Out to the Ball Game
A Springtime Story

Characters: Jiggs (right hand)
Miggs (left hand)

Props: baseball
mitten
Halloween mask

> You can use a tennis ball or some other ball instead of the baseball.
>   In place of a mitten, you can use a paper cutout in the shape of a mitten.
>   You can make a mask by cutting eyeholes out of a paper plate and drawing a nose and mouth.

Preparation: Put mitten on stage or in your lap. Set ball on top of it and mask next to it.

Jiggs: *(sings raucously center stage)* "Take me out to the ball game. Take me out to the crowd."

Miggs: *(runs in stage left and pushes Jiggs to stage floor or in your lap)* You'd better lie down, Jiggs. Where does it hurt?

Jiggs: *(stands up)* I'm not in pain.

Miggs: Then why were you bellowing in agony?

Jiggs: I wasn't. I was singing. *(sings)* "Take me out to the ball game. . . ."

Miggs: *(puts hand over Jiggs's mouth)* Please don't sing.

Jiggs: But I always sing when I'm excited.

Miggs: Why are you excited?

Jiggs: It's baseball time! I've been waiting for this new season to start ever since they played the World Cereal last fall.

Miggs: That's World Series.

Jiggs: Right. And now I can follow my favorite teams again.

Miggs: Which teams do you like?

Jiggs: First of all, there's the Chicago Underwear.

Miggs: That's the Chicago **WHITE SOX.**

Jiggs: Yeah, I knew it had something to do with stuff you wear. I also like the Minnesota Twits.

Alternative Action: If Miggs is a movable mouth puppet, shake its head vigorously.

Miggs: That's the Minnesota **TWINS!**

Jiggs: Yeah. And I always root for the New York Yankee Doodle Dandies.

Miggs: The New York **YANKEES.**

Jiggs: Them, too. I especially like the team whose name sounds so good: The Baltimore Oreos.

Miggs: They're **NOT** named after cookies, Jiggs.

Jiggs: Oh. Are they the Cupcakes, or the Doughnuts, or the Fruit Pies?

Miggs: No, Jiggs, they're the Orioles.

Jiggs: Orioles? What kind of food is that?

Miggs: It's not a food. Orioles are birds.

Jiggs: Oh. Well, it's a good team anyway, even if it isn't named after something good to eat. But my favorite team of all is the Chicago Cub Scouts.

Miggs: You mean, the Chicago **CUBS.** Do you collect baseball cards?

Jiggs: You bet! I have cards for all my favorite players.

Miggs: I hate to hear what you're going to do to their names.

Jiggs: There's Boo-Boo Jackson.

Miggs: **BO** Jackson.

Jiggs: He's good, too. There's also José Can You See?

Miggs: José Can**SE**co.

Jiggs: Right. And Kirby Hockey Puck.

Miggs: That's Kirby **PUCKETT.**

Jiggs: Don't forget Blueberry Bonds.

Miggs: **BARRY** Bonds.

Jiggs: And Sammy So-so.

Miggs: Sammy **SOSA.**

Jiggs: There's also Fred McGruff.

Miggs: Fred **McGRIFF.** McGruff is a dog.

Jiggs: I didn't know dogs played baseball.

Miggs: They don't.

Jiggs: Then why are you talking about McGruff?

Miggs: *(groans)* I have a feeling you don't know much about baseball.

Note: As players retire and new ones rise to prominence, you might want to change the names of Jiggs's favorite team members.

Jiggs: Sure I do. I know you play it on an emerald.

Miggs: That's **DIAMOND.**

Jiggs: Diamonds, emeralds, what's the difference? They're both jewels.

Miggs: Do you even know the idea of the game?

Jiggs: Sure. You want to win, win, win, win, win, so you can play in the World Cereal Bowl.

Miggs: That's World Series. Do you know how to win in baseball?

Jiggs: Of course. You try to score lots of touchdowns.

Miggs: Touchdowns are for football, Jiggs. In baseball you want to get hits.

(Jiggs hits Miggs on arm three times.)

Miggs: *(rubs arm)* Ouch! Why did you do that?

Jiggs: You said you wanted hits. Shall I hit you again?

Miggs: *(leaps back)* No! You're supposed to hit the ball, not the players.

Jiggs: *(hits ball three times, picks it up, and holds it out to Miggs)* Do you want to give it a few whacks now?

Miggs: *(takes ball and puts it down)* That's not the way to hit a baseball, Jiggs. You should choke up on the bat first and then hit it.

Jiggs: *(aghast)* Choke the bat? That's mean! *(turns and calls off-stage)* S.P.C.A.! S.P.C.A.! Miggs is being cruel to animals!

Miggs: *(turns Jiggs around)* I'm not choking an animal, Jiggs. Baseball bats are wooden sticks.

Jiggs: Oh. *(turns and calls offstage)* Forget it, S.P.C.A. I made a mistake.

Miggs: Now, Jiggs, after the players hit the ball—**WITH THE BAT**—they run around and tag the bases.

Jiggs: *(punches Miggs in arm)* Tag! You're it!

Miggs: *(rubs arm)* Ouch! Not **THAT** kind of tag. The players step on all the bases before stealing home.

Jiggs: Uh-oh! I'd better go home and lock all my doors and windows. *(turns to go)*

Miggs: *(pulls Jiggs back)* Why?

Jiggs: I don't want people stealing my home! *(starts running off stage right)*

Miggs: *(pulls Jiggs back)* Relax, Jiggs. No one is going to rob you. Stealing home just means the runner tries to touch home plate before the catcher catches the ball.

Alternative Action: If your Miggs puppet doesn't have arms, Jiggs can hit it on the side of its head.

Jiggs: Speaking of catcher, that's the position I'd like to play, because I want to stand behind the old home saucer.

Miggs: That's home **PLATE.**

Jiggs: Home plate, home saucer, what's the difference? Anyway, I have everything I need to be a catcher. I have a mask *(picks up mask, waves it, and puts it down)* and a catcher's mitten. *(picks up mitten and waves it around)*

Miggs: That's **MITT,** not mitten. *(takes mitten and throws it offstage)* And this Halloween mask *(picks it up and waves it)* won't do you any good. *(throws it offstage)* You need a proper catcher's mask to protect your face from getting hit by the ball.

Jiggs: You mean I could get hurt?

Miggs: Yes.

Jiggs: Then I don't want to be the catcher.

Miggs: O.K., you can be the shortstop.

Jiggs: But I'm not short. Can I be the tallstop?

Miggs: There's no such thing as a tallstop, Jiggs, but you can be the pitcher.

Jiggs: How can I do that? You pour water into a pitcher, and then you pour it out of the pitcher. But if you pour water into me, I'm just going to swallow it. I really don't think anybody will want it back after that, do you?

Miggs: I'm not talking about water pitchers, Jiggs. I'm talking about the pitcher who throws the ball at the batter.

Jiggs: Ooh, what a mess!

Miggs: What do you mean?

Jiggs: Don't you know? If you throw a ball into a bowl of cake batter, it's going to splatter all over. Yuck!

Miggs: Jiggs, nobody is going to throw a ball into cake batter. The pitcher throws to the catcher behind home plate.

Jiggs: Maybe I shouldn't be the pitcher then. I can't throw well.

Miggs: Then try playing in the outfield. Can you catch flies?

Jiggs: What do you think I am, a frog? I don't catch bugs with my tongue.

Miggs: You don't have to.

Jiggs: Good. Because bugs would taste awful. *(gags)*

Miggs: Catching flies means grabbing the ball before it hits the ground.

Jiggs: These terms are so confusing, I think I'll just be a coach.

Miggs: You can't be a coach, Jiggs. Coaches have to know a lot about the game.

Jiggs: If a pumpkin can do it, I can do it.

Miggs: What do you mean? Pumpkins don't coach baseball.

Jiggs: Sometimes they do. Cinderella had a pumpkin for a coach.

Miggs: Cinderella had a different kind of coach. She didn't play baseball.

Jiggs: I should say she didn't. She kept running away from the ball, and that's no way to play the game.

Miggs: Jiggs, I'm tired of trying to explain baseball to you. Why don't you go to the library and read a book about it?

Jiggs: That sounds like a good idea. See you later. *(exits stage right, singing)* "Take me out to the ball game. Take me out to the crowd."

Miggs: *(addresses audience)* Why don't you go to the library, too? If you don't want to read about baseball, you can find a good book about something else. The library has lots of good books on all kinds of subjects, and the people who work there can help you find what you want. Good-bye for now. *(exits stage left)*

Books about Baseball

Day, Alexandra. *Frank and Ernest Play Ball.* Scholastic, 1990.

Hanft, Philip. *Never Fear, Flip the Dip Is Here.* Dial, 1991.

Joyce, William. *Dinosaur Bob: And His Adventures with the Family Lazardo.* HarperCollins, 1988.

Kovalski, Maryann. *Take Me Out to the Ballgame.* Scholastic, 1993.

Norworth, Jack. *Take Me Out to the Ballgame.* Simon & Schuster, 1992.

Parish, Peggy. *Play Ball, Amelia Bedelia.* HarperCollins, 1972.

· Teague, Mark. *The Field Beyond the Outfield.* Scholastic, 1992.

Welch, Willy. *Playing Right Field.* Scholastic, 1995.

The Valentine Party

Characters: Jiggs (right hand)
Miggs (left hand)

Props: canvas tote bag
can of mixed nuts
can of hot chocolate
box of cookies

Note: Empty cans and boxes will be easier to carry. If you lack any of the props, make substitutions. Because things fall out of the bag a different way each time you perform the skit, pick items up in whatever order is easiest.

Preparation: Put cans and box into bag and set on floor to your left.

Jiggs: *(enters stage right, crosses to stage left, and calls)* Yoo hoo, Miggs. Are you home?

Miggs: *(enters stage left)* You're too early. My Valentine party isn't until this afternoon.

Jiggs: I know. I came over early, so I could help you get ready.

Miggs: Then go home. You always mess things up when you try to help.

Jiggs: I won't today. Please let me put up the decorations.

Miggs: No. When you blew up balloons for my last party, you kept blowing and blowing *(blows)* until you got so dizzy, you passed out. *(faints)*

Jiggs: Then I'll just hang streamers today.

Miggs: *(stands up)* No. Last time you did that, you draped them around the rungs of the chairs. Most of our guests tripped on them *(falls forward)* and skinned their noses. Ouch! *(stands up and rubs nose)*

Jiggs: If you don't want me to help with the decorations, let me make the refreshments.

Miggs: No way! That would be worse! Don't you remember what happened when you made lemonade for my beach party last summer?

Jiggs: *(hangs head)* Yeah, I made a little mistake.

Miggs: *(knowingly)* Uh-huh. You thought the salt was the sugar. Do you remember how the lemonade tasted?

Jiggs: Well . . . , it wasn't the best.

Miggs: **THAT'S** putting it mildly. It was so bad, everybody got sick on it. *(gags)*

Jiggs: So I'll just make the cake today.

Miggs: No! You burned the last cake you baked.

Jiggs: Only a little.

Miggs: A **LITTLE?** There was so much smoke, the neighbors called the fire department. And when we finally pulled the cake out of the oven, it looked like a lump of coal.

Jiggs: I can do better this time.

Miggs: No, Jiggs. I'm going to the store now, and I don't want you touching anything while I'm gone.

Jiggs: Please let me go to the store for you.

Miggs: No. You always forget what I want and bring back all the wrong things.

Jiggs: I'll remember and bring all the right things today.

Miggs: No!

Jiggs: You **HAVE** to let me shop for you. You don't have time to put up the decorations, make the refreshments, **AND** go to the store in time for the party.

Miggs: Rats! You're right. You can go to the store.

Jiggs: *(shows excitement)* Oh, boy! Oh, boy! What do you want me to get?

Miggs: *(admonishes)* You'd better write it down, Jiggs. You know how you always forget.

Jiggs: I won't forget. Now just tell me.

Miggs: O.K., I want Hawaiian Punch.

Jiggs: *(hits Miggs on the arm or behind the ear)* Aloha!

Miggs: *(rubs arm or ear)* Ouch! What was that all about?

Jiggs: Aloha is a Hawaiian greeting.

Miggs: I know. But why did you hit me?

Jiggs: You said you wanted Hawaiian punch. *(hits Miggs)* Aloha.

Miggs: *(rubs arm or ear)* Ouch! I didn't want **THAT** kind of punch.

Jiggs: I thought that was a strange request. What kind **DID** you want?

Miggs: The kind you drink.

Jiggs: Oh. I don't think I can get that for you.

Miggs: Why not?

Jiggs: Don't you know? Hawaii is very far away. I don't think I can get **ALL** the way to Hawaii *(moves as far right as possible)* and **ALL** the way back *(moves back to center stage)* in time for your party.

Miggs: You don't **HAVE** to go to Hawaii to get Hawaiian Punch. You can buy it in cans down at the grocery store. *(points to right)*

Jiggs: I learn something new every day. What else do you want?

Miggs: *(admonishes)* I want you to write this down, Jiggs. You know how you always forget.

Jiggs: I won't forget, so just tell me.

Miggs: Very well. I want conversation hearts.

Jiggs: Wow! I've never heard a heart talk before! In the movie we saw for science class, the heart just went, "lub-dub, lub-dub, lub-dub."

Miggs: I don't want **REAL** hearts, Jiggs. I want candy hearts with little messages on them like "Sweetheart," "I like you."

Jiggs: I like you, too. But I wouldn't go so far as to call you sweetheart. That's too mushy.

Miggs: I **WASN'T** calling you sweetheart. I was giving you an example of the messages written on the hearts.

Jiggs: Oh. Do you want anything else?

Miggs: *(admonishes)* Yes, and you'd better write it down. You know how you always forget.

Jiggs: I won't forget. Just tell me.

Miggs: O.K., I want strawberry ice cream.

Jiggs: I like vanilla better.

Miggs: But strawberry is pink and looks nice for Valentine's Day.

Jiggs: How about if I get vanilla and some red food coloring?

Miggs: No, Jiggs. *(admonishes)* And come right back from the store. When I sent you for ice cream last summer, you stopped at the library on the way home.

Jiggs: Yeah, and I had a lot of fun that day. I saw a puppet show, read a new magazine, and checked out a lot of good books.

Miggs: Yes, but by the time you got home, the ice cream had melted.

Jiggs: It **WAS** a little on the soft side, wasn't it?

Miggs: We were sipping it through straws!

Jiggs: That won't happen today, because it's colder now.

Miggs: Well, come straight home anyway.

Jiggs: All right. I'm going now. *(turns to leave)*

Miggs: *(pulls Jiggs back)* Before you go, repeat what I told you, so I know you'll buy the right things.

Jiggs: You want *(hits Miggs on arm or behind ear)* aloha, hearts that talk, vanilla ice cream, and red food coloring.

Miggs: *(warningly)* Jiggs!

Jiggs: Just kidding. You really want a can of Hawaiian Punch, a bag of candy hearts, and *(says distastefully)* **STRAW-BERRY** *(gags)* ice cream.

Miggs: That's right.

Jiggs: See? I told you I'd remember. Good-bye. *(turns to leave)*

Miggs: *(pulls Jiggs back)* Wait. You didn't get a bag.

Jiggs: They'll give me a plastic bag at the store.

Miggs: But it's better for the environment to use canvas bags. *(exits stage left, returns with bag, and holds it out)*

(Jiggs takes bag and exits stage right.)

Miggs: *(addresses audience)* I hate to trust Jiggs, but I **AM** busy. I'd better go bake the cake. *(exits stage left)*

Jiggs: *(enters stage right with bag, puts bag onstage or in your lap, faces stage left, and calls)* I'm back.

Miggs: *(enters stage left)* Did you remember to get the right things?

Jiggs: *(nods vigorously)* You're going to be very proud of me.

Miggs: Hmmmmm, let's see . . . *(Miggs and Jiggs each grab a corner at the bottom of the bag, turn it upside down, and shake out the props. Miggs picks up the can of hot chocolate.)* a can of hot chocolate, *(Jiggs puts head next to it and nods vigorously. Miggs puts down the chocolate and picks up the can of nuts.)* a can of mixed nuts, *(Jiggs puts head next to it and nods vigorously. Miggs puts the nuts down and holds up cookies.)* and a box of cookies. *(Jiggs puts head next to it and nods vigorously. Miggs puts down cookies and faces Jiggs.)* I told you you should write it down, Jiggs. You forgot the marshmallows.

Puppeteer: Did Miggs ask Jiggs to buy marshmallows? Moral of the story: Don't send either Miggs or Jiggs to the store for you.

Books for Valentine's Day

Bauer, Caroline Feller. *Valentine's Day: Stories and Poems.* HarperCollins, 1993.

Brown, Marc. *Arthur's Valentine.* Little, Brown, 1980.

Carlson, Nancy. *Louanne Pig in The Mysterious Valentine.* Puffin, 1987.

DeGroat, Diane. *Roses Are Pink, Your Feet Stink.* Morrow, 1996.

Matthews, Liz. *Teeny Witch and the Perfect Valentine.* Troll, 1991.

Modell, Frank. *One Zillion Valentines.* Greenwillow, 1981.

Prelutsky, Jack. *It's Valentine's Day.* Greenwillow, 1983.

Sharmat, Marjorie Weinman. *The Best Valentine in the World.* Holiday, 1982.

Stevenson, James. *Happy Valentine's Day, Emma!* Greenwillow, 1987.

Books about Forgetting

Arnold, Tedd. *Ollie Forgot.* Dial, 1988.

Birdseye, Tom. *Soap! Soap! Don't Forget the Soap!: An Appalachian Folk Tale.* Holiday, 1993.

Cole, Joanna. *Aren't You Forgetting Something, Fiona?* Parents, 1984.

Hutchins, Pat. *Don't Forget the Bacon!* Greenwillow, 1976.

Help! Help! Help!
A Variation of "The Boy Who Cried Wolf"

Characters: Miggs (left hand)
Jiggs (right hand)
Honey Bear (left hand)

> If you don't have a bear, use some other character with a sweet tooth.

Props: basket (or bowl)
honey cakes

> You can draw a pile of honey cakes on a sheet of cardboard that fits into your basket or bowl. When you put the cutout into the basket or bowl, make sure some of the cakes show above the rim.

Introduction: Before presenting this skit to school-aged children, you could say something like "This skit might remind you of another story you've heard. Think about that while you're watching it."

Miggs: *(carries basket of honey cakes while looking all around the stage)* Now where can I hide these so Honey Bear can't eat them while I'm cleaning the living room?

Jiggs: *(calls from offstage)* Yoo hoo, Miggs. May I come in?

Miggs: *(puts down basket at center stage or in your lap, faces stage right, and calls)* Sure, Jiggs.

Jiggs: *(enters stage right)* I know I'm too early for your party, but I was so excited, I just couldn't stay away any longer.

Miggs: I'm glad you came. I was worried about the honey cakes.

Jiggs: Do you want me to taste them and make sure they're all right for your company? I'd be happy to. *(bends over basket)*

Miggs: *(pushes Jiggs back)* No, Jiggs! I don't want you to eat them; I want you to watch them.

Jiggs: *(looks down at cakes and then back at Miggs)* Watch them, huh? What are they going to do, some sort of trick?

Miggs: No, but I need you to keep your eye on them for me while I'm out cleaning the living room.

Jiggs: That sounds like a silly thing to do, but here goes. *(bends over and puts eye on cakes)*

Miggs: *(pulls Jiggs's head up)* That's not what I meant, Jiggs. I just want you to keep watch and make sure Honey Bear doesn't come and eat all the cakes while I'm out cleaning the living room.

Jiggs: I couldn't stop Honey Bear all by myself!

Miggs: You don't have to. If you see him, holler, and I'll run in and help you chase him off.

Jiggs: Whoop! Whoop! Whoop! Whoop!

Miggs: *(holds hands over ears and cringes)* Stop, Jiggs! You're hurting my ears!

Jiggs: You want me to be your burglar alarm, so I have to practice sounding like one. Whoop! Whoop! Whoop!

Miggs: *(puts hand over Jiggs's mouth or closes it firmly)* No, you don't. All you have to do is yell, "Help!"

Jiggs: *(pulls away from Miggs)* But it's more fun to make noise! Whoop! Whoop! Whoop!

(Miggs puts hand over Jiggs's mouth or closes it firmly.)

Jiggs: *(pulls away)* You sure know how to take all the fun out of things.

Miggs: I'm going out to the living room now. You keep watch for Honey Bear. *(turns to leave)*

Jiggs: Whoop! Whoop! Who . . .

(Miggs turns around and looks at Jiggs. Jiggs quickly closes mouth tightly or claps hands over it. Miggs exits stage left.)

Jiggs: *(looks down into basket)* Mmmmm. These honey cakes sure look good. It would be a shame if Honey Bear ate them before the party. *(addresses audience)* I wonder if Miggs could get in here fast enough to save the cakes if Honey Bear really did come. I'd better check. *(shouts loudly)* Help! Help! **HELP!**

(Miggs runs in stage left and looks all around.)

Jiggs: Are you looking for something?

Miggs: Yes. Where's Honey Bear?

Jiggs: I don't know. I haven't seen him for a **LOOOONG** time.

Miggs: You mean, he's not here?

Jiggs: No.

Miggs: Then why did you call me?

Jiggs: I wanted to see if you could get here fast enough to save the cakes if Honey Bear really did come.

Miggs: Are you satisfied now that I could?

Alternative Action: If Miggs is a movable mouth puppet, shake its head vigorously.

Note: Have Miggs simply yell "Stop" if the puppet does not have movable arms.

Jiggs: You bet! You're so fast, you ought to try out for the Olympic track team.

Miggs: *(with irritation)* That will have to wait. Right now I'm cleaning the living room. *(leans toward Jiggs)* Or **TRYING** to. *(Miggs turns and exits stage left.)*

Jiggs: *(watches Miggs leave)* Miggs sounded a little crabby. I wonder why. *(looks down at cakes, sighs, looks around while humming, looks down at cakes, sighs, looks around while humming, looks down at cakes, and sighs)* This is **BORING!** *(collapses)* I wish something would happen. *(stands up)* Hey! I could make something happen. *(yells loudly)* Help! Help! **HELP!**

Miggs: *(runs in stage left and looks all around)* Where's Honey Bear?

Jiggs: I already told you. I haven't seen him for a long time.

Miggs: Then why did you get me out here if you don't need my help?

Jiggs: But I **DO** need your help before I die from boredom just sitting here with nothing to do.

Miggs: You **HAVE** something to do. **YOU'RE** guarding the honey cakes while **I** clean the living room. *(leans toward Jiggs and says angrily)* Now do **YOUR** job, so I can do **MINE!** *(stomps off stage left)*

Jiggs: *(watches Miggs leave)* Ooooo! Miggs is **REALLY** mad. I didn't mean to make my friend mad. I'd better get Miggs in here so I can apologize. *(yells loudly)* Help! Help! **HELP!**

Miggs: *(runs in stage left, looks all around, and then looks right at Jiggs and speaks with irritation)* I don't see Honey Bear. Does that mean you got me out here for no good reason again?

Jiggs: Oh no. I had a very good reason. I wanted to apologize for making you mad.

Miggs: If you're **REALLY** sorry, you'll promise not to call me again unless Honey Bear actually comes.

Jiggs: I promise.

Miggs: All right. I accept your apology. *(admonishes)* **BUT DON'T CALL ME AGAIN UNLESS HONEY BEAR ACTUALLY COMES.** *(stomps off stage left)*

(Take off Miggs. Put on Honey Bear.)

Jiggs: *(addresses audience)* I hope Miggs doesn't stay mad the rest of the day. The party won't be any fun at all if my best friend is mad at me.

Honey Bear: *(enters stage left, holding nose in air and sniffing loudly)* I smell honey cakes. *(crosses to basket)* Yum!

Jiggs: *(pushes Honey Bear away from basket)* No, Honey Bear! Those aren't for you.

Honey Bear: **ALL** honey cakes are for me! *(pushes Jiggs away from basket, bends over it, and starts chewing on the cakes and making loud eating noises)*

Jiggs: *(loudly)* Help! Help! **HELP!** *(Honey Bear chews on the cakes and makes loud eating noises.)*

Jiggs: *(frantically)* Help! Help! **HELP!** *(Honey Bear chews on the cakes and makes loud eating noises.)*

Jiggs: *(desperately)* Help! Help! **HELP!**

Honey Bear: *(picks cakes up in mouth, makes loud eating noises, and then drops them behind the stage or in tote bag at your feet, burps and looks at Jiggs)* Those were good. Got any more?

Jiggs: No.

Honey Bear: Then I'll be going. Got to find more honey cakes. *(burps and exits stage left)*

(Take off Honey Bear. Put on Miggs.)

Jiggs: *(looks in basket, picks it up, turns it upside down and shakes it, then puts it down and addresses audience)* Boy, he didn't even leave any crumbs. Miggs is really going to be mad now.

Miggs: *(enters stage left and talks while crossing to basket)* I finished cleaning the living room, so I'll put the honey cakes on the coffee . . . *(Miggs looks down at basket and then over at Jiggs. This happens several times. Miggs sticks head into basket, picks it up, and looks underneath it. Finally, Miggs puts down basket and looks at Jiggs.)* Where are the honey cakes?

Jiggs: *(turns away, hangs head, and mumbles)* Honey Bear ate them.

Miggs: Quit kidding around and tell me what you did with the honey cakes.

Jiggs: *(turns to Miggs)* I **TOLD** you! Honey Bear came and ate them. Didn't you hear me calling you?

Miggs: Yes.

Jiggs: *(angrily)* Then why didn't you come in and help?

Miggs: I thought you were just trying to get my attention again.

Jiggs: But I had promised I wouldn't call you unless Honey Bear actually came.

Alternative Action: If Honey Bear's mouth doesn't open, move his head up and down near the honey cakes.

Miggs: I know, but why should I believe you? You fool around so much, I never know when you're telling the truth.

Jiggs: *(turns away and hangs head)* I guess I'd better be more careful from now on, huh?

Miggs: That's a good idea. Right now, though, you'd better go to the store and use your allowance to buy more honey cakes for the party.

Jiggs: But if I have to spend my own money, I won't have enough to buy that new toy I've been saving for.

Miggs: I'm sorry, Jiggs, but when you make a mistake, you have to do something to correct it.

Jiggs: Oh, all right. *(turns to go)*

Miggs: And hurry back, so you don't miss the party.

Jiggs: *(turns back)* You mean, you still want me to come?

Miggs: Of course. You make me mad sometimes, but you're still my best friend. *(hugs Jiggs)*

Jiggs: *(turns away and hangs head)* Aw, gee!

Miggs: *(pushes Jiggs off stage right)* Now hurry down to the store. *(Jiggs exits stage right.)*

Miggs: *(watches Jiggs leave and calls)* Watch out for Honey Bear on your way home!

Follow-up

Ask the children what story they thought about during the skit. Accept all answers. When someone says, "The Boy Who Cried Wolf," tell children the author got the idea for the skit from that famous Aesop fable. Encourage them to write their own variations on familiar stories or to read some of the titles listed for "Little Blue Riding Hood" and "The Three Little Pigs."

Versions of the "The Boy Who Cried Wolf"

Schecter, Ellen. *The Boy Who Cried Wolf.* Bantam, 1994.

Vozar, David. *Yo, Hungry Wolf!: A Nursery Rap.* Doubleday, 1993.

Books about Honesty

Carlson, Nancy. *Harriet and the Garden.* Lerner, 1982.

Elliott, Dan. *Ernie's Little Lie.* Random, 1992.

Sharmat, Marjorie Weinman. *A Big Fat Enormous Lie.* Dutton, 1986.

Books about Bears and Their Food

Berenstain, Stan, and Jan Berenstain. *Big Honey Hunt.* Beginner Books, 1962.

Kwitz, John, ill. *Winnie the Pooh and the Honey Tree.* Disney, 1993.

McCloskey, Robert. *Blueberries for Sal.* Viking, 1948.

Milne, A. A. *Winnie-the-Pooh.* Dutton, 1988.

Wood, Don. *Little Mouse, the Red Ripe Strawberry and the Big Hungry Bear.* Childs Play, 1990.

Jiggs Plays a Trick

Characters: Jiggs (right hand)
Miggs (left hand)

Props: book called *Sneaky Tricks to Fool Your Friends*
big leaf
little leaf
two cutouts in the shape of the number *3*

Notes: The library where I worked had two books of practical jokes, *Sneaky Tricks to Fool Your Friends* by E. Richard Churchill and *The Surprise Book* by Laurence B. White, both of which have gone out of print. If you have different books, substitute the title of one of these for *Sneaky Tricks to Fool Your Friends.* If you don't have any books with practical jokes, you might want to revise the skit. Jiggs might open it by setting out the props and telling the audience, "I'm getting ready to play some little tricks on Miggs today." When Miggs comes over and asks what they can do, Jiggs will announce plans to play some tricks. At the end, Miggs can go home to think of a few jokes to play on Jiggs, and the latter can address the audience with "Maybe you'd like to try these tricks on your family or friends someday. Good luck if you do. 'Bye."

You could perform this skit around April Fool's Day along with "The Mysterious Visitors."

Preparation: Open book so it stands up in the center of the stage with its cover facing the audience. Set leaves side by side at stage left. Put the numbers at stage right.

Jiggs: *(reads, laughs, and addresses audience)* That's a good one. *(reads, laughs, and addresses audience)* I'll have to remember this one. *(reads, laughs, and addresses audience)* I love it!

Miggs: *(enters stage left and walks over to Jiggs)* What's so funny?

Jiggs: This book I got from the library. *(taps the cover)*

Miggs: *(looks at cover and reads)* Sneaky Tricks to Fool Your Friends, eh? You're wasting your time with this book, Jiggs.

Jiggs: No, I'm not. Reading is never a waste of time, because it helps us learn lots of cool things.

Miggs: I know. And it's fun, too. But **THIS** particular book is a waste of your time. *(lays book flat on stage)*

Jiggs: Why do you say that?

Miggs: I'm the friend you're trying to fool, right?

Jiggs: Right!

Miggs: Then the book is definitely a waste of your time, because you could never fool me.

Jiggs: Are you sure?

Miggs: Positive.

Jiggs: May I go ahead and try?

Miggs: Sure. Just don't hold your breath.

Jiggs: O.K. Do you see that big leaf down there?

Miggs: Of course. What about it?

Jiggs: I bet you can't bend over and pick it up without saying anything.

Miggs: Of course, I can. *(bends over to pick up leaf. Jiggs pinches Miggs's bottom. Miggs jumps up.)* Ouch!

> **Alternative Action:** (with movable mouth puppet) Jiggs bites.

Jiggs: You said something!

Miggs: Only because you pinched me!

> **Alternative Dialogue:** (with movable mouth Jiggs) . . . you bit me!

Jiggs: I fooled you! You have to admit that I fooled you.

Miggs: That was just a fluke. You couldn't do it again.

Jiggs: Mind if I try anyway?

Miggs: If you must.

Jiggs: O.K. Now put the big leaf on top of the little leaf.

Miggs: No way! You'll pinch me again.

> **Alternative Dialogue:** bite

Jiggs: No, I won't. *(gags)* You taste terrible.

> **Note:** Omit this last sentence if Jiggs pinched Miggs.

Miggs: Promise?

Jiggs: Cross my heart and hope to die.

> **Note:** If your puppet has movable arms, move your thumb, so it looks as if Jiggs is crossing its heart.
> **Alternative Dialogue:** fold your hands

Miggs: All right. But close your mouth as tightly as you can. *(Jiggs does so.)* And step back. *(Jiggs moves slightly to stage right.)* A little more. *(Jiggs moves closer to stage right.)* A little more. *(Jiggs moves to far right of stage. Miggs moves toward big leaf, but keeps turning to look at Jiggs. Finally, Miggs picks up the big leaf and sets it down on the little leaf.)* I did it. And you didn't trick me.

Jiggs: That wasn't the trick.

Miggs: Then what **IS** the trick?

Jiggs: I bet I can pick up the little leaf without ever touching the big leaf.

Miggs: You cannot.

Jiggs: Yes, I can. In fact, I already have.

Miggs: No, you haven't. The little leaf is still under the big leaf.

Jiggs: Are you sure?

Miggs: Of course. *(picks up big leaf and looks down at it)* See? The little leaf is right there. *(points)*

Jiggs: *(picks up little leaf, waves it in Miggs's face, and then puts it down on the stage or in your lap)* I picked up the little leaf without ever touching the big leaf. I fooled you!

Miggs: For the last time. You won't be able to trick me again.

Jiggs: That's what you think, Smarty-pants. What are one and one?

Miggs: Two.

Jiggs: Very good. What are two and two?

Miggs: *(sounds bored)* Four.

Jiggs: Very, very good. What are three and three?

Miggs: *(sounds irritated)* Six.

Jiggs: Very, very **WRONG.** Three and three make eight.

Miggs: No, they don't.

Jiggs: *(picks up a number and holds it so it faces audience)* Yes, they do. What's this?

Miggs: A three.

Jiggs: *(gives it to Miggs)* Right. *(picks up the other three, and holds it out)* What's this?

Miggs: That's a three, too.

Jiggs: Yes, and three and three make eight. See? *(holds the three upside down and backward next to the number Miggs is holding and then puts it down)* I fooled you! I fooled you!

Miggs: *(throws the number offstage in disgust)* You won't trick me again today.

Jiggs: How can you be so sure?

Miggs: Because I'm leaving. *(turns to go)*

Jiggs: Going home to sulk?

Miggs: *(turns back)* No. I'm going to the library and get a book of tricks for myself. *(exits stage left)*

Jiggs: *(addresses audience)* Miggs and I like to go to the library and learn new things. I hope you do, too. Well, see you later. *(exits stage right)*

Books with or about Tricks

Aardema, Verna. *Borreguita and the Coyote.* Knopf, 1991.

Cobb, Vicki, and Kathy Darling. *Bet You Can! Science Possibilities to Fool You.* Avon, 1983.

———. *Bet You Can't! Science Impossibilities to Fool You.* Lothrop, 1980.

McMullan, Jim, and Kate McMullan. *Hey Pip-squeak!* HarperCollins, 1995.

Wolff, Patricia Rae. *The Toll-Bridge Troll.* Harcourt, 1995.

See also the books listed for the skits "Rabbit Makes Trouble," "Brer Wolf Plays House," and "Only Two Hops."

It's Not Fair!

A Variation of "Tops or Bottoms"

Characters: Miggs (left hand)
Jiggs (right hand)

Props: hoe
watering can
carrot
leafy top part of carrot
packet with picture of corn
ear of corn
roots of corn

> You can cut all the props out of cardboard or use the real things.

Miggs: *(hoes, sets down hoe, wipes brow)* Whew! *(picks up hoe and hoes)* Hoeing is hard work. I wish I could get somebody to do it for me.

Jiggs: *(enters stage right)* Hi, Miggs. What are you doing?

Miggs: Right now I'm hoeing the garden. After that, I'm going to plant vegetables. *(addresses audience, laughs, and turns to Jiggs)* If you help me, I'll give you half of everything we grow.

Jiggs: *(shows happiness)* I'd like that. *(hangs head)* But I don't know how to grow vegetables.

Miggs: *(addresses audience, laughs, and turns to Jiggs)* I'll tell you exactly what to do. First, though, you must decide if you want the tops or the bottoms of the vegetables.

Jiggs: *(thinks)* Hmmmmm . . . I guess I'll take the tops. A lot of delicious things grow above the ground.

Miggs: Tops it is. Now here's what you do. *(hoes in demonstration and then hands hoe to Jiggs)* You try.

Jiggs: *(takes hoe and hoes)* Is this all right?

Miggs: *(congratulates Jiggs)* It's splendid. *(yawns)* I'm going inside to take a little nap. Keep up the good work. *(exits stage left)*

Puppeteer: All summer long Jiggs worked in the hot sun, hoeing *(Jiggs hoes)*, watering *(Jiggs picks up watering can and pretends to water)*, and weeding. *(Jiggs bends over and pretends to pull out weeds.)*

Jiggs: *(wipes forehead)* Whew! Raising vegetables is hard work.

Puppeteer: Finally it was time to divide the harvest. *(With your left hand, lay the carrot and the leafy top part of it on the stage or in your lap.)*

Miggs: *(enters stage left, looks down at carrots, and congratulates Jiggs)* You did a great job. These carrots look delicious.

Jiggs: Yes, they do. I can't wait to eat some. Mmmmm.

Miggs: *(hands leafy top part to Jiggs)* Here's your half. *(picks up carrot and hugs it)* This is mine.

Jiggs: *(drops leafy top part and wails)* I can't eat leaves!

Miggs: Then why did you ask for the tops?

Jiggs: I thought I'd get something good to eat, not a bunch of old leaves.

Miggs: Stop complaining. You got just what you asked for. I'm going in for supper now. Enjoy your meal. *(exits stage left with carrot)*

Jiggs: *(pretends to take a bite and then throws leaves away)* Yuck! I did all that work for nothing! *(stomps off stage right)*

Puppeteer: Spring came again.

(Miggs enters stage left and start hoeing. Then Jiggs enters stage right.)

Miggs: Hi, Jiggs. Did you come to help me again this year?

Jiggs: No! I'm never going to help you again!

Miggs: Why not?

Jiggs: Because you gave me nothing but leaves after all my hard work last year. It wasn't fair!

Miggs: It was fair as fair can be. You had told me you wanted the tops, so that's exactly what I gave you. If you prefer, however, I'll let you have the bottoms this time.

Jiggs: I **DO** want the bottoms. **YOU** can get stuck with the tops.

Miggs: *(shakes Jiggs's hand)* It's a deal! *(picks up packet of seeds and hands it to Jiggs)* Here are the seeds. *(addresses audience, laughs, and turns to Jiggs)* We're growing corn this year. *(exits stage left)*

Puppeteer: Once again, Jiggs worked hard all summer long.

Jiggs: *(Jiggs pretends to hoe, plant, water, and weed. Every now and then Jiggs wipes brow and exclaims.)* "Whew!"

Alternative Action: If Miggs is a movable mouth puppet, it can nod at the carrot.

Puppeteer: Then harvest time came.

Miggs: *(enters stage left)* Is it time to divide the crop yet, Jiggs?

Jiggs: Yes, and this time it's **MY** turn to feast. Mmmmm. *(grabs ear of corn)*

Miggs: *(admonishes)* Hold on, Jiggs. You wanted the bottoms this year. *(picks up roots and sets them down in front of Jiggs)* This is your share. *(grabs corn away from Jiggs and sets it down behind self)* This is mine.

Jiggs: Yuck! I don't want to eat roots! *(picks them up and throws them offstage)*

Miggs: Then why did you pick bottoms?

Jiggs: I didn't know I'd only get roots. It isn't fair. I did all that work for nothing again.

Miggs: It is **SO** fair, because you got **EXACTLY** what you asked for. Now, let's talk about next year's garden.

Jiggs: Yes, let's! Next year it will be **YOUR** *(pokes Miggs in stomach)* turn to work in the garden and **YOUR** *(pokes Miggs in stomach)* turn to pick tops or bottoms. Which do you want?

Miggs: *(thinks)* Uh . . . tops. . . . No, bottoms. . . . No, tops. . . . No, bottoms. . . .

Jiggs: Is bottoms your final choice?

Miggs: *(sounds indecisive)* Yes. . . . No. . . . Yes. . . . No. . . . Yes.

Jiggs: *(shakes Miggs's hand)* It's a deal. *(pokes Miggs in stomach)* **YOU** get the bottoms. I get the tops. And we're going to raise lots of vegetables that grow above the ground, like pumpkins, tomatoes, squash, and cucumbers. *(laughs)* He who laughs last, laughs best.

Books about Gardening

Caseley, Judith. *Grandpa's Garden Lunch.* Greenwillow, 1990.

Ernst, Lisa Campbell. *Miss Penny and Mr. Grubbs.* Macmillan, 1991.

Koscielniak, Bruce. *Bear and Bunny Grow Tomatoes.* Knopf, 1993.

Krauss, Ruth. *The Carrot Seed.* HarperCollins, 1989.

Parkinson, Kathy. *Enormous Turnip.* Albert Whitman, 1985.

Stevens, Janet. *Tops & Bottoms.* Harcourt, 1995.

Stevenson, James. *Grandpa's Too-Good Garden.* Greenwillow, 1989.

Wiesner, David. *June 29, 1999.* Houghton, 1992.

Wolf, Janet. *The Rosy Fat Magenta Radish.* Little, Brown, 1990.

The Mysterious Visitors

Characters: Jiggs (right hand)
Miggs (left hand)

Props: dust cloth   mouse mask
plate   rabbit mask
three cookies tiger mask

Small boxes make good, sturdy masks when you cut off the bottom panels. Find three that fit over your puppet's head. (Graham cracker boxes worked well with my Miggs.) Because they shouldn't interfere with moving Miggs's arms, you might need to cut off the lower parts of the boxes until they cover only the puppet's head down to its chin.

Cover the mouse and rabbit masks with brown paper. (You can cut open a grocery bag.) Draw heads, complete with ears, cut them out, and glue them onto the front of the boxes.

Cover the tiger mask with yellow paper. Draw a face and stripes on the front. Draw half circles for ears in the upper corners.

Note: If you like, you can share this for April Fool's Day. See the alternative dialogue.

Preparation: Put plate of cookies at stage right or on table at your right. Put mouse mask on Miggs. Put the rabbit and tiger masks upside down on the floor to your left with the faces turned toward you. When the time comes to change masks, turn Miggs upside down and shake your hand until the mask the puppet is wearing falls off. Plunge the puppet's head down into the next mask and then hold the puppet up. (If you have trouble with this, plan to get help before the skit by asking an adult or older child to sit on your left side and take the old masks off and put the new ones on.)

Jiggs: *(dusts all over and then puts cloth down)* There! Now my house is clean enough for company.

Puppeteer: Bong, bong, bong.

Jiggs: I finished just in time. Miggs is coming over at three o'clock today.

Puppeteer: Ding dong.

Jiggs: There's Miggs now. I hope my friend likes the new kind of cookie I bought at the bakery this morning. *(crosses to stage left)*

Miggs: *(enters stage left in mouse mask)* Excuse me, but I'm lost. Could you please tell me how to get to 1107 Rodentia Avenue?

Jiggs: Of course, little mousie. Just go to the corner, turn left, and walk about a mile until you get to the cheese factory.

Miggs: *(dismayed)* A mile? I'm so tired, I was hoping it was closer.

Jiggs: Would you like to come in and rest awhile?

Miggs: Yes, please.

(Miggs and Jiggs move to center stage.)

Jiggs: I'll even give you a cookie for extra energy. *(Jiggs crosses to plate, picks up cookie, and takes it to Miggs.)*

Miggs: Thank you. *(takes cookie and eats)*

Jiggs: Have you come from far away?

Miggs: Oh, yes. I live 'way out in the country.

Jiggs: Then what brings you all the way to the city?

Miggs: I'm going to visit my cousin. And I'd better be going now because she's probably wondering where I am.

(Miggs and Jiggs start walking to stage left.)

Jiggs: I hope you enjoy your visit.

Miggs: I'm sure I will. My cousin has told me what a wonderful place the city is. Good-bye. *(exits stage left)*

(Take off mouse mask. Put on rabbit mask.)

Jiggs: *(addresses audience)* I hope she gets to her cousin's house safely. The city can be a dangerous place for a little mousie.

Puppeteer: Ding dong.

Jiggs: I'll bet that's Miggs. *(turns to stage left)*

Miggs: *(enters stage left, wearing rabbit mask; jumps up and down, waving arms)* Help, help! Mr. McGregor is chasing me!

Jiggs: *(pulls Miggs toward center stage)* You can hide in here.

Miggs: *(collapses)* I'm beat. Mr. McGregor can sure run fast! *(pants)*

Jiggs: Why is he chasing you?

Miggs: *(stands up)* He caught me eating vegetables in his garden. I don't know why that made him mad. I only ate a few, and he has lots! What a grouch!

Jiggs: Even when people have a lot of something, you should never take anything from them without their permission.

Miggs: *(disgustedly)* You sound like my mother. She's always telling me, *(raises voice to mimic his mother)* "Stay away from Mr. McGregor's garden."

Jiggs: Why don't you listen to your mother?

Miggs: Mr. McGregor's vegetables taste so good, I can't stop eating them. Mmmmm.

Jiggs: I have something you'll probably like even better. *(crosses to plate, picks up cookie, and takes it to Miggs)*

Miggs: *(takes cookie and eats)* Mmmmm. That was good. . . . Say, what time is it?

Jiggs: About 3:30.

Miggs: Then I'd better get hopping, before Mom gets hopping mad. She wants me home by 3:30. I hope Mr. McGregor is gone.

Jiggs: I'll check. *(Jiggs moves beyond stage left and looks all around. Returns to center stage)* The coast is clear.

Miggs: Good. *(hops to stage left)* Thanks for the cookie. Thanks for hiding me, too.

Jiggs: You're welcome. *(admonishes)* Now stay away from Mr. McGregor's garden.

Miggs: I will. But I may not stay away from his cookie jar. *(laughs and hops off stage left)*

(Take off rabbit mask. Put on tiger mask.)

Jiggs: *(addresses audience)* It's getting late. I hope nothing has happened to Miggs.

Puppeteer: Ding dong.

Jiggs: Good. My friend is finally here. *(crosses to stage left)*

Miggs: *(enters stage left, wearing tiger mask and growling)* I'm hungry, and I'm going to gobble you up. Grrrr.

Jiggs: *(shakes)* P-please d-don't eat m-me. I-I'll g-give y-you a c-cookie.

Miggs: What's a cookie?

Jiggs: S-something g-good t-to eat.

Miggs: You look good to eat. Mmmmm.

Jiggs: B-but I-I d-don't h-have m-molasses in m-me. C-cookies d-do.

Miggs: Then give me a cookie. **NOW!**

(Still shaking, Jiggs crosses to plate, picks up cookie, and takes it to Miggs.)

Miggs: *(grabs cookie and eats noisily)* That was good. Give me another.

Jiggs: *(shakes)* I-I d-don't h-have anym-more. Y-you c-could b-buy s-some at the b-bakery.

Miggs: I will. Then maybe I'll come back and eat **YOU** for dessert. *(exits stage left, growling)*

(Take off tiger mask.)

Jiggs: *(addresses audience, still shaking)* I'd better make sure all my doors and windows are locked in case that tiger comes back.

Puppeteer: Ding dong.

Jiggs: *(faces stage left and calls)* Go away!

Miggs: *(from offstage)* But you invited me to come over this afternoon.

Jiggs: Is that you, Miggs?

Miggs: *(from offstage)* It sure isn't Santa Claus.

Jiggs: Then come on in.

(Miggs enters stage left.)

Jiggs: *(sighs and wipes brow)* Whew! It really **IS** you.

Miggs: Were you expecting somebody else?

Jiggs: I was afraid you were that tiger coming back to eat me.

Miggs: Tigers don't live around here, Jiggs. Besides, tigers don't eat people.

Jiggs: This one was going to. It said . . .

Miggs: "I'm hungry, and I'm going to gobble you up. Grrrr!"

Jiggs: Yes, that's just what it said, and that's just the way it sounded! How did you know?

Miggs: Because **I** was the tiger.

Jiggs: You're not a tiger. You're a _____.

Miggs: I know, but I was wearing a mask and pretending to be a tiger. I pretended to be the mouse and the rabbit, too.

Jiggs: Why?

Miggs: I got bored cleaning out my closet. When I ran across my old Halloween masks, I thought it would be fun to come over and try to fool you.

Jiggs: Well, you sure scared me with that tiger mask.

Miggs: I'm sorry.

(Jiggs moves up close and looks at Miggs from every angle.)

Note: Fill in the appropriate name of your puppet.

Alternative Dialogue: It's April Fool's Day, so I wanted to play a little joke on you.

Miggs: What are you doing?

Jiggs: I'm trying to figure out if you're wearing another mask, or if this is your **REAL** face.

Miggs: You know very well it's my real face. You see it all the time.

Jiggs: That means it's your real face, all right. If you had a better-looking one, you'd want to wear it all the time.

Miggs: That wasn't a nice thing to say.

Jiggs: *(laughs)* I know. I just wanted to play a little joke on you, because you played one on me.

Alternative Dialogue: April Fool!

Miggs: Are we even now?

Jiggs: Yes, so let's go down to the bakery and get some cookies. You ate all the other ones. *(Miggs and Jiggs exit stage left.)*

Books about Jiggs's Mysterious Visitors

Brett, Jan. *Town Mouse, Country Mouse.* Putnam, 1994.

Cauley, Lorinda B. *Town Mouse and the Country Mouse.* Putnam, 1990.

Potter, Beatrix. *The Tale of Peter Rabbit.* Warne, 1987.

Stevens, Janet. *Town Mouse and the Country Mouse.* Holiday, 1987.

Book for April Fool's Day

Brown, Marc. *Arthur's April Fool.* Little, Brown, 1985.

Books about Wearing Costumes

Allard, Harry. Miss Nelson series. Houghton Mifflin.

Allen, Pamela. *Belinda.* Viking, 1993.

Brooks, Ben. *Lemonade Parade.* Albert Whitman, 1992.

Chevalier, Christa. *Spence Isn't Spence Anymore.* Albert Whitman, 1985.

Polacco, Patricia. *Babushka Baba Yaga.* Putnam, 1993.

Schindel, John. *"Who Are You?"* Simon & Schuster, 1991.

Schneider, Howie. *No Dogs Allowed.* Putnam, 1994.

Books about Mistaken Identity

McKean, Thomas, *Hooray for Grandma Jo!* Crown, 1994.

Wildsmith, Brian. *Bear's Adventure.* Pantheon, 1982.

The Amazing Jiggs

Characters: Jiggs (right hand)
Miggs (left hand)

Props: piece of paper   dish towel
pencil   stuffed rabbit (or rabbit cutout)
magician's hat   a few playing cards

> If you don't have a magician's hat, you can make one by removing the lid from a coffee can or similar cylindrical container and covering it with black paper. Apply glue all around the rim of the can and lay a black paper circle on top of it to make a brim. The circle should be about two to three inches wider than the can with a circle about one quarter of an inch smaller than the can cut from its center. (You might prefer using felt instead of paper, so the brim won't tear when Jiggs puts the hat over Miggs's head.)

Preparation: Tie a string around the rabbit's ears and put it inside the hat with the string hanging out in back. Put dish towel in hat on top of rabbit. Put hat at stage right or on a table at your right. Put the playing cards, the pencil, and the paper to the left of the hat. The cards should be facedown.

(Jiggs stands to the left of the hat, looking down into it.)

Miggs: *(enters stage left)* Hi, Jiggs.

Jiggs: *(turns to face Miggs)* Don't call me Jiggs.

Miggs: But that's your name.

Jiggs: Not anymore. I am now The **AMAZING** Jiggs, the Magician.

Miggs: When did you become a magician?

Jiggs: Yesterday. I read a book of magic tricks at the library. Would you like me to astound, amaze, and mystify you?

Miggs: How are you going to do that?

Jiggs: I shall start by reading your mind. *(picks up paper and gives it to Miggs)* Write something on this paper. Then, without ever having seen what you wrote, I'll tell you what's on the paper.

Miggs: *(puts paper down)* You can't do that!

Jiggs: I can, and I will. Now write something on the paper.

Miggs: Oh, all right, but you'll have to turn around first. *(Jiggs does so. Miggs picks up pencil, writes on paper, and puts pencil down on the stage or in your lap.)* O.K., Jiggs, I've written something.

Jiggs: *(still turned away)* Then step on it.

Miggs: *(surprised)* What?

Jiggs: Step on it. Then I can't see what you wrote.

Miggs: I guess that makes sense. *(stands on paper)*

Jiggs: *(turns around)* Are you ready for me to tell you what's on the paper?

Miggs: **IF** you can.

Jiggs: Of course, I can. Your feet are on the paper! *(laughs)*

Miggs: That wasn't magic, Jiggs. Magic is pulling scarves and rabbits out of hats.

Jiggs: I can do that, too. Watch. *(faces hat and waves arms around)* Abracadabra. Scarf, appear. *(reaches in, pulls out dish towel, waves it around with a flourish and puts it down on the stage or in your lap)* Ta da!

Miggs: *(points)* That isn't a scarf; it's just an old dish towel. *(throws it offstage)*

Jiggs: Use your imagination. I'm just getting started and haven't had a chance to collect fancy props yet. Now, for my next trick, I will pull a rabbit out of the hat. *(faces hat and waves arms)* Abracadabra. Rabbit, appear. *(grabs rabbit's string, pulls rabbit out of hat, grabs its ears, waves it around with a flourish, and puts it down)* Ta da! *(turns to Miggs)* Why aren't you clapping?

Miggs: That wasn't real magic either. You had the rabbit and the dish towel in the hat all along.

Jiggs: I did not. I made them appear by saying the magic words.

Miggs: Then why didn't you let me see the hat before you did the trick?

Jiggs: Hey! You were standing only a few inches away from it. If you couldn't see the hat, you must need glasses.

Miggs: But you didn't let me see the **INSIDE** of the hat.

Jiggs: Now I will. *(picks up hat and puts it upside down over Miggs's head)*

Miggs: *(shakes to make hat spin around)* Help, it's dark in here! Get me out!

Alternative Action: With a movable mouth puppet, move Jiggs in small circles whenever directions call for arm waving.

Jiggs: *(takes hat off Miggs and puts it down)* Now that you've seen the hat, we can go on to my next trick.

Miggs: What's that?

Jiggs: I shall make the rabbit disappear. *(waves arms)* Abracadabra. Rabbit, disappear. *(picks up hat, drops it down on top of rabbit, and spreads arms out)* Ta da!

Miggs: You didn't make the rabbit disappear.

Jiggs: You don't see it, do you?

Miggs: No, because the hat is covering it up. But if I pick the hat up . . . *(reaches for hat)*

Jiggs: *(shouts quickly and waves arms)* Abracadabra. Rabbit, appear.

Miggs: *(picks up hat, sets it aside, picks up rabbit, waves it under Jiggs's nose, and puts it down)* See, the rabbit was here all along.

Jiggs: No, it wasn't. When you picked up the hat, I said the magic words to make the rabbit reappear.

Miggs: *(addresses audience)* Do you believe that? *(turns back to Jiggs)* Neither do I.

Jiggs: *(addresses audience)* Whose side are you on anyway? *(turns to Miggs and points to cards)* Pick a card, any card, and I'll tell you what it is.

Miggs: You mean, you'll **TRY.** Now turn around. *(Jiggs does so. Miggs turns over a card, looks at it, and puts it facedown on the stage or in your lap.)* O.K., Jiggs, what card did I pick?

Jiggs: *(with conviction)* The ace of spades!

Miggs: No.

Jiggs: The jack of clubs!

Miggs: No.

Jiggs: The queen of hearts.

Miggs: No.

Jiggs: *(doubtfully)* The two of diamonds? *(Miggs shakes head.)* The three of diamonds? *(Miggs shakes head. Continue up to the six of diamonds.)*

Miggs: *(exasperated)* Give up, Jiggs. You're just guessing!

Jiggs: *(sounds genuinely surprised)* How did you know?

Miggs: *(shakes head)* Jiggs, you amaze me.

Jiggs: *(triumphantly)* I told you my magic would amaze you.

Miggs: Your magic isn't what amazes me. It's how you always manage to do everything wrong.

Jiggs: I do **NOT** do everything wrong!

Miggs: What do you do that's right?

Jiggs: When I want to learn about something, like how to do magic, I always go to the library and get a book about it. Isn't that the right thing to do?

Miggs: It certainly is. I'm amazed you do something so smart.

Jiggs: *(triumphantly)* I told you! I am The **AMAZING** Jiggs! *(claps)* Let's hear a round of applause. *(bows to each corner of the audience and turns to leave)*

Miggs: Where are you going?

Jiggs: To the library. I want to learn how to draw. Then I can be a great artist as well as an amazing magician. *(exits stage right)*

Miggs: *(addresses audience and shakes head)* Jiggs **IS** amazing because I never know what my friend will come up with next. The library is amazing, too, because you can learn all kinds of cool stuff there. Be sure to visit it next time you want to learn something. Well, good-bye for now. *(exits stage left)*

Stories about Magic

Balian, Lorna. *The Sweet Touch.* Humbug, 1994.

De Paola, Tomie. Strega Nona series.

Dubowski, Cathy W. *Pretty Good Magic.* Random, 1987.

Galdone, Paul. *The Magic Porridge Pot.* Clarion, 1979.

Himmelman, John. *Amanda and the Witch Switch.* Puffin, 1987.

Houck, Eric L., Jr. *Rabbit Surprise.* Crown, 1993.

Howe, James. *Rabbit Cadabra!* Morrow, 1993.

Lester, Helen. *The Wizard, the Fairy, and the Magic Chicken.* Houghton, 1983.

———. *The Revenge of the Magic Chicken.* Houghton, 1990.

Slater, Teddy, retel. *Walt Disney's The Sorcerer's Apprentice Storybook and Magic Tricks.* Disney, 1993.

Detective Jiggs Takes the Case

Characters: Jiggs (right hand)
Miggs (left hand)
Honey Bear (left hand)

Props: badge that says "Junior Detective"
box marked "Junior Detective Kit"
poncho

pair of child's sunglasses
party hat
cookbook

The badge can be a shield cut from yellow paper with the words "Junior Detective" written on it.

You can fashion the detective kit out of a box with a hinged lid (like a cigar box). If you don't have such a box, take an empty graham cracker box or other similar-sized carton. Tape the open flaps shut and cut around the front of it on three edges. Leave the front attached to the rest of the box on its fourth side to make a hinged lid for Jiggs to open and close. Cover the box with brown paper and write "Junior Detective Kit" on it. Place the box so the opening is at the top and the hinge of the lid is at the bottom. Make a handle by taping the ends of a 12″ to 15″ piece of yarn to either side of the box.

The poncho can be a rectangle of felt or other material. Cut a hole in the middle of it so you can slide it over Jiggs's head.

If you don't have sunglasses (or they won't stay on Jiggs's face), cut some lenses and frames out of paper. Cut a piece of yarn long enough to fit around Jiggs's head and attach the ends to either side of the glasses so you can slip them over the puppet's head.

Make a party hat by cutting a half circle out of a bright color of construction paper and making a cone out of it by gluing, taping, or stapling the edges together. Draw polka dots on it with markers or crayons.

If you prefer, you can rewrite the script to allow Jiggs to wear different disguises.

Preparation: Pin detective badge on Jiggs. Put poncho, sunglasses, and hat in box.

SCENE 1: ON THE STREET

(Jiggs enters stage right, carrying box so audience can't see the writing, and crosses stage with head down.)

Jiggs: *(looks around)* There must be some clues here somewhere, and I'll find them. My keen, sharp detective eyes miss nothing.

Miggs: *(enters stage left and crosses to right. Jiggs bumps into Miggs.)* Watch where you're going!

Jiggs: *(puts case down)* I'm sorry. I didn't see you.

Miggs: What are you doing?

Jiggs: Looking for clues. That's what detectives do.

Miggs: You're not a detective.

Jiggs: Yes I am. My Junior Detective Kit came in the mail yesterday. See my badge? *(jumps up close to Miggs and points to badge)* It proves I can solve mysteries now.

Miggs: Wearing a badge doesn't mean you can solve mysteries.

Jiggs: Maybe not, but I've also read most of the detective stories at the library. I'm all ready for my first case. Where are you going?

Miggs: To the store. I need to buy frozen dinners for our supper.

Jiggs: When you invited me over for dinner last week, you said you were going to cook something special.

Miggs: I'd planned to, but now my cookbook is gone. I can't cook without it.

Jiggs: What happened to your cookbook?

Miggs: I don't know. I left it on the kitchen table when I went to bed last night, but when I woke up this morning, it was gone.

Jiggs: The Mystery of the Missing Cookbook will be my first case. I'll go to your house right now and solve it. *(picks up box and carries it off stage left)*

Miggs: And I'll go to the store and buy those frozen dinners. *(exits stage right)*

(Take off Miggs.)

SCENE 2: MIGGS'S KITCHEN

Jiggs: *(Jiggs enters stage left, crosses to center stage, puts down box, and addresses audience.)* If the cookbook was here last night but gone this morning, then somebody must have stolen it. I'll have to find the thief. But how? *(thinks)* Hmmmmm. . . . I know. Criminals always return to the scene of the crime, so I'll just wait here for the thief to walk through that door. *(looks toward stage left for awhile and then addresses audience)* I wonder why the thief isn't coming. *(thinks)* Hmmmmm. . . . I know. The thief knows I'm a detective, so I'll have to disguise myself. *(holds up box)* Good thing I brought along my Junior Detective Kit. *(opens box and looks inside)* Aha! *(pulls out poncho, closes box, and waves poncho around)* This poncho is just the thing to cover up my detective badge. *(Put poncho over Jiggs's head.)* The thief will be here any minute now.

(turns toward stage left. After awhile, Jiggs sighs and addresses audience.) The thief must still be able to recognize me. I wonder how. . . . *(thinks)* Hmmmmm. . . . I know. It must be because of my keen, sharp detective eyes that miss nothing. I'd better cover them up. *(opens box and looks inside)* Aha! *(pulls out sunglasses, closes box, and waves sunglasses around)* These sunglasses will do the trick. *(Put sunglasses on Jiggs. Jiggs faces stage left.)* At any moment, I'll be able to see the thief walk through that door—well, sort of. It's a little hard to see anything with these dark glasses on.

(Jiggs hums for awhile and then addresses audience.) That thief is smarter than I thought if he can recognize me in these disguises. But I am even smarter, so I will put on another disguise. *(opens box and peeks inside)* Aha! I'll put on this party hat. *(pulls out hat, closes box, and waves hat around)* Since everybody loves a party, the thief is sure to come in any minute. *(Put party hat on Jiggs. Jiggs faces stage left for awhile, hums, and then addresses audience.)*

(Put on Honey Bear.)

Jiggs: I can't understand why the thief isn't coming. Now that I'm wearing all these disguises, he can't possibly know who I am. I'm not even sure myself.

Honey Bear: *(enters stage left carrying cookbook, and puts it down on the stage or in your lap)* Hi, Jiggs.

Jiggs: How do you know who I am, Honey Bear?

Honey Bear: Only you would wear such a silly outfit. Don't you know it's too late to go trick-or-treating?

Jiggs: I am **NOT** trick-or-treating. I am solving The Mystery of the Missing Cookbook.

Honey Bear: What a coincidence. I happened to find a cookbook just this morning.

Jiggs: Where?

Honey Bear: *(points)* On the kitchen table here. It had recipes using honey, so I decided to borrow it.

Jiggs: Where is the cookbook now?

Honey Bear: Right here. I've copied all the recipes with honey, so now I'm returning it to Miggs. *(picks up book and holds it out to Jiggs)*

Jiggs: *(grabs book)* I'll take that.

Honey Bear: Good-bye. I'm going home to bake now. *(exits stage left)*

Alternative Dialogue: too early (depending on time of year)

Jiggs: *(waves book and addresses audience)* Aha! I've solved The Mystery of the Missing Cookbook. Miggs will have to agree I'm a good detective now, don't you think?

Puppeteer: If you'd like to be a detective, you'll find plenty of mysteries to solve at the library. Check some out soon.

Books about Detectives

Benchley, Nathaniel. *The Strange Disappearance of Arthur Cluck.* HarperCollins, 1067.

Christelow, Eileen. *Gertrude, the Bulldog Detective.* Houghton, 1992.

Delton, Judy. *Brimhall Turns Detective.* Lerner, 1983.

Hurd, Thacher. *Mystery on the Docks.* HarperCollins, 1983.

Levy, Elizabeth. Something Queer series. Hyperion and Dell.

Sharmat, Marjorie Weinman. Nate the Great series. Putnam.

Yolen, Jane. Piggins series. Harcourt.

PART THREE

Skits from the Library's Shelves

A Monkey for Lunch
A Jataka Fable from India

Characters: Crocodile (left hand)
Monkey (right hand)

> If you have a bear but no monkey, you might try pinning a long tail on it and passing it off as a primate.

Introduction: Hold Monkey behind your back. Ask audience to pretend you're a tree with a river running in front of it.

Crocodile: *(addresses audience)* Hmmmmm, what shall I have for lunch? Usually I eat birds and fish, but I'd rather have something different today. *(thinks)* Hmmmmm, a fried monkey heart would be good, but how could I get one? *(looks up)* Monkeys live 'way up there in the trees, but crocodiles *(looks down)* live 'way down here in the water. *(raises and lowers head quickly as if shrugging)* Oh, well. I'll look for a monkey anyway. Finding one may help me think of a way to catch it.

Puppeteer: The crocodile swam downstream *(Crocodile swims toward stage right)* until he saw a monkey sitting at the top of a tree. *(Bring Monkey out from behind your back and hold it as high as you can at stage right.)*

Monkey: *(moves head as if eating, rubs stomach, spreads arms wide, and says)* Ahhhhh.

Puppeteer: The monkey was eating a banana.

Crocodile: *(looks up and calls)* Hello, Monkey.

Monkey: *(looks down and calls)* Hello, Crocodile.

Crocodile: *(still looking up)* I hope I'm not interrupting your breakfast.

Monkey: *(still looking down)* No. I ate breakfast fifteen minutes ago. The banana was just a snack.

Crocodile: *(still looking up)* If you eat snacks right after breakfast, you must really like food.

Monkey: *(still looking down)* I certainly do. *(rubs stomach)* Especially anything sweet.

Crocodile: *(addresses audience, laughs evilly, and then looks back up at Monkey)* If you like sweet things so much, what are you doing up there in that tree when on the other side of the river *(points stage left),* the mangoes grow sweeter than honey?

Monkey: *(claps hands)* I'd love to go *(hangs head),* but I can't swim. *(wipes tear from eye and sniffs)*

Crocodile: *(addresses audience, laughs evilly, and then looks up at Monkey)* I can. *(very slyly)* Climb on my back, and I'll take you there.

Monkey: *(claps hands)* Oh, boy! That's very nice of you. *(As you slowly lower your arm, Monkey pretends to climb down tree. Then she leaps onto Crocodile's back, and Crocodile swims toward stage left.)*

Monkey: *(spreads arms wide)* Whee! This is fun. You swim very well, Crocodile.

Crocodile: I **DIVE** even better. *(addresses audience and laughs evilly)*

Puppeteer: When he said that, Crocodile dove to the bottom of the river. Monkey had to hold on for dear life. *(Wrap Monkey's arms around Crocodile's neck as you lower the puppets behind the stage or down toward the floor and bring them up again.)* When they surfaced, Monkey had swallowed so much water, she was coughing and choking.

Monkey: *(coughs)* Please don't do that again, Crocodile *(coughs),* or I'll drown. *(Monkey spreads arms and collapses dramatically onto Crocodile's back.)*

Crocodile: *(turns head back to address Monkey)* **THAT'S** what I want. You didn't **REALLY** think I was taking you to eat mangoes, did you?

Monkey: Well, yes.

Crocodile: Fool! It's not **YOUR** appetite I'm worried about; it's **MINE.** *(sinisterly)* I want to eat your heart.

Monkey: Well, why didn't you say so in the first place? If I'd known that, I would have brought my heart along.

Crocodile: You mean, you don't carry it around all the time?

Monkey: No. We monkeys never do. *(sways)* We swing through the trees so much, our hearts would burst *(spreads arms wide)* if we did. *(bends forward, puts one hand confidingly to mouth, and speaks near Crocodile's ear)* I left mine in the tree back there. *(points to stage right)* If you take me back, I'll get it for you.

Note: Move your wrist from side to side so Monkey seems to swing a little.

Puppeteer: So Crocodile went swimming back very fast. *(Crocodile quickly swims toward stage right.)* But Monkey shot up the tree even faster. *(climbs quickly)*

Note: Quickly raise your right arm.

Monkey: *(looks down and calls)* If you want it *(beckons)*, come and get it. *(laughs and exits stage right)*

Puppeteer: That made Crocodile **VERY** angry. But he was determined to catch that monkey anyway.

Note: Make a fist inside the puppet and shake it a little.

Crocodile: *(addresses audience)* But how? I couldn't trick her like that again, not for a million mangoes. If she wanted to cross the river *(looks down),* she'd just use these stepping stones here. *(addresses audience)* Stepping stones! That gives me a **WONDERFUL** idea. If I lie here on this biggest rock *(pretends to lie on a rock),* **VERY** still and **VERY** quiet, the monkey will think that I am part of the rock. And when she climbs on my back *(snaps)*, **I'LL GET HER!** *(laughs evilly)*

Puppeteer: So Crocodile lay on that biggest rock, **VERY** still and **VERY** quiet. After awhile, along came Monkey.

Monkey: *(enters stage right, rubbing stomach)* Oh, boy, oh, boy, oh, boy, I can almost taste those mangoes now. *(taps head)* **WHY** didn't I think of using these stepping stones before?

Puppeteer: Then she stopped.

Monkey: *(addresses audience)* Don't look now, but *(points)* I think that's that crocodile. I'd better find out for sure. *(faces Crocodile and calls)* Hello, Rock.

Puppeteer: She listened *(Monkey listens),* but she didn't hear anything. So she called again.

Monkey: *(calls)* Yoo hoo, Rock!

Puppeteer: She listened *(Monkey listens),* but she still didn't hear anything. So she called again.

Monkey: *(calls)* What's the matter, Rock? Why don't you talk to me the way you do every night?

Crocodile: *(addresses audience)* If this rock talks to the monkey every night, I'd better answer her now or she'll think something's wrong. *(calls)* Hello, Monkey.

Monkey: *(laughs)* I thought it was you, Crocodile. Well, nice chatting with you, but I'd best be running along. Good-bye. *(Monkey runs to stage right and pretends to climb tree.)*

Note: Raise your arm as high as you can.

Puppeteer: Monkey scampered for home, and Crocodile realized he'd never be smart enough to catch her. *(Move Crocodile to stage left.)* So Crocodile went home and had birds and fish for lunch *(pretends to eat)* and never bothered Monkey again.

Folk Tales from India

Backstein, Karen. *The Blind Men and the Elephant.* Scholastic, 1992.

Brown, Marcia. *Once a Mouse.* Simon & Schuster, 1972.

Galdone, Paul. *The Monkey and the Crocodile.* Houghton, 1979.

Gurney, Eric. *The King, the Mice, and the Cheese.* Random, 1986.

Martin, Rafe. *Foolish Rabbit's Big Mistake.* Putnam, 1985.

Newton, Pam. *The Stonecutter.* Putnam, 1990.

Books about Monkeys

Collins, David R. *Ceb's Amazing Tail.* Modern Curriculum, 1987.

Christelow, Eileen. *Five Little Monkeys Sitting in a Tree.* Houghton, 1991.

Galdone, Paul. *Turtle and the Monkey.* Houghton, 1990.

McKissack, Patricia. *Monkey-Monkey's Trick.* Random, 1988.

Myers, Walter Dean. *How Mr. Monkey Saw the Whole World.* Doubleday, 1996.

Perkins, Al. *Hand, Hand, Fingers, Thumb.* Random, 1969.

Rey, H. A. Curious George series. Houghton.

Sierra, Judy. "The Monkey and the Crocodile" and "Counting Crocodiles." In *The Flannel Board Storytelling Book.* Wilson, 1987.

Slobodkina, Esphyr. *Caps for Sale.* HarperCollins, 1947.

Books about Crocodiles

Dumbleton, Mike. *Dial-a-Croc.* Orchard, 1991.

Gomi, Taro. *The Crocodile and the Dentist.* Millbrook, 1994.

Jorgensen, Gail. *Crocodile Beat.* Simon & Schuster, 1989.

Waber, Bernard. Lyle series. Houghton.

The Urge to Scratch
An African Folk Tale

Characters: Monkey (left hand)
Rabbit (right hand)

If you have a bear but no monkey, you might try pinning a long tail on it and letting it pass for a primate.

(Monkey scratches back of head with left paw.)
(Rabbit lifts nose, sniffs loudly, and turns head from side to side.)
(Monkey scratches under right arm.)
(Rabbit lifts nose, sniffs loudly, and turns head from side to side.)
(Monkey scratches stomach with right paw.)
(Rabbit lifts nose, sniffs loudly, and turns head from side to side.)
(Monkey scratches under left arm.)

Rabbit: *(crossly)* Do you **HAVE** to keep scratching? It's very annoying.

Monkey: It's no more irritating than the way **YOU** keep wrinkling up your nose and turning your silly head from side to side.

Rabbit: Maybe I **HAVE** been twitching my nose and turning my head, but I could easily stop.

Monkey: Ha! But I know **I** could stop scratching at any time. *(raises paw to neck but stops quickly and claps hands together)*

Rabbit: Wanna bet?

Monkey: Yes! I'll bet **I** can keep still for the rest of the afternoon, but **YOU'LL** keep sniffing and turning your head.

Rabbit: Well, I'll bet that **I** can keep still for the rest of the afternoon, but **YOU'LL** continue to scratch.

Monkey: You're on. *(shakes Rabbit's paw)* We'll start **NOW**.

(Monkey and Rabbit stand still for a bit, facing the audience. Then each slowly turns toward the other. As soon as one realizes the other is watching, both quickly turn back toward the audience. Repeat this several times.)

Rabbit: *(addresses audience)* I wish I could turn my head all the way around, because I have this terrible feeling that something dreadful is sneaking up behind me.

(Rabbit slowly turns toward Monkey as Monkey slowly turns toward Rabbit. Both turn back quickly to face audience.)

Monkey: *(addresses audience)* My skin feels so dry and itchy, I can't stand it. If only I could scratch without Rabbit seeing.

(Monkey slowly turns toward Rabbit, as Rabbit slowly turns toward Monkey. Both quickly turn back to face audience.)

Rabbit: *(thinks and then addresses audience)* I have an idea. *(taps head with one paw, then turns to face Monkey)* You know, I'm very comfortable and easy in my mind, but I **AM** a little bored. May I tell you a story to make the time go faster?

Monkey: Sure. Go ahead.

Rabbit: Once upon a time I was walking through the forest. *(listens)* When I came to a clearing without any trees or bushes to hide me, I heard a noise off to my left. I turned around *(turns left and shows horror)* and saw a hyena running right at me! Then I heard something off to my right. *(listens)* I looked over there *(turns right and shows horror)* and saw another hyena coming at me! A minute later, I heard noises behind me. *(listens)* Once again I turned around *(turns to face you and shows horror)* and saw hyenas surrounding me on every side! *(turns all the way around)*

Monkey: *(shows excitement)* Let **ME** tell a story now! Please!

Rabbit: Very well.

Monkey: Once upon a time I was walking through a village. *(swings from side to side while humming)* Some nasty little children started throwing stones at me. *(makes throwing motion)* One rock hit me on my ear. *(touches ear)* Another one hit me on my neck. *(touches neck)* The third stone hit me in the stomach *(touches stomach),* and a fourth one grazed me on the arm. *(touches arm).* Pretty soon rocks were pelting me all over. *(Paws fly as they point to different parts of body.)*

Rabbit: *(laughs)* I know why you're telling your story that way.

Monkey: And I know why **YOU** told your story the way **YOU** did. *(laughs)*

(Monkey and Rabbit laugh and roll around onstage or in your lap. Then they stop and stand up.)

Monkey: I haven't lost the bet yet.

Rabbit: Neither have I. We were both just telling stories the way they should be told.

Monkey: That's true. But you have to admit: It's very hard to break a bad habit.

Rabbit: It certainly is.

Alternative Action: If rabbit is a movable mouth puppet, cock its head from side to side.

Monkey: So let's not worry about it anymore. You can sniff and turn your head whenever you want.

Rabbit: *(hugs Monkey)* Thank you. *(lifts nose, sniffs loudly, and turns head from side to side)* Why don't you go ahead and scratch if you feel like it?

Monkey: *(hugs Rabbit)* Thank you. *(scratches and sighs)* **AHHHHH.**

(Monkey scratches and Rabbit turns head from side to side during last line.)

Puppeteer: To this very day, rabbits and monkeys never keep still for very long, unless they are sleeping.

(Rabbit and Monkey collapse and make snoring sounds.)

Books about Breaking Habits

Berenstain, Stan, and Jan Berenstain. *Berenstain Bears and the Bad Habit.* Random, 1987. (nail-biting)

Keller, Holly. *Geraldine's Blanket.* Greenwillow, 1984.

Murphy, Jill. *Last Noo-Noo.* Candlewick, 1995. (pacifier)

Books about Monkeys

See the books listed for the skit "A Monkey for Lunch."

Books about Rabbits

See the books listed for the skits "Only Two Hops," "Brer Wolf Plays House," "Rabbit Makes Trouble," and "Peter Rabbit."

How the Bear Lost Its Tail
A Native American Legend

Characters: Bear (left hand)
Fox (right hand)

Although Native Americans told this pourquoi, or "Why?," story with a fox, any puppet could trick Bear.

Props: tail (cut from paper or fake fur about 16 to 18 inches long)
pin

Preparation: Pin the tail on the bear.

Bear: *(enters stage left and looks around at left of stage)* Oh, dear. Nothing here either. It's hard to find any in the winter.

Fox: *(enters stage right and addresses audience)* I'm so bored, I'd like to do something to stir up a little excitement. *(notices Bear and crosses to stage left)* What are you looking for?

Bear: Something to eat. But I'm not having much luck, because of all the ice and snow. *(sighs)* I've searched all morning, but I can't find even a single nut or berry or root or bug.

Fox: *(distastefully)* Roots? Bugs? Yuck! *(gags)* Why don't you eat fish instead? Mmmmm.

Bear: *(claps)* I'd love to, but *(hangs head)* I don't know how to catch them.

Fox: *(addresses audience, laughs nastily, and turns back to Bear)* Then this is your lucky day because I will gladly teach you.

Bear: *(looks up)* You will?

Fox: There's nothing I'd rather do today. *(addresses audience, laughs nastily, and turns back to Bear)* Come on. Follow me to the river. *(points to right)*

(Puppets move a little to the right.)

Fox: *(looks down behind stage or into space between your legs)* See this hole in the ice?

Bear: *(looks down)* Uh-huh.

Fox: If you want to catch fish, put your tail in it.

Bear: *(shivers)* Brrrrr! It's freezing down there.

Alternative Actions: If you're performing in the open, hold Fox behind your back and have Bear look under your chair, behind your back, etc. If you have space to move, walk around the room and have Bear look into wastebaskets and other unlikely places. As you walk back to your chair, bring Fox out from behind your back.

Alternative Action: If you're performing in the open and wearing slacks, part your knees slightly.

Note: Raise your arm to lift Bear above "hole" and then lower it to make the tail go down behind the stage or between your legs. Then raise your arm up again very quickly to make Bear pull his tail out of the icy water.

Fox: Well, of course. *(looks around)* You can see how the river's almost solid ice.

Bear: It's too cold to stick my tail down there. Couldn't I just lower a stick into the water?

Fox: Not if you want to catch fish. Fish won't bite a stick, but they will bite your tail. Fish like the taste of fur.

Bear: I didn't know that.

Fox: There are a lot of things **BEARS** don't know. But we foxes are very clever and sly. *(addresses audience, laughs nastily, turns back to Bear, and says very slyly)* **TRUST** me.

Bear: *(looks down at "hole," scratches head while shaking it, and says doubtfully)* I don't know.

Fox: Of course, it's all up to you. If you don't **WANT** any fresh, juicy fish *(smacks lips or rubs stomach)*, if you **WANT** to be hungry, *(puts ear next to Bear's stomach)* if you **WANT** your stomach to rumble like thunder . . . **DON'T** put your tail in the hole. It makes no difference to me.

Bear: *(pats stomach)* I **AM** hungry. . . . *(sighs)* Here goes.

Bear: *(shivers)* Brrrrr! *(jumps a little)* Ouch! Something pinched my tail.

Fox: Excellent. That means the fish are biting already.

Bear: *(jumps a little)* Ouch!

Fox: You're lucky. The fish are really biting today.

Bear: *(jumps a little)* Ouch!

Fox: You're going to eat well tonight.

Bear: *(jumps a little)* Ouch!

Fox: Tomorrow, too.

Bear: *(jumps a little)* Ouch!

Fox: You're going to feast for a week.

Bear: *(jumps a little)* Ouch!

Fox: You're doing great. Since you don't need me anymore, I'll be running along. *(turns to go)*

Bear: Thank you for teaching me how to catch fish.

Fox: *(turns back)* You don't need to thank me. When you think you have enough fish, give your tail a good, hard **PULL.** *(pretends to pull and runs off stage right, laughing loudly)*

Note: Raise your arm to lift Bear above "hole" and slowly bring it down to lower tail behind stage or between your legs. Bear ends up sitting on stage or on your legs, with about one-third of his tail not caught between your knees.

Bear: *(watches Fox go and then addresses audience)* He must be laughing because he's happy he helped me. What a nice guy! *(shivers)* Brrrrr! *(jumps a little)* Ouch! I'm cold, and my tail hurts. But I'd better not think about that. I'll think about how good the fish will taste instead. Mmmmm, fish. . . . *(jumps a little)* Ouch! Mmmmm, fish. . . . *(jumps a little)* Ouch! Mmmmm, fish. . . . *(jumps a little)* Ouch! *(shivers)* I'm so cold, and my tail hurts so bad, I can't stand it any longer. I have to go.

    (Bear tries to walk away, but his tail holds him back. He pulls at it a little and then falls forward.) Ouch! *(rubs nose and looks around from his prone position)* Oh, no! The river's frozen solid, and my tail's caught in the ice. *(and says angrily)* That fox tricked me! No wonder he was laughing! *(Bear tries to pull away from the ice, pants and grunts.)*

Bear: *(turns around, looks down, and says very sorrowfully)* Ohhhhh . . . my beautiful tail is gone forever. *(cries)*

Puppeteer: That is why bears today have short, stumpy tails *(turn Bear around to show audience and point to tail if you're performing in the open)* and why they hibernate all winter. *(Lay Bear on the stage or in your lap so he looks as if he's sleeping.)* Now they never again have to go out and look for food when there isn't any.

Note: If you're performing in the open, your legs will hold his tail in place as Bear strains away from it. If you're using a stage, hold the tail with your free hand. As Bear struggles, bend your wrist down, so the puppet leans forward. Move your whole arm forward in different directions. When you're ready to end skit, remove the pin holding Bear's tail in place with your right hand and lift Bear up with your left hand.

Books about Tails

Abolafia, Yossi. *Fox Tale.* Greenwillow, 1991.

Brown, Marc. *The Silly Tail Book.* Parents, 1983.

Burton, Marilee. *Tail Toes Eyes Ears Nose.* HarperCollins, 1988.

Dubanevich, Arlene. *Tom's Tail.* Puffin, 1992.

Ernst, Lisa Campbell. *Walter's Tail.* Simon & Schuster, 1992.

Hogrogian, Nonny. *One Fine Day.* Simon & Schuster, 1971.

Jennings, Linda. *Tom's Tail.* Little, Brown, 1995.

Peet, Bill. *Spooky Tail of Prewitt Peacock.* Houghton, 1979.

Potter, Beatrix. *The Tale of Squirrel Nutkin.* Warne, 1987.

Seuss, Dr. "Gertrude McFuzz." in *Yertle the Turtle & Other Stories.* Random, 1958.

Stevens, Janet. *How the Manx Cat Lost Its Tail.* Harcourt, 1990.

Books about Hibernation

Dabcovich, Lydia. *Sleepy Bear.* Dutton, 1982.

Dodd, Lynley. *Wake Up, Bear.* Gareth Stevens, 1988.

Lemieux, Michele. *What's That Noise?* Morrow, 1985.

Oppenheim, Joanne. *Could It Be?* Bantam, 1990.

Native American *Why* Stories

Bruchac, Joseph. *The Great Ball Game.* Dial, 1994.

Connolly, James E., ed. *Why the Possum's Tail Is Bare: And Other North American Indian Nature Tales.* Stemmer, 1992.

Esbensen, Barbara J. *The Star Maiden.* Little, Brown, 1988.

Goble, Paul. *The Great Race.* Simon & Schuster, 1985.

———. *Iktomi and the Boulder.* Orchard, 1988.

Hausman, Gerald. *How Chipmunk Got Tiny Feet: Native American Animal Origin Stories.* HarperCollins, 1995.

McDermott, Gerald. *Raven.* Harcourt, 1993.

Rodanas, Kristina. *Dance of the Sacred Circle.* Little, Brown, 1994.

Siberell, Anne. *Whale in the Sky.* Dutton, 1982.

Van Laan, Nancy. *Rainbow Crow.* Knopf, 1989.

Books about Bears and Fishing

Asch, Frank. *Just Like Daddy.* Simon & Schuster, 1984.

Gliori, Debi. *Willie Bear and the Wish Fish.* Macmillan, 1995.

Books about Animals in Winter

See the books listed for the skit "Something Good to Eat."

Only Two Hops

A Brer Rabbit Story

Characters: Little Cricket (right hand)
Brer Rabbit (left hand)
Brer Fox (right hand)

Patterns for Little Cricket and Resting Cricket appear in appendix B.
    If your rabbit doesn't have a tail, you can make one for it out of cotton balls or pompoms and pin it to the appropriate place. If you don't have a rabbit, any puppet can play this part. Any other puppet can play Brer Fox.

Props: resting cricket (attached to cardboard ring)

(Move Little Cricket up and down at center stage.)

Puppeteer: One day Little Cricket was fiddling by the side of the road when Brer Rabbit came hopping by.
(Brer Rabbit enters stage left.)

Little Cricket: Howdy, Brer Rabbit. Where are you going?

Brer Rabbit: To town. I've heard the restaurant there serves scrumptious food.

Little Cricket: Mmmmm. May I come, too?

Brer Rabbit: No. You're too little to travel so far.

Little Cricket: *(argues)* I am not!

Brer Rabbit: *(argues)* You are, too!

Little Cricket: *(argues)* I am not!

Brer Rabbit: *(argues)* You are, too!

Little Cricket: *(argues)* I am not!

Brer Rabbit: *(argues)* You are, too.

Little Cricket: *(argues quickly)* I am not! I am not! I am not! In fact, I could get to town faster than you could.

Brer Rabbit: Don't be ridiculous. I could beat you hopping on one foot.

Little Cricket: *(argues)* You could not!

Brer Rabbit: *(argues)* I could, too!

Little Cricket: *(argues)* You could not!

Brer Rabbit: *(argues)* I could, too!

Little Cricket: *(argues)* You could not!

Brer Rabbit: *(argues)* I could, too!

Little Cricket: *(argues quickly)* No, you couldn't! No, you couldn't! No, you couldn't! How long do you think it will take you to get to town?

Brer Rabbit: *(thinks)* Oh, about two hours.

Little Cricket: Two hours? I could get to town, eat a seven-course meal, and be back in less time than that.

Brer Rabbit: *(argues)* You could not!

Little Cricket: *(argues)* I could, too!

Brer Rabbit: *(argues)* You could not!

Little Cricket: *(argues)* I could, too!

Brer Rabbit: *(argues)* You could not!

Little Cricket: *(argues quickly)* Yes, I could! Yes, I could! Yes, I could!

Brer Rabbit: Wanna bet?

Little Cricket: Yes!

Brer Rabbit: Very well then, I'll race you to the restaurant. If you beat me by even an inch, I'll buy your dinner.

Little Cricket: That sounds good to me.

Brer Rabbit: But since **I'LL** win, **YOU'LL** have to buy **MY** dinner. I'm going to order one of everything on the menu.

Little Cricket: We'll just see about that!

Brer Rabbit: We certainly shall. See you later, alligator, much later! *(hops toward stage right, laughing)*

(Put down Little Cricket.)

Puppeteer: Brer Rabbit didn't know it, but Little Cricket jumped onto his tail.

(Slide resting cricket over Brer Rabbit's tail. Put on Brer Fox.)

Brer Rabbit hopped off briskly, never realizing he was giving his opponent a free ride. *(Brer Rabbit hops toward stage right.)*

Brer Fox: *(enters stage right)* Howdy, Brer Rabbit. Where are you off to in such a hurry?

Brer Rabbit: I'm racing Little Cricket to town. That silly insect bet she could beat me. Isn't that a joke?

Brer Fox: *(looks at Brer Rabbit's tail, addresses audience, laughs, and turns back to Brer Rabbit)* Not really. I saw her pass by a long time ago. You'd better run fast if you want to catch up.

(Take off Brer Fox.)

Puppeteer: Brer Rabbit ran and ran and ran and ran. *(Puppet runs very fast from left to right and from right to left several times.)* Of course, no matter how fast he was going, Little Cricket was traveling at the very same speed. When Brer Rabbit got to the restaurant, he collapsed in the road. *(Puppet collapses and pants.)*

(Resting cricket moves off tail and up, over, and down toward stage right to simulate leaping)

Little Cricket leaped off Brer Rabbit's tail and landed on the mat in front of the restaurant.

(Put down resting cricket. Hold up little cricket.)

She yawned and stretched as if she'd been waiting for a long time.

Note: Extend your arm toward the audience and shake the puppet to simulate yawning and stretching.

Little Cricket: What took you so long, Brer Rabbit? Did you stop for a nap along the way?

Brer Rabbit: No! *(suspiciously)* How did you get here so fast?

Little Cricket: I'm such a fantastic jumper, I got here in only two hops.

Brer Rabbit: I don't believe that, but I'll stick to my end of the bargain anyway. Let's go inside, and I'll buy your dinner.

Little Cricket: Good. I'm so hungry, I'm going to order one of everything on the menu. You'd better get some alphabet soup.

Brer Rabbit: Why?

Little Cricket: So you can eat your words. *(laughs)*

(Brer Rabbit and Little Cricket exit stage right.)

Books about Races, Bets, and Contests

Climo, Shirley. *King of the Birds.* HarperCollins, 1991.

Connolly, James E., ed. "How the Turtle Beat the Rabbit" and "The Race Between the Crane and the Hummingbird." In *Why the Possum's Tail Is Bare: And Other North American Indian Nature Tales.* Stemmer, 1992.

Granowsky, Alvin. *Friends at the End.* Raintree Steck-Vaughn, 1996. (a contemporary version of "The Tortoise and the Hare" from the Hare's point of view)

Lowell, Susan. *Tortoise and the Jackrabbit.* Northland, 1994.

Mogensen, Jan. *The Tiger's Breakfast.* Interlink, 1991.

Stevens, Janet. *Tortoise and the Hare.* Holiday, 1984.

Thomas, Jane Resh. *Wheels.* Houghton, 1986.

VanSchuyver, Jan M. "Tortoise and the Hare." In *Storytelling Made Easy with Puppets.* Oryx, 1993.

Vozar, David. *M. C. Turtle and the Hip-hop Hare: A Nursery Rap.* Doubleday, 1995.

Books about Crickets

Carle, Eric. *A Very Quiet Cricket.* Putnam, 1990.

Howe, James. *I Wish I Were a Butterfly.* Harcourt, 1987.

Lobel, Arnold. "The Crickets." In *Mouse Taloc.* HarperCollins, 1977.

Maxner, Joyce. *Nicholas Cricket.* HarperCollins, 1989.

Books about Brer Rabbit

Dickinson, Susan. *Brer Rabbit and the Peanut Patch.* Forest House, 1990.

Faulkner, William J. *Brer Tiger and the Big Wind.* Morrow, 1995.

Hayward, Linda. *Hello, House.* Random, 1988.

———. *All Stuck Up.* Random, 1990.

Jaquith, Priscilla. *Bo Rabbit Smart for True: Tall Tales from the Gullah.* Putnam, 1994.

Lester, Julius. *Further Tales of Uncle Remus.* Dial, 1990.

———. *Last Tales of Uncle Remus.* Dial, 1994.

———. *More Tales of Uncle Remus.* Dial, 1988.

———. *The Tales of Uncle Remus.* Dial, 1987.

Parks, Van Dyke. *Jump.* Harcourt, 1986.

———. *Jump Again.* Harcourt, 1987.

———. *Jump on Over.* Harcourt, 1989.

Weiss, Jacqueline. *Young Brer Rabbit and Other Trickster Tales of the Americas.* Stemmer, 1985.

Books about Tricky Rabbits

See the books listed for the skit "Brer Wolf Plays House."

Brer Wolf Plays House
A Brer Rabbit Story

Characters: Brer Rabbit (left hand)
Brer Wolf (right hand)

If you don't have a wolf, the puppets you use for Brer Bear or Brer Fox could fill in for the title character. You could also substitute any other animal that eats rabbits, for example, a crocodile, a lion, or a cat.

Props: house with a door that opens and closes
(cardboard) tree

You can make the house out of a cardboard box, such as the ones books come in. Cut the flaps off the top. Cover the box with white paper and stand it up on one of its short sides. Draw on windows and a door. Cut along the door on three sides so it will open and close.

Preparation: Put house at center stage with door open. Put tree at stage right.

Brer Rabbit: *(comes out from behind house, closes door firmly, looks around, and stretches)* It's such a beautiful day, I think I'll go for a walk. *(hops off stage left, singing)* "Oh, what a beautiful morning. Oh, what a beautiful day."

Brer Wolf: *(comes out from behind tree and addresses audience)* Now that Brer Rabbit is gone, I'll go into his house and wait for him to come home. When he steps inside that door, *(snaps)* I'll get him. *(laughs)*

(Brer Wolf opens door and walks behind house, leaving door open.)

Brer Rabbit: *(hops in stage left, patting stomach)* Now that I've worked up an appetite, I'll go inside for lunch. *(stops, looks at door, and addresses audience)* Hmmmm, I know I closed the door, but it's open now. That means somebody's in my house. I'd better stay out here until I find out who it is. *(turns to house and calls)* Hello, House! *(listens awhile and then calls)* Hello, House! *(listens awhile and then calls)* Hey, House! Has the cat got your tongue?

Brer Wolf: *(comes out from behind house on right side and addresses audience)* Uh-oh! Brer Rabbit is getting suspicious. *(faces house)* Talk to Brer Rabbit, House!

Brer Rabbit: *(calls)* What's the matter, House? Why aren't you saying, "Howdy, Brer Rabbit"?

Note: Hold Brer Wolf so audience can't see him.

Brer Wolf: *(looks at house and then addresses audience)* I guess the house isn't going to answer tonight, so I'll have to say it myself. *(calls in very low voice)* Howdy, Brer Rabbit.

Brer Rabbit: *(laughs and addresses audience)* That sounds like Brer Wolf. I think I'll have a little fun with him. *(faces house and calls)* You must have a cold, House. Your voice sounds awfully low.

Brer Wolf: *(calls in very high voice)* Howdy, Brer Rabbit.

Brer Rabbit: Now it sounds too high. What's the matter with you?

Brer Wolf: *(calls in regular voice)* Howdy, Brer Rabbit.

Brer Rabbit: *(laughs and beckons)* You might as well come out, Brer Wolf. I recognize your voice.

Brer Wolf: *(stomps out from behind house on left side)* Rats! You've tricked me again!

Brer Rabbit: Why don't you go home and practice sounding like a house, Brer Wolf?

Brer Wolf: I'll go home, you varmint, but I'll think of a way to catch you. You'll be sorry you fooled me, Brer Rabbit; you just wait and see. *(stomps off stage left)*

Brer Rabbit: *(addresses audience)* I'll have to wait a looooong time, because anyone who thinks houses talk isn't smart enough to ever catch me. Brer Wolf will be lucky to catch cold. *(laughs, hops behind house, and pokes head out through door)* 'Bye.

Books about Tricky Rabbits

Aardema, Verna. *Rabbit Makes a Monkey of Lion: A Swahili Tale.* Dial, 1989.

DeSpain, Pleasant. "Dancing Wolves." In *Twenty-Two Splendid Tales,* vol. 1. August House, 1994.

Han, Suzanne C. *Rabbit's Escape.* Holt, 1995.

Johnson, Tony. *The Tale of Rabbit and Coyote.* Putnam, 1994.

McDermott, Gerald. *Zomo the Rabbit.* Harcourt, 1992.

Mayo, Gretchen Will. *Big Trouble for Tricky Rabbit!* Walker, 1994.

———. *Here Comes Tricky Rabbit.* Walker, 1994.

Mora, Francisco X. *Coyote Rings the Wrong Bell.* Children's Pr., 1991.

Shannon, George. *Dance Away!* Greenwillow, 1982.

Shute, Linda. *Rabbit Wishes.* Lothrop, 1995.

Stevens, Janet. *Tops & Bottoms.* Harcourt, 1995.

Books about Brer Rabbit

See the books listed for "Only Two Hops."

Books about Foiled Foxes and Wolves

See the books listed for "Brer Fox Eats the Wash."

African Trickster Tales

See the books listed for "Rabbit Makes Trouble."

Brer Fox's (Not So) Great Idea
A Brer Rabbit Story

Characters: Brer Wolf (left hand)
Brer Fox (right hand for Scene 1 and left hand for Scene 3)
Brer Rabbit (right hand)

Brer Bear could fill in for either Brer Fox or Brer Wolf if you don't have both of these puppets. You could also substitute a lion, a crocodile, or some other creature that might eat rabbits.

Props: handkerchief
bed

You could use a little pillow or baby blanket folded into a small rectangle for a bed.

SCENE 1: IN THE FOREST

Brer Wolf: You know who really makes me mad?

Brer Fox: No. Who?

Brer Wolf: Brer Rabbit, that's who! That pesty varmint's always playing tricks on us.

Brer Fox: Yeah! He's always making fools out of us!

Brer Wolf: Yeah! We have to do something about it!

Brer Fox: Yeah! But what?

Brer Wolf: I don't know. We'll have to give the matter some serious consideration.

Brer Fox: You mean, think about it?

Brer Wolf: Yeah! *(thinks)* Hmmmmm.

Brer Fox: *(thinks)* Hmmmmm . . . *(jumps up and down several times)* I know! I know! I have an idea!

Brer Wolf: *(bobs head up and down while watching Brer Fox)* Then tell me. Don't just jump up and down, making me dizzy. *(moves in small circles and collapses)*

Brer Fox: *(pulls Brer Wolf up)* Here's the plan. I'll go home, jump into bed, and pretend to die. *(collapses)*

Brer Wolf: What good will that do?

Brer Fox: *(jumps up)* You'll go tell Brer Rabbit I'm dead. Since he won't believe you, he'll hop over to my house to check for himself. When he sees me lying in bed, he'll tippy-toe up *(tiptoes)* to get a better look. When he gets close . . .

Brer Wolf: *(snaps)* **YOU'LL GET HIM!** *(laughs)*

Brer Fox: *(laughs)*

Brer Wolf: What a great idea! Now go home, jump into bed, and pretend to die. I'll go to Brer Rabbit's house and tell him the **SAD** news. *(laughs)*

(Brer Fox laughs and then exits stage right.)
(Brer Wolf exits stage left.)

(Take off Brer Fox. Put on Brer Rabbit.)

SCENE 2: ON THE ROAD TO BRER RABBIT'S HOUSE

Brer Wolf: *(addresses audience)* Here I am on the road to Brer Rabbit's house. *(looks toward stage right and then addresses audience)* I think I see that varmint coming now. I'd better act sad. *(cries loudly and artificially)*

Brer Rabbit: *(hops in stage right, carrying handkerchief; crosses to Brer Wolf; wipes Brer Wolf's eyes)* What's the matter?

Brer Wolf: Haven't you heard? *(cries)*

Brer Rabbit: *(wipes Brer Wolf's eyes)* Heard what?

Brer Wolf: The sad news! *(cries)*

Brer Rabbit: *(wipes Brer Wolf's eyes)* What sad news?

Brer Wolf: The sad news about Brer Fox! *(cries)*

Brer Rabbit: *(wipes Brer Wolf's eyes)* What about Brer Fox?

Brer Wolf: He's dead! *(cries)*

Brer Rabbit: *(wipes Brer Wolf's eyes)* What? Brer Fox is dead?

Brer Wolf: Yes. He died this morning. Hadn't you heard?

Brer Rabbit: Not a word.

Brer Wolf: Maybe I'm the only one who knows. I'd better go tell his friends. *(cries)*

Brer Rabbit: *(wipes Brer Wolf's eyes and then holds handkerchief out)* Would you like to take my handkerchief?

Brer Wolf: Thank you. I'll need it. *(takes handkerchief and exits stage left, crying)*

(Take off Brer Wolf. Put on Brer Fox.)

Brer Rabbit: *(watches Brer Wolf leave, rubs chin, and addresses audience thoughtfully)* This sounds like some sort of trick to me. I'd better go over to Brer Fox's house and see what's up. *(hops off stage left)*

(Put bed at stage left.)

SCENE 3: BRER FOX'S HOUSE

Brer Fox: *(staggers, coughs, staggers, and collapses on bed; after a slight pause, stands up, laughs evilly, and addresses audience)* Now that I'm "dead," I'll just wait for Brer Rabbit to come along. *(collapses on bed; after a slight pause, stands up, laughs evilly, and addresses audience)* He won't believe I'm dead, so he'll come tippy-toeing up to my bed for a closer look. *(tiptoes)* When he comes close . . . *(snaps)* I'll get him! *(laughs and then listens)* I think I hear that varmint now. *(collapses on bed)*

Brer Rabbit: *(enters stage right slowly and addresses audience)* Here I am, just outside Brer Fox's house. I'd better check to make sure there aren't any traps. *(looks all around and then addresses audience)* I guess it's safe to go a little closer. *(takes two small hops toward Brer Fox, stops, and points while addressing audience)* There's Brer Fox. *(leans forward and tilts his head first to one side and then to the other; addresses audience)* He looks pretty dead to me, but I don't know. *(raises voice a little)* You can't tell for sure a fox is **REALLY** dead until he starts shaking his left front leg. *(looks at Brer Fox; Brer Fox shakes left front leg.)*

Brer Rabbit: *(laughs)* You can't fool me, Brer Fox. 'Bye. *(turns and runs off stage right)*

Brer Fox: *(stands up)* Rats! That varmint tricked me again!

Alternative Action: If Brer Rabbit is a movable mouth puppet, cock his head from side to side.

Alternative Dialogue: If your fox puppet doesn't have arms that move, Brer Rabbit can say, ". . . dead until his mouth drops open."
Alternative Action: Drop Brer Fox's mouth open.

Books about Playing Dead

DeSpain, Pleasant. "Reynard and the Fisherman." In *Twenty-Two Splendid Tales,* vol. 1. August House, 1994.

Hartley, Deborah. *Up North in Winter.* Dutton, 1986.

Kimmel, Eric A. *Four Dollars & Fifty Cents.* Holiday, 1990.

Books about Brer Rabbit

See the books listed for the skit "Only Two Hops."

Books about Foiled Foxes and Wolves

See the books listed for the skit "Brer Fox Eats the Wash."

African Trickster Tales

See the books listed for the skit "Rabbit Makes Trouble."

Books about Tricky Rabbits

See the books listed for the skit "Brer Wolf Plays House."

Who's Really Better?
A Jataka Fable from India

Characters: Elephant (left hand)
Monkey (right hand)
Wise Woman (left hand)

If you have a mouse but no elephant, try putting a trunk (a gray sock or strip of material) over its nose. If you have a bear but no monkey, try pinning a long tail on it. Any puppet could play Wise Woman's part.

Props: (cardboard) tree
mango (cutout)

Tear off a strip of tape about two to three inches long and make a loop out of it by bringing the ends together. Use this to loosely attach a mango cutout to your cardboard tree. Velcro would work, too.

SCENE 1: IN THE FOREST

Monkey: *(sings saucily)* "Nanny, nanny, boo-boo. You can't do what I do."

Elephant: What do you mean?

Monkey: I'm nimble and quick, so I can climb trees and swing by my tail. You can't.

Elephant: I wouldn't want to. It's better to be big and strong.

Monkey: *(argues)* No, it's not!

Elephant: *(argues)* Yes, it is!

Monkey: *(argues)* No, it's not!

Elephant: *(argues)* Yes, it is!

Monkey: *(argues)* No, it's not!

Elephant: *(argues)* Yes, it is!

Monkey: *(argues)* No, it's not! You just don't want to admit it, but I'm really better than you are.

Elephant: *(argues)* No, you're not!

Monkey: *(argues)* Yes, I am!

Elephant: *(argues)* No, you're not!

Monkey: *(argues)* Yes, I am!

Note: Move your arm from side to side to make Monkey swing.

Elephant: *(argues)* No, you're not!

Monkey: *(argues)* Yes, I am!

Elephant: I'm not going to waste any more time arguing with you because I know I'm better, and that's that! *(stomps off stage left)*

(Take off Elephant. Put on Wise Woman.)

Monkey: Humph! I'm really better than that old Elephant, but what can I do to convince him? *(thinks)* I know. I'll ask the Wise Woman to tell him how much better I am. He'll have to believe her, because everyone respects her great knowledge and wisdom. *(crosses to stage left and calls)* Wise Woman! Are you there?

Wise Woman: *(enters stage left)* Yes, Monkey? What brings you here?

Monkey: I want you to settle an argument for me. Go to Elephant's house and tell him I'm better than he is. I've already told him, but he won't believe me.

Wise Woman: What makes you think that I think you're better than Elephant?

Monkey: You're so wise, you must know a monkey is obviously far superior to a mere elephant.

Wise Woman: Before I tell Elephant anything, you'll have to prove to me that you're better.

Monkey: *(cockily)* Piece of cake! What do you want me to do?

Wise Woman: Go to the island in the middle of the river. Pick a mango from the tree there and bring it back to me.

Monkey: *(shakes Wise Woman's hand)* You got it! Now don't go away. I'll be right back. *(runs off stage right)*

Wise Woman: *(addresses audience)* I'm not so sure about that. *(exits stage left)*

(Take off Wise Woman. Put on Elephant.)

SCENE 2: AT THE RIVER

Monkey: *(enters stage left and looks down)* Oh, dear, the current in the river is very strong. If I try to swim in it, I'll probably drown. *(cries)*

Elephant: *(enters stage left behind Monkey)* Aha! I see you've finally realized I'm better than you are.

Monkey: *(turns around and says indignantly)* I did not!

Elephant: Then why are you crying?

Monkey: Because I'll probably drown if I try to cross the river. *(cries)*

Elephant: Then stay on the shore.

Monkey: I can't. I have to get to the island and pick a mango from the tree there. Wise Woman said that would prove I'm better than you.

Elephant: If picking a mango will prove which of us is the better, then **I'LL** pick one myself. The current won't bother **ME**, because **I'M** big and strong. Climb on my back, so you can come along and watch how superior I am.

(Monkey climbs onto Elephant's back. Elephant swims across stage and exits stage right.)

(Put up tree near stage right but not at the very edge. Leave room for the monkey to stand there later.)

SCENE 3: ON THE ISLAND

(Elephant enters stage left and swims to center stage. Monkey hops off Elephant's back and lands in front of the tree.)

Elephant: *(pushes Monkey back)* Out of my way! I'm going to pick the mango now.

(Monkey goes behind tree and reappears on right side of it.)

(Elephant reaches up, but mango is too high. He jumps up and down, holding his arm up, trying to reach the mango.)

Alternative Action: If Elephant is a movable mouth puppet, open and close his mouth as you make him jump.

Monkey: *(laughs and sings)* "Nanny, nanny, bo-bo. You can't pick the mango."

Elephant: Yes, I can. I'll get a running start, and then I can jump higher. *(Elephant walks to stage left, turns around, and runs to center stage. He jumps forward and falls flat on his face.)*

Elephant: *(stands up; rubs nose)* Ouch!

Alternative Action: For a movable mouth puppet, wrinkle its nose.

Monkey: *(laughs)* Why don't you just admit you can't get it?

Elephant: Because I can! I'll just knock down the whole stupid tree. *(Elephant leans over, puts head against tree trunk, and pretends to push very hard. Finally he collapses and pants.)*

Monkey: *(crosses over, leans over, and puts face in Elephant's)* Give up? *(stands up)* Then **I'LL** get the mango.

Elephant: *(stands up and says very scornfully)* Don't be silly! If **I** can't knock the tree down, **YOU** certainly can't.

Monkey: I don't have to. I can just climb right up and pick the fruit. *(Monkey climbs up tree, picks mango, and climbs back down.)*

Monkey: *(waves mango in Elephant's face and sings)* "Nanny, nanny, boo-boo. You couldn't do what I do." Now I'll take this back to the Wise Woman to prove I'm better than you are.

Elephant: How are you going to cross the river?

Monkey: Same way I got here, of course.

Elephant: Aha! You got here because **I** brought you. That proves **I'M** better, so **I'LL** take the mango to her. *(pulls fruit out of Monkey's hands)*

Monkey: You will not! *(pulls fruit out of Elephant's hands)* **I'LL** take it back, because **I'M** the one who actually picked it.

(Elephant grabs mango, and the two engage in a tug of war.)

Elephant: You couldn't have picked it without my help!

Monkey: Well, you couldn't have gotten it without me!

Elephant: *(lets go of mango)* Did you hear what we just said? I couldn't have gotten the mango without you, but you couldn't have picked it without my help in getting here.

Monkey: That's true. It's good to be quick and nimble, but it's also good to be big and strong.

Elephant: Right! And by working together, we can do things neither of us could do alone.

Monkey: You know . . . working together is good, but eating together is even better. Let's share this mango. *(puts mango down)* *(Both animals bend over and eat. Then they stand up.)*

Elephant: Mmmmm, that was delicious.

Monkey: It certainly was.

Elephant: It's good to agree with you on something, my friend.

Monkey: I couldn't agree with you more, friend. *(hugs Elephant)*

Note: Bend your left wrist back and your right wrist forward. Then bend your right wrist back and your left wrist forward. Repeat this several times. If your puppets don't have movable arms, eliminate the tug of war.

Books about Elephants

Caple, Kathy. *Biggest Nose.* Houghton, 1985.

Cole, Joanna. *Aren't You Forgetting Something, Fiona?* Parents, 1984.

Giannini, Enzo. *Zorina Ballerina.* Simon & Schuster, 1993.

Kipling, Rudyard. *The Elephant's Child* (any version)

Mogensen, Jan. *The Tiger's Breakfast.* Interlink, 1991.

Peet, Bill. *The Ant and the Elephant.* Houghton, 1980.

———. *Ella.* Houghton Mifflin, 1964.

———. *Encore for Eleanor.* Houghton, 1981.

Seuss, Dr. *Horton Hatches the Egg.* Random, 1940.

———. *Horton Hears a Who.* Random, 1954.

Smath, Jerry. *But No Elephants.* Parents, 1979.

Thaler, Mike. *Never Mail an Elephant.* Troll, 1993.

Books about Bragging

Mogensen, Jan. *The Tiger's Breakfast*. Interlink, 1991.

Seuss, Dr. "The Big Brag." In *Yertle the Turtle & Other Stories*. Random, 1958.

"The Tortoise and the Hare" (any version, see the books listed for the skit "Only Two Hops")

Wilhelm, Hans. *The Big Boasting Battle*. Scholastic, 1995.

Folk Tales from India and Books about Monkeys

See the books listed for the skit "A Monkey for Lunch."

The Fox and the Crane
An Aesop Fable

Characters: Fox (right hand)
Crane [Bird with Long Beak] (left hand)

> You could substitute any animal for the fox if you substitute the word *trick* for *outfox*. (See the alternative dialogue.)

Props: two plates
two tall vases

> Bud vases work well. If you don't have any, use pop bottles or just cut some vases out of light cardboard and tape them to small boxes or blocks to make them stand.

SCENE 1: FOX'S HOUSE

(Fox puts two plates down on the stage or in your lap.)

Crane: *(calls from offstage)* Yoo hoo, Fox! May I come in?

Fox: *(beckons)* Please do.

(Crane enters stage left.)

Fox: I'm so glad you could come to lunch today, I fixed chili. *(points to plates)* I know that's one of your favorite dishes.

Crane: *(looks at plates)* Mmmmm. It looks good.

Fox: It tastes even better. Sit down and eat.

(Fox bends over and licks the plate noisily.)

Crane: *(looks down at plate and then addresses audience)* Fox knows I can't eat off a plate with this long beak. But I'll fix him for being so rude.

Fox: *(straightens up and addresses audience)* Mmmmm. That was certainly delicious. *(turns to Crane)* Why aren't you eating? *(addresses audience)* As if I didn't know. *(laughs evilly)*

Crane: It's much too spicy for my taste. You're not a very good cook, I'm afraid.

Fox: I may not be good at cooking, but I'm **VERY** good at playing tricks.

Crane: You shouldn't be so quick to fool folks. Somebody may trick you someday.

Fox: Ha! Nobody could ever trick me!

Crane: Are you sure?

Fox: So sure, I'd eat my words if anyone did.

Crane: Well, I'm sure I couldn't outfox a fox *(addresses audience, laughs, and then turns back to Fox),* but I know I can out-cook one. If you come to my house at noon tomorrow, you can taste for yourself how good my chili is.

Fox: I'll be there! Mmmmm!

Crane: Good. I'll see you then. *(exits stage left)*

Fox: I'm glad she didn't get mad about my little joke. Well, I'd better do these dishes now. *(picks up plates and carries them off stage right)*

SCENE 2: CRANE'S HOUSE

(Crane sets two tall vases on the stage or in your lap.)

Fox: *(calls from offstage)* Yoo hoo, Crane, I'm here.

Crane: *(beckons)* Then come on in.

(Fox enters stage right.)

Crane: Please sit down. *(points to vases)* Everything's ready.

Fox: Good. *(pats stomach)* I'm starved.

Crane: *(pushes vase toward Fox)* Then dig in. *(addresses audience)* **IF** he can! *(laughs)*

(Crane sticks the tip of beak in a vase and eats.)

Fox: *(tries to stick nose in vase, but bumps it)* Ouch! *(rubs nose, sticks nose in vase again, but bumps it)* Ouch! *(rubs nose and addresses audience)* Rats! I can't get my tongue inside this skinny vase. Crane must be paying me back for tricking her yesterday. *(tries to stick nose in vase, bumps it, and rubs it)* Ouch!

Crane: *(turns to Fox)* Mmmmm, wasn't that good?

Fox: How should I know? I never even got to taste it.

Crane: That's why it's time for dessert.

Fox: What are we having?

Crane: I thought you'd like some alphabet soup.

Fox: I'd prefer chocolate cake.

Crane: But don't you remember? You said you'd eat your words if anyone ever outfoxed you.

Alternative Dialogue: Use "trick" for "outfox" and name the alternative animal if using one.

Alternative Action: If Fox is a movable mouth puppet, wrinkle his nose.

Alternative Dialogue: . . . tricked you.

Fox: *(sighs)* You've got me there, so I'll eat the soup. But you'll have to serve it in something I can put my tongue in. *(tries to stick nose in the vase and bumps it)* Ouch! *(rubs nose)*

Books with Fables

Bierhorst, John. *Dr. Coyote.* Simon & Schuster, 1987.

Kraus, Robert. *Fables Aesop Never Wrote.* Viking, 1994.

Lobel, Arnold. *Fables.* HarperCollins, 1980.

Miller, Edna. *Mousekin's Fables.* Prentice-Hall, 1982.

Yolen, Jane. *A Sip of Aesop.* Scholastic, 1995.

Books about Tricksters Being Tricked

Abolafia, Yossi. *Fox Tale.* Greenwillow, 1991.

Cushman, Doug. *Possum Stew.* Dutton, 1990.

Galdone, Paul. *What's in Fox's Sack?* Houghton, 1982.

See also the books listed for the skits "Brer Fox Eats the Wash" and "Rabbit Makes Trouble."

Something Good to Eat
A Chinese Fable

Characters: Rabbit (right hand)
Raccoon (right hand)
Cow (left hand)
Pig (left hand)

You can use any puppets you have for this Chinese fable.

Props: two turnips (or cardboard cutouts)
"snow" (bag of cotton balls, air-popped popcorn, white confetti, or Styrofoam packing material)

Preparation: Hold the bag of "snow" in your lap. Whenever a puppet mentions the weather, raise your free hand as high as you can and drop a handful of "snow" on the puppet.

Put turnips at center stage.

Rabbit: *(enters stage right, addresses audience, and shivers)* Brrrrr! It's cold! And with all this snow on the ground, it's hard to find food. *(looks around)* Oh, yum! Turnips! *(eats one noisily)* Mmmmm, that was good. Now I'll eat the other one.

(bends over, pauses, and then straightens up) Maybe my friend, Raccoon, doesn't have anything to eat on this cold and snowy day. I shall take my other turnip to him. *(picks up turnip, carries it to stage left, puts it down on the stage or in your lap, and calls)* I have a present for you, Raccoon. Come and get it. *(After a pause, Rabbit addresses audience.)* I guess Raccoon isn't home, so I'll leave the turnip here on his doorstep. *(hops off stage right)*

(Take off Rabbit. Put on Raccoon.)

Raccoon: *(enters stage right and speaks while crossing to stage left)* I can't believe I was lucky enough to find something to eat on such a cold and snowy day, but those potatoes were delicious. Mmmmm. *(arrives at stage left, looks down at turnip, and addresses audience)* Now how did this turnip get here? *(pats stomach)* It looks very good, but I'd better not eat it myself. I've already had potatoes. Maybe my friend, Cow, has nothing to eat. *(picks up turnip, carries it across stage, puts it down on the stage or in your lap, faces stage right, and calls)* Yoo hoo! Anybody home? *(after a pause, addresses audience)* I guess not, so I'll leave the turnip here on the doorstep. *(exits stage left)*

(Take off Raccoon. Put on Cow.)

Cow: *(enters stage left and speaks while crossing to stage right)* Mmmmm, those leaves were good. I can't believe I was able to find something so delicious on such a cold and snowy day. *(arrives at stage right and looks down)* Now how did this get here? *(pats stomach)* It looks good, but I'm full. Besides, my friend, Pig, probably couldn't find anything to eat during this snowstorm. I'll take the turnip to her. *(picks up turnip, carries it to stage left, puts it down on the stage or in your lap, and calls)* Special delivery, Pig! *(after a while, addresses audience)* Pig must not be home. I guess it will be okay to just leave the turnip on the door-step. *(exits stage right)*

(Take off Cow. Put Pig on left hand. Put Rabbit on right hand after Pig has talked about the snowy day.)

Pig: *(enters stage right and speaks while crossing to stage left)* Mmmmm, that was the best cabbage I ever ate. I was awfully lucky to find it on such a cold and snowy day. *(arrives at stage left and looks down)* What's this doing here? I like turnips, but it wouldn't be fair for me to eat this one. After all, I had that scrumptious cabbage, but my friend, Little Rabbit, probably doesn't have anything to eat today. I'll take this to her. *(picks up turnip)*

(Lay Rabbit at stage right with her back to Pig.)

Pig: *(carries turnip across stage, puts it down behind the sleeping puppet, and addresses audience)* I don't want to wake Little Rabbit, so I'll just leave this here. *(puts hand in front of mouth)* Shhhhh. *(tiptoes off stage left)*

Rabbit: *(stands up, yawns, stretches, and then looks down at turnip)* I must be dreaming. That looks like a turnip. *(eats it and addresses audience)* Mmmmm. If that was a dream, it was the best-tasting one I've ever had.

Books about Turnips

Parkinson, Kathy. *Enormous Turnip.* Albert Whitman, 1985.

Sierra, Judy. "The Turnip" and "The Goat in the Turnip Field." In *The Flannel Board Storytelling Book.* Wilson, 1987.

Books about Animals in Winter

Brett, Jan. *The Mitten.* Putnam, 1990.

Dabcovich, Lydia. *Sleepy Bear.* Dutton, 1982.

Keller, Holly. *Geraldine's Big Snow.* Greenwillow, 1988.

Minarik, Else Holmelund. "What Will Little Bear Wear?" In *Little Bear.* HarperCollins, 1957.

Pfister, Marcus. *Hopper.* North-South, 1991.

Singer, Bill. *The Fox with Cold Feet.* Parents, 1980.

Stoeke, Janet Morgan. *A Hat for Minerva Louise.* Dutton, 1994.

Tresselt, Alvin. *The Mitten.* Lothrop, 1964.

Van Leeuwen, Jean. *Oliver & Amanda and the Big Snow*. Dial, 1995.

Warren, Jean, comp. "The Rabbit Who Ate the Snowman's Nose." In *Short Short Stories*. Warren, 1987.

Skit about Animals in Winter

See the skit "How the Bear Lost Its Tail."

Books about Rabbits and Vegetables

See the books listed for the skit "Peter Rabbit."

Rabbit Makes Trouble
An African Trickster Tale

Characters: Raccoon (left hand)
Bear (right hand)
Rabbit (left hand for Scene 1 and first part of Scene 2; right
hand for second part of Scene 2)

> You could use other animals who like fish and honey. You could also
> revise the skit slightly to include animals that like different foods.

Props: (cardboard) tree
fish
jar of honey

> You can cut both fish and jar from paper. You could also use a small
> bottle, such as the kind vitamins come in, for the honey.

Preparation: Set tree at center stage.

SCENE 1: BY THE TREE

*(Raccoon enters stage left, carrying fish; crosses to tree; and puts
down fish.)*

*(Bear enters stage right, carrying honey; crosses to tree; and puts
down honey.)*

Raccoon: Good afternoon, friend. You're right on time for our
meeting.

Bear: So are you. *(looks down at fish)* I see you had a good day of
fishing.

Raccoon: I certainly did. As usual, I caught more than I can eat, so
this is for you. *(picks up fish and holds it out toward Bear)*

Bear: *(takes fish and puts it down in front of himself)* Thanks. I
have something for you, too, because I found a very fine
bee tree today. It had enough honey to give us both a
feast. *(picks up honey and holds it out toward Raccoon)*

Raccoon: Thank you. *(takes honey and puts it down in front of self)*
Mmmmm. I'm glad you're good at finding honey.

Bear: I'm glad **YOU'RE** good at catching fish.

Raccoon: Now let's go home and get good at eating!

Bear: Great idea! See you tomorrow.

Raccoon: Yes, same time, same place. 'Bye.

Bear: 'Bye.

(Raccoon picks up honey and exits stage left. Bear picks up fish and exits stage right.)

(Take off Raccoon. Put on Rabbit.)

Rabbit: *(hops out from behind tree and addresses audience)* I'm glad I stopped to rest behind this tree today. Now that I know Bear and Raccoon exchange goodies every afternoon, I can think of a way to got oome for myoclf. *(thinks)* Hmmmm. I know. I'll come back tomorrow and carry out my plan. *(hops off stage left)*

SCENE 2: BY THE TREE ON THE NEXT DAY

Rabbit: *(hops in stage left, crosses to tree, and addresses audience)* I'm a little early for the meeting. I hope the others don't get here at the same time.

(Bear enters stage right, carrying honey, and crosses to tree.)

Rabbit: Hello, Bear. What's in the jar?

Bear: *(puts jar down)* Some honey for my friend, Raccoon.

Rabbit: Uh-oh! You'd better not give that to him.

Bear: Why not? Raccoon loves my honey.

Rabbit: Not anymore. When I saw him just a few minutes ago, he told me your honey gave him a terrible stomachache yesterday. He was sick all night long.

Bear: I'm sorry to hear that.

Rabbit: Not as sorry as you'll be when Raccoon catches up with you. He's planning to scratch your eyes out.

Bear: Uh-oh!

Rabbit: He'll probably come looking for you here any minute now. Better run home and lock your door.

(Bear turns around and runs off stage right.)

(Take off Bear.)

Rabbit: *(addresses audience and laughs)* My plan is working! I'll hide the honey behind the tree and wait for Raccoon. *(picks up honey and hops behind tree)*

(Take off Rabbit. Put Raccoon on left hand. Put Rabbit on right hand.)

(Rabbit hops out from behind tree and looks toward stage left.)

(Raccoon enters stage left, carrying fish, and crosses to tree.)

Rabbit: Good-bye, Raccoon.

Raccoon: *(puts down fish)* I'm not going anywhere.

Rabbit: Then you're really brave!

Raccoon: What do you mean?

Rabbit: If Bear were as angry with me as he is with you, I'd be running away so fast you'd eat my dust.

Raccoon: Bear isn't angry with me.

Rabbit: Oh yes, he is! Only a few minutes ago, he was here looking for you and saying he wanted to sink his teeth into you!

Raccoon: Why?

Rabbit: He choked on the bones in that fish you gave him yesterday and almost died!

Raccoon: *(shows horror)* That's awful! No wonder he's angry.

Rabbit: He's not angry, he's furious! *(admonishes)* You'd better go home immediately and stay there until Bear's had plenty of time to cool off.

(Raccoon runs off stage left.)

Rabbit: *(picks up fish, addresses audience, and laughs)* It looks as if I'll eat well tonight. Mmmmm. *(hops behind tree, picks up honey, and hops off stage left)*

(Take off Rabbit. Put on Bear. Remove tree.)

SCENE 3: ABOUT A WEEK LATER

Raccoon: *(enters stage left, carrying fish; sets fish down at center stage; and wipes brow)* Whew! I'm so tired from fishing, I think I'll lie down and rest. *(lies down facing stage left)*

Bear: *(enters stage right, looking all around)* Now where did that bee go? *(crosses stage while looking all around and trips over Raccoon)*

Raccoon: *(jumps up)* Hey! *(turns around)* Oh, it's you.

Bear: Yes. Are you still angry with me?

Raccoon: You're the one who's angry. Rabbit told me how you wanted to bite me.

Bear: He did?

Raccoon: Uh-huh. He told me you were mad because you'd choked on the fish I gave you.

Bear: Then he's tricked us both. He said you were mad because you'd gotten really sick on the honey I gave you.

Raccoon: I don't know **WHY** we ever believed him. We know what a troublemaker he is.

Bear: Let's promise ourselves we won't ever let him break up our friendship again.

Raccoon: It's a deal! *(shakes Bear's hand)*

Bear: Would you like to come honey-hunting with me? I've been following a bee all day, and I think it went that way. *(points off stage left)*

Raccoon: I'll be happy to . . . as long as you accept this present from me. *(picks up fish and holds it out to Bear)*

Bear: With pleasure. Now let's go. *(takes fish)*

(Raccoon puts paw around Bear, and they exit stage left.)

Alternative Action: If Raccoon is a movable mouth puppet, have him lean against Bear as they exit.

African Trickster Tales

Aardema, Verna. *Anansi Finds a Fool.* Dial, 1992.

———. *Rabbit Makes a Monkey of Lion.* Dial, 1989.

———. *Who's in Rabbit's House?* Dial, 1979.

Hadithi, Mwenye. *Crafty Chameleon.* Little, Brown, 1987.

———. *Tricky Tortoise.* Little, Brown, 1992.

Kimmel, Eric A. *Anansi and the Talking Melon.* Holiday, 1994.

———. *Anansi Goes Fishing.* Holiday, 1991.

Knutson, Barbara. *Sungura and Leopard.* Little, Brown, 1993.

McDermott, Gerald. *Zomo the Rabbit.* Harcourt, 1992.

McKissack, Patricia. *Monkey-Monkey's Trick.* Random, 1988.

Books about Tricky Rabbits

See the books listed for the skits "Only Two Hops" and "Brer Wolf Plays House."

Moon Rock Soup
A Variation of "Stone Soup"

Characters: Person (right hand)
Alien (left hand)

> Person can be either male or female and of any age. If you don't have any people, you could substitute any type of puppet. If the puppet is male, change the pronoun references accordingly for the lines marked with an asterisk (✱) in the right-hand column.

Props:

stove	potatoes
pan with spoon leaning against side of it	container of milk
	peas
rock	carrots
sack of flour	bowl

> The stove can be a rectangle of white Styrofoam or a white gift box such as shirts come in. Draw four circles on it with a black marker to make burners.
>
> You can cut the sack of flour, container of milk, potatoes, and peas and carrots out of paper or cardboard.
>
> If you remove the label and cap, a small white bottle (such as vitamins come in) could serve as a gallon of milk.

Preparation: Set stove at stage right.

Person: *(enters stage right, carrying pan with spoon in it; sets pan on stove)* I'd better start the soup now, so it will be done by suppertime.

Puppeteer: *Ding dong.*

Person: *(faces stage left and calls)* Who's there?

Alien: *(from offstage)* An alien from outer space.

Person: *(addresses audience and laughs)* It must be the girl next door. She just loves to play jokes. *(faces stage left and calls)* Come on in, Nicky.

Alien: *(enters stage left)* My name is not Nicky. It is Eep.

Person: *(claps)* Great costume, Nicky. Be sure to save it for Halloween.

Alien: I am not Nicky. I am Eep, an alien from outer space.

Person: *(laughs)* I love your sense of humor, dear. *(pats Alien's arm and then looks at it from head to toe)* What on earth did you do to make yourself taller?

Alien: I did nothing on earth. I am a creature from another planet. *(Person jumps back and screams.)*

Alien: Do not be alarmed. I did not come to harm you.

Person: *(suspiciously)* Why **DID** you come?

Alien: My spaceship ran out of fuel.

Person: Then you shouldn't be here. You should go to the gas station down the street.

Alien: My spaceship runs on vegetable soup instead of gas. Do you have any?

Person: No. I don't have any food at all. And even if I did, I wouldn't give it to an alien who's come to invade the planet.

Alien: I did not come to invade your planet. I got lost on my way to Mars and had to land here when I ran out of fuel.

Person: That's too bad, but you'll just have to get your vegetable soup somewhere else. I don't have anything for you here.

Alien: You don't have any food in your cupboards at all?

Person: That's what I said, isn't it? Do you have trouble hearing?

Alien: No. *(taps its ear with one hand)* I can hear a pin drop—on velvet—from fifty feet away.

Person: Then hear this: *(leans toward Alien, puts mouth next to its ear, and shouts)* **GET OUT!**

(Alien jumps back, holds hands to ears, and shakes.)

Person: Why aren't you leaving?

Alien: I'd like to give you something before I go.

Person: What?

Alien: Something very special. I'll run out to my spaceship and fetch it for you. *(exits stage left)*

Person: *(addresses audience)* I hope that alien isn't up to something. I have plenty of food in the house, but I don't want to give any to some creature from outer space.

Alien: *(enters stage left, carrying rock)* Here is your present. Keep it forever, and you'll always have something to eat.

Person: What do you mean? I can't eat a rock.

Alien: No, but you can make soup with it.

Person: You can't make soup with a rock.

Alien: That is true of earth rocks, but moon rocks make very good soup. Would you like me to show you?

Person: Yes, please.

Alien: Does that pan on your stove have water in it?

Person: Yes.

Alien: Good. Then I'll put the rock in and let it boil. *(crosses to pan and drops rock into it)*

(Person and Alien stand awhile and look at pan.)

Person: *(looks at Alien)* Well?

Alien: Well, what?

Person: Is it done yet?

Alien: Let me taste. *(Person picks up spoon and holds it to Alien's mouth, and Alien slurps.)* Not bad. But this is an awfully small stone, so the soup is a little thin. Too bad we don't have a speck of flour to add to it.

Person: *(puts hand on Alien's arm)* Wait. I might have some flour here somewhere. *(exits stage right)*

Alien: *(addresses audience)* That is what I thought.

Person: *(enters stage right, carrying flour; pretends to pour some into pan, puts down sack, stirs soup, and then holds spoon to Alien's mouth)* How does it taste now?

Alien: *(makes slurping sounds)* Much better. It would be even nicer if we could add a few potatoes, but we can do without them.

Person: *(holds up arm)* Wait. I just remembered where some potatoes might be. *(exits stage right)*

Alien: *(addresses audience)* I'll bet she could remember where a lot of things are.   *

Person: *(enters stage right, carrying potatoes; puts them in pan, stirs, and then holds spoon to Alien's mouth)* Taste it now.

Alien: *(makes slurping sounds)* It's coming along nicely, but it's too bad we can't pour in a little milk.

Person: Maybe we can. If I look **VERY** carefully in my refrigerator, I **MIGHT** be able to find some milk. *(exits stage right)*

Alien: *(addresses audience)* I bet she doesn't have to look too hard.   *

Person: *(enters stage right, carrying milk; pretends to pour some in the pan, puts container down, stirs, and then holds the spoon to the Alien's mouth)* Is this better?

Alien: *(makes slurping sounds)* Much. If we could add some peas and carrots, this would be a truly super soup.

Person: Maybe I could find a **FEW** vegetables somewhere. *(exits stage right)*

Alien: *(addresses audience)* She will probably find more than just a few.

Person: *(enters stage right, carrying vegetables; drops them into pan, stirs, and holds spoon up to Alien's mouth)* How does it taste now?

Alien: *(makes slurping sounds)* Delicious. Why don't you see for yourself? *(Alien takes spoon from Person, turns it around, dips it into pan, and holds it up to Person's mouth.)*

Person: *(slurps)* Mmmmmm. It's magnificent. It's marvelous. *(hugs self)* It's . . . out of this world!

Alien: If you pour a little into a bowl, I will carry it out to my spaceship. You can eat the rest.

Person: *(exits stage right, reenters with bowl, and puts bowl down; picks pan up, tilts it as if pouring soup into bowl, puts pan down, picks up bowl, and holds it out)* Will this be enough?

Alien: *(looks into bowl)* Definitely. My spaceship gets very good mileage. Thank you for the soup. *(takes bowl from Person)*

Person: Thank you for teaching me how to make it.

Alien: I was glad to do it, because if you remember what I showed you, you will always have something to eat.

Person: I'll remember. And I'll keep the rock forever.

Alien: Then good-bye, Earthling. If you're ever in outer space, please look me up.

Person: I will. Good-bye, Space Creature.

(Alien exits stage left with bowl.)

Person: *(addresses audience)* I'd better write that recipe down before I forget. I'll call it . . . *(thinks)* Otherworldly Vegetable Soup. Good-bye. *(exits stage right)*

*

Versions of "Stone Soup"

Brown, Marcia. *Stone Soup.* Simon & Schuster, 1947.

McGovern, Ann. *Stone Soup.* Simon & Schuster, 1986.

Van Rynbach, Iris. *Stone Soup.* Greenwillow, 1988.

Books about Soup

Croll, Carolyn. *Too Many Babas.* HarperCollins, 1979.

Everitt, Betsy. *Mean Soup.* Harcourt, 1995.

Galdone, Paul. *Magic Porridge Pot.* Houghton, 1979.

Meddaugh, Susan. *Hog Eye.* Houghton, 1995.

Sachar, Louis. *Monkey Soup.* Knopf, 1992.

Stevenson, James. *Yuck!* Greenwillow, 1984.

Temple, Frances. *Tiger Soup: An Anansi Story from Jamaica.* Orchard, 1994.

Vaughan, Marcia K. *Wombat Stew.* Silver Burdett, 1985.

Books about Aliens

Asch, Frank, and Vladimir Vagin. *Insects from Outer Space.* Scholastic, 1995.

Bradman, Tony. *It Came from Outer Space.* Dial, 1992.

Brown, Marc. *Arthur's First Sleepover.* Little, Brown, 1994.

Leedy, Loreen. *Blast Off to Earth!* Holiday, 1992.

McNaughton, Colin. *Here Come the Aliens!* Candlewick, 1995.

Sadler, Marilyn. *Alistair in Outer Space.* Simon & Schuster, 1984.

Peter Rabbit

Characters: Mother Rabbit (left hand)
Peter Rabbit (right hand)
Mr. McGregor (left hand)

Props: vegetables
watering can
bed
cup

You can make Mr. McGregor's garden out of an egg carton. Remove the lid and cut slits in it. (You can also paint it brown or cover it with brown paper.) Cut vegetables out of colored paper or a seed catalog and insert them into the slits.

You can make a watering can by taping a sheet of construction paper to a metal bookend, box, or wooden block so it stands on one of its short sides. Cut a handle and spout out of the same color of paper and attach them to the appropriate places.

Note: The skit "Something Good to Eat" is also about a rabbit eating vegetables. Peter Rabbit appears as a character in the skits "The Mysterious Visitors," "Storybook Characters Look for Work," and "Wanted: A Whiz of a Wiz."

SCENE 1: OUTSIDE THE RABBITS' HOUSE

Mother Rabbit: *(stands center stage, faces stage right, and calls)* Peter! Peter Rabbit!

Peter Rabbit: *(hops in stage right and crosses to Mother)* What do you want, Mommy?

Mother Rabbit: I'd like you to go to the woods and pick blackberries for supper tonight.

Peter Rabbit: How about if I pick lettuce and radishes instead? They taste better. Mmmmm.

Mother Rabbit: Lettuce and radishes are good, but I'm afraid you can't find any in the woods.

Peter Rabbit: I could find plenty in Mr. McGregor's garden.

Mother Rabbit: *(shows horror)* Peter Weston Rabbit! Don't you **DARE** go into Mr. McGregor's garden! You'll end up in a pie if he catches you!

Peter Rabbit: *(boastfully)* He couldn't ever catch me because I can run really fast. Watch! *(runs to stage right and back to Mother)*

Mother Rabbit: I don't **CARE** how fast you can run! *(admonishes)* You are **NOT** to go anywhere near that garden. Do you understand?

Peter Rabbit: Yes, Mommy.

Mother Rabbit: Good. Now run along to the woods for the blackberries. I'm going to buy buns and bread at the baker's. *(kisses Peter's cheek, turns, and exits stage left)*

(Take off Mother. Put on Mr. McGregor.)

Peter Rabbit: *(addresses audience)* Mommy's just an old worrywart. Nothing could ever happen to me, so I'll go over to Mr. McGregor's and have a little snack. *(hops off stage right)*

SCENE 2: MR. MCGREGOR'S GARDEN

Setup: Put vegetables near stage left.

Peter Rabbit: *(hops in stage right and looks at vegetables)* Mmmmm, they sure look good. *(hops over to vegetables, bends over them, and pretends to eat)*

Mr. McGregor: *(enters stage left)* Stop, thief!

(Peter screams, turns around, and runs toward stage right. Mr. McGregor chases him. When they reach stage right, they turn around and run toward stage left. Repeat this action several times. They finally exit stage left.)

Note: Cross your arms on every turn, so Peter always runs in front of Mr. McGregor.

SCENE 3: INSIDE TOOL-SHED

Setup: Take down vegetables. Put watering can at center stage.

Peter Rabbit: *(enters stage left and wipes brow)* Whew! I'll hide in here until I catch my breath. If I jump into this watering can, Mr. McGregor will never find me. *(He jumps up, over, and down behind the watering can. Then he sticks his head up to address the audience.)* Brrrrr! *(shivers)* It's cold and wet in here. I hope I don't have to hide in this can very long. *(ducks down out of sight)*

Mr. McGregor: *(enters stage left and looks around)* I saw that varmint hop in here. Now where did he go? *(looks all around, even under stage)*

Peter Rabbit: *(from inside can)* Ah, ah, ah, ah-choo!

Mr. McGregor: There he is! *(turns toward can)*

(Peter jumps out of can and runs toward stage right.)

Mr. McGregor: *(chases Peter)* Stop, thief! *(runs by the watering can and knocks it off the stage)*

(As they did in Scene 2, Peter and Mr. McGregor run back and forth across the stage several times. They finally exit stage right.)

(Take off Mr. McGregor. Put on Mother.)

SCENE 4: ON THE ROAD

Peter Rabbit: *(enters stage right and wipes brow)* Whew! That was close, but I'm safe outside now. Ah, ah, ah, **AH-CHOO!** *(puts hand to head)* I don't feel very good. I'd better go home. *(hops slowly across stage and exits stage left)*

Alternative Action: If Peter is a movable mouth puppet, have him hang his head.

SCENE 5: INSIDE THE RABBITS' HOUSE

Setup: Put bed near stage left.

Peter Rabbit: *(enters slowly stage right and calls wearily)* I'm home.

Mother Rabbit: *(enters stage left)* Good. I was getting worried about you.

Peter Rabbit: Ah, ah, ah, **AH-CHOO!**

Mother Rabbit: Oh, dear, you're catching cold. I'd better get you some camomile tea. *(exits stage left, returns with cup, and holds it out to Peter)* Drink some of this now.

Peter Rabbit: No! I hate camomile tea! *(turns away)*

Mother Rabbit: But it's very good for colds. *(firmly)* Now drink it.

Peter Rabbit: *(sighs)* Oh, all right. *(turns back)*

Mother Rabbit: *(sets cup down)* That wasn't so bad now, was it?

Note: Tilt your right wrist slightly back and raise your left arm a little, so Mother can hold the cup to Peter's mouth.

Peter Rabbit: Yuck! *(wipes hand across mouth)*

Alternative Action: If Peter is a movable mouth puppet, have him gag.

Mother Rabbit: Come to bed now, Peter. *(grabs his hand and leads him to bed)*

Peter Rabbit: But it isn't eight o'clock yet.

Mother Rabbit: I know, but sick little rabbits need extra sleep. *(pushes him down on bed)*

Peter Rabbit: *(stands up)* I don't want to go to sleep.

Mother Rabbit: *(pushes him back and says firmly)* Good-night. *(kisses him and exits stage left)*

Peter Rabbit: *(stands up and addresses audience)* I'm never going into Mr. McGregor's garden again. It's too much trouble.

Books about Peter Rabbit and Beatrix Potter

Ada, Alma Flor. *Dear Peter Rabbit.* Simon & Schuster, 1994.

Collins, David R. *The Country Artist.* Lerner, 1989.

Potter, Beatrix. *Tale of Benjamin Bunny.* Warne, 1987.

————. *Tale of Peter Rabbit.* Warne, 1987.

Terrio, Bob. *Peter Rabbit and His Friends.* Forest House, 1994.

Wallner, Alexandra. *Beatrix Potter.* Holiday, 1995.

Books about Rabbits, Vegetables, and Gardens

Ernst, Lisa Campbell. *Miss Penny and Mr. Grubbs.* Simon & Schuster, 1991.

Hoban, Tana. *Where Is It?* Simon & Schuster, 1974.

LeTord, Bijou. *Rabbit Seeds.* Dell, 1993.

Modesitt, Jeanne. *Vegetable Soup.* Simon & Schuster, 1988.

Brer Fox Eats the Wash

A Brer Rabbit Story

Characters: Mrs. Duck (right hand for Scene 1 and first part of Scene 2 but left hand for last part of Scene 2)
Brer Fox (left hand)
Brer Rabbit (left hand)
Bis Dog (right hand)

If you don't have a duck puppet, substitute any animal that could be prey. If you lack a fox, you could substitute some other meat-eating animal. Any animal puppet could play Brer Rabbit.

Props:

rock	two boxes of laundry detergent
tree	bed and blanket
washtub	bundle of washing
handkerchief (or similar-sized piece of material)	

The tree and rock can be cut from cardboard and taped to metal bookends or wooden blocks to make them stand.

You can make a washtub by cutting the bottom two inches off a cylindrical container (such as an oatmeal box) and covering it with gray paper or aluminum foil.

If you don't have miniature boxes of laundry detergent, wrap colored paper around small boxes (such as the ones used for bars of soap, gelatin, or baking soda) and write an appropriate brand name on them.

A little pillow can serve as a bed, as can a baby blanket folded in a small rectangle. A piece of material can serve as a blanket.

To make the bundle of washing, put a bunch of cotton or crumpled facial tissue in the middle of a large handkerchief or square of material, bring the corners together, and tie a knot.

Preparation: Put the rock at extreme left of stage with the tree next to it. Leave some space between the rock and the tree so Brer Rabbit can stand there. Put the washtub at far right of stage and the box of laundry detergent next to it.

SCENE 1: MRS. DUCK'S YARD

Mrs. Duck: *(stands in front of washtub with her back to tree and rock; holds the handkerchief in her bill and dips it up and down into the washtub as she sings to the tune of "Here We Go Round the Mulberry Bush")* This is the day to wash the sheet, wash the sheet, wash the sheet. This is the day to wash the sheet to get it very clean. *(looks into tub)* I need more suds. *(picks up the box and holds it upside down over the tub while shaking it up and down vigorously, then throws it away)* Drat! This box is empty. I'll have to go inside and get another one. *(exits stage right)*

Brer Fox: *(enters from behind tree, addresses audience, and laughs evilly)* Mmmmm. She looks tasty. I think I'll come back tonight when she's asleep. I'll grab her out of bed, carry her home, and cook her for dinner tomorrow. Mmmmm. Right now I'd better go to the library and look up a recipe for roast duck. *(exits stage left)*

(Take off Brer Fox. Put on Brer Rabbit.)

(Brer Rabbit steps out from behind rock.)

Mrs. Duck: *(enters stage right, carrying laundry detergent and sits down)* Hello, Brer Rabbit. What were you doing behind that rock?

Brer Rabbit: *(hops behind tree to get to Mrs. Duck)* Resting. I was walking home from my cousin's house and got tired.

Mrs. Duck: Would you like to come inside and have some tea?

Brer Rabbit: No, thank you. I just want to warn you: I overheard Brer Fox say he's going to sneak into your house tonight and snatch you out of bed.

Mrs. Duck: Why?

Brer Rabbit: I'm afraid he wants to take you home to eat.

(Mrs. Duck starts to cry.)

Brer Rabbit: *(comforts her)* Don't cry, Mrs. Duck. Your washing is wet enough already.

Mrs. Duck: *(indignantly)* How can you make jokes at a time like this?

Brer Rabbit: I'm sorry if I offended you; I was trying to cheer you up.

Mrs. Duck: How can I be cheery when I'm about to become roast duck? *(cries)*

Brer Rabbit: *(comforts her)* Don't you worry, Mrs. Duck. Brer Fox is **NOT** going to eat you.

Mrs. Duck: But how can I protect myself? Brer Fox is bigger and stronger than I am.

Brer Rabbit: But he's not smarter, so we're going to trick him. Put a bundle of laundry in your bed tonight, cover it with a blanket, and hide in your closet. It will be so dark when Brer Fox comes into your room, he'll think the washing is you.

Mrs. Duck: But what happens when he gets close to the bed and sees it's only laundry? Won't he start looking for me?

Brer Rabbit: No, because Sis Dog will be hiding under the bed and chase him off.

Mrs. Duck: Are you sure she'll help?

Brer Rabbit: Positive! She likes to trick Brer Fox as much as I do. I'll go talk to her right now. You get your laundry ready. *(exits stage left)*

(Take off Brer Rabbit. Put on Brer Fox.)

Mrs. Duck: Oh, dear. Oh, dear. *(picks up handkerchief and exits stage right)*

SCENE 2: MRS. DUCK'S BEDROOM

Mrs. Duck: *(enters stage left, carrying bundle and shaking; crosses to bed, puts bundle on it, covers washing with blanket, and addresses audience)* I'd better go hide in the closet now. I hope this works. I'm so scared, I can't stop shaking. *(exits stage left, shaking)*

(Take off Mrs. Duck. Put on Sis Dog.)

Brer Fox: *(enters stage left, puts paw to lips, and addresses audience)* Shhhhh. I don't want to wake Mrs. Duck. Mmmmm. She's so nice and plump, she'll make a wonderful meal. *(tiptoes to bed and pounces on bundle)*

(Sis Dog leaps up from behind bed, barking and growling.)

(Brer Fox screams, drops bundle, and runs off stage left.)

(Take off Brer Fox. Put on Mrs. Duck.)

Sis Dog: *(stands by bed, faces left, and calls)* You can come out now, Mrs. Duck.

Mrs. Duck: *(pokes her head out at stage left, looks around, and asks timidly)* Is Brer Fox gone?

Sis Dog: He's gone, all right. And he was so scared, I don't think he'll ever come back.

Mrs. Duck: *(runs to Sis Dog and kisses her)* Thank you, oh, thank you. You saved my life!

Sis Dog: You're very welcome. It was fun to play a trick on mean old Brer Fox.

Mrs. Duck: Brer Rabbit likes to trick Brer Fox, too.

Setup: Take down all props. Put bed a little to the right of center stage. Put blanket next to it.

Sis Dog: I bet tomorrow he tells everybody that Brer Fox tried to steal your laundry for dinner.

Mrs. Duck: That ought to make people laugh. It's pretty funny to think about Brer Fox eating a sheet. *(laughs)*

Sis Dog: It certainly is. *(laughs)*

Mrs. Duck: Speaking of eating, would you like to go out to the kitchen with me for a midnight snack?

Sis Dog: That sounds good. I'm so hungry, I could almost eat a sheet myself.

(Sis Dog and Mrs. Duck exit stage right.)

Books about Foiled Foxes and Wolves

Edwards, Pamela Duncan. *Four Famished Foxes and Fosdyke.* HarperCollins, 1995.

Fox, Mem. *Hattie & the Fox.* Simon & Schuster, 1987.

French, Vivian. *Red Hen & Sly Fox.* Simon & Schuster, 1995.

Hutchins, Pat. *Rosie's Walk.* Simon & Schuster, 1968.

Isami, Ikuyo. *Fox's Egg.* Lerner, 1989.

Kasza, Keiko. *Wolf's Chicken Stew.* Morrow, 1987.

Leverich, Kathleen. *The Hungry Fox and the Foxy Duck.* Parents, 1979.

Marshall, James. "Miss Jones." In *Rats on the Roof: And Other Stories.* Dial, 1991.

Roy, Ron. *Three Ducks Went Wandering.* Ticknor & Fields, 1987.

Silverman, Erica. *Don't Fidget a Feather!* Macmillan, 1994.

Vaughan, Marcia K. *Wombat Stew.* Silver Burdett, 1985.

Books about Brer Rabbit

See the books listed for the skit "Only Two Hops."

Books about Tricky Rabbits

See the books listed for the skit "Brer Wolf Plays House."

Books about African Tricksters

See the books listed for the skit "Rabbit Makes Trouble."

The Three Little Pigs

Characters: Mother Pig (left hand)
Pig (who plays all three little pigs and goes on right hand)
Wolf (left hand)

Props:

bundle of straw	stick house
straw house	three or four bricks
bundle of sticks	brick house

To make the bundle of straw, cut yellow paper or posterboard into many skinny strips about three inches long. You could also cut up yarn or the straws of an old broom. Hold the "straws" together with a rubber band.

The bundle of sticks can be real twigs, toothpicks, or skinny strips of brown paper held together with a rubber band.

Use small wooden blocks or small boxes (such as the kind paper clips or matches come in) covered with red paper for the bricks.

The straw house can be a sheet of yellow paper; the stick house, a sheet of brown paper; and the brick house, a sheet of red paper. Draw a door and a couple of windows on each house. The brick house must be very sturdy, so tape it to a metal bookend or wooden block. The wolf must be able to knock over the other houses, so attach them to small, empty boxes.

SCENE 1: HOME OF THREE PIGS AND MOTHER

(Both pigs stand center stage.)

Pig: Good-bye, Mom, I'm leaving now.

Mother Pig: Oh, Wilbur, do you really think you should?

Pig: Of course. I'm old enough to be on my own.

Mother Pig: But I'll worry about you all the time. I'm afraid the Big Bad Wolf will get you.

Pig: You don't need to worry. I can take care of myself.

Mother Pig: Mothers always worry. Now brush your teeth after every meal, get plenty of sleep, and don't forget to write.

Pig: *(exasperated)* Good-**BYE,** Mom. *(kisses her and exits stage right)*

Mother Pig: Oh, my baby . . . *(exits stage left, crying)*

(Take off Mother. Put on Wolf.)

SCENE 2: ON THE ROAD

Pig: *(enters stage right and crosses to middle of stage singing)* I'm on my own; I'm on my own. *(addresses audience)* I guess the first thing to do is build myself a house. *(looks down and sees straw)* I can use this straw and build right here. *(drops straw backstage, picks up house, and sets it on stage)* There! My very own home, sweet home, the place where I can stay up as late as I want, eat candy between meals, and **NEVER** make my bed. I love it!

Puppeteer: Grrr.

Pig: Uh-oh! That sounds like the Big Bad Wolf. I'd better run inside where it's safe. *(runs behind house)*

Wolf: *(enters stage left, holding nose in air and sniffing loudly)* Mmmmm, I smell a pig. *(runs his nose up and down the side of the house, sniffing loudly)* It seems to be in this house. *(calls)* Little Pig, Little Pig, let me come in.

Pig: *(from behind house)* Not by the hair of my chinny chin chin.

Wolf: Then I'll huff *(exhales loudly)*, and I'll puff *(exhales loudly)*, and I'll blow your house in.

(Wolf blows, and the house falls down.)

Pig: *(runs off stage right, crying)* Mommy!

Wolf: *(watches Pig leave and addresses audience)* Rats! Peanut butter for dinner again.

(Take off Wolf. Put on Mother.)

SCENE 3: HOME OF THREE PIGS AND MOTHER

(Both pigs stand center stage.)

Pig: 'Bye, Mom. I'm leaving now.

Mother Pig: I don't think you should go, Oliver.

Pig: *(exasperated)* **MOM,** I'm a big pig now. It's time for me to have my own place.

Mother Pig: But you know what happened to Wilbur. Your poor brother's been hiding in the closet ever since the Big Bad Wolf blew his house down last year.

Pig: That won't happen to me, because **I'M** going to build a stronger house.

Mother Pig: I hope so, dear. Now take care of yourself. Eat plenty of veggies, don't snack between meals, and don't forget to write.

Pig: I'll send you a postcard as soon as I'm settled. *(kisses Mother)* Good-bye, Mom. *(exits stage right)*

Setup: Put bundle of straw at center stage.

Note: With your left hand, hold the straw house up to the stage.

Note: Throughout, as you make Wolf blow, move him next to the house and have him knock it over.

Setup: Take down straw house.

Mother Pig: *(watches him leave)* There goes another one of my babies. *(exits stage left, crying)*

(Take off Mother. Put on Wolf.)

SCENE 4: ON THE ROAD

Pig: *(enters stage right and talks while crossing to center stage)* Now that I'm on my own, I ought to build myself a house. *(looks down and sees sticks)* I'll use these sticks. *(drops sticks backstage, takes house, and sets it on the stage)*

Pig: Ah, home! The place where I can sleep as late as I want, leave my stuff wherever I want, and never have to eat spinach or broccoli.

Puppeteer: Grrr.

Pig: Uh-oh! That sounds like the Big Bad Wolf! I'd better run inside where it's safe. *(runs behind house)*

Wolf: *(enters stage left, holding nose in air and sniffing loudly)* Mmmmm, I smell a little pig. *(runs nose up and down the side of the house, sniffing loudly)* It smells as if the piggy is in this house. *(calls)* Little Pig, Little Pig, let me come in.

Pig: *(from behind house)* Not by the hair of my chinny chin chin.

Wolf: Then I'll huff *(exhales loudly)*, and I'll puff *(exhales loudly)*, and I'll blow your house in.

(Wolf blows, and house falls down.)

Pig: *(runs off stage right, crying)* Help!

Wolf: *(watches Pig leave and then addresses audience)* Darn! I sure am getting tired of peanut butter.

(Take off Wolf. Put on Mother.)

SCENE 5: HOME OF THE THREE PIGS AND MOTHER

Pig: 'Bye, Mom. I'm leaving now.

Mother Pig: Do you **REALLY** think you should, Amanda?

Pig: Of course. Every pig has to leave home sometime.

Mother Pig: But look what happened to your brothers. The Big Bad Wolf scared them so badly, they haven't come out from under the bed in years.

Pig: Well, that old windbag can't scare me; I'm going to build my house with bricks.

Mother Pig: That's a good idea, dear. Now be polite to your elders, wash behind your ears every day, and write to me once a week.

Setup: Put bundle of sticks at center stage.

Note: With your left hand, hold the stick house up to the stage.

Setup: Take down stick house.

Pig: I will. *(kisses Mother)* Good-bye, Mom. I love you. *(exits stage right)*

Mother Pig: *(watches her leave)* Oh, my baby! *(exits stage left, crying)*

(Take off Mother. Put on Wolf.)

SCENE 6: ON THE ROAD

Pig: *(enters stage right, crosses to bricks, and looks at them)* These bricks are just what I need to build a house that wolf can't blow down. *(Pig piles blocks on top of each other near the edge of the stage. Pig takes house and sets it on stage in front of blocks.)* This is a wonderful house that will last for a hundred years. My children can live here, and my grandchildren, and my great-grandchildren, and my great-great grandchildren.

Setup: Put the bricks at center stage.

Note: With your left hand, hold the brick house up to the stage.

Puppeteer: Grrr.

Pig: Uh-oh. I'd better go inside, or I won't live long enough to have great-great grandchildren! *(runs behind house)*

Wolf: *(enters stage left, holding nose in air and sniffing loudly)* Mmmmm. I smell a succulent piglet. *(runs nose up and down the side of the house)* The little porker must be inside. *(calls)* Little Pig, Little Pig, let me come in.

Pig: *(from behind house)* Not by the hair of my chinny chin chin.

Wolf: That's what they all say. But I'll huff *(exhales loudly),* and I'll puff *(exhales loudly),* and I'll blow your house in.

Pig: *(from behind house)* Go ahead and try, you old windbag!

Wolf: You'll be sorry you said that. Nobody calls me names and gets away with it.

(Wolf blows very hard several times. Finally, he collapses and pants.)

Pig: *(from behind house)* Nyaah, nyaah, nyaah, nyaah, nyaah. You can't get me!

Wolf: *(jumps up)* Oh, yes, I can! I'll climb down your chimney, like Santa Claus. *(climbs up side of house and stands on top of chimney)* Ho, ho, ho! Down I go!

(Wolf disappears behind chimney, screams, jumps up out of chimney, lands on stage, and runs off stage left.)

Pig: *(comes out from behind house on right side, laughing, and addresses audience)* I guess I fixed him with that kettle of boiling water. He'll be too afraid to come back and mess with me. I'd better go home and tell everybody the good news. *(dances off stage right singing)* "Who's afraid of the Big Bad Wolf, the Big Bad Wolf, the Big Bad Wolf?"

Variations of "The Three Little Pigs"

Allen, Jonathan. *Who's at the Door?* Morrow, 1993.

Celsi, Teresa Noel. *The Fourth Little Pig.* Raintree Steck-Vaughn, 1990.

Lowell, Susan. *The Three Little Javelinas.* Northland, 1992.

Scieszka, Jon. *The True Story of the Three Little Pigs.* Viking, 1989.

Trivizas, Eugene. *The Three Little Wolves and the Big Bad Pig.* Simon & Schuster, 1993.

Books about Pigs, Foxes, and Wolves

Meddaugh, Susan. *Hog Eye.* Houghton, 1995.

Palatini, Margie. *Piggie Pie.* Houghton, 1995.

Rayner, Mary. *Garth Pig Steals the Show.* Dutton, 1993.

————. *Mr. and Mrs. Pig's Evening Out.* Simon & Schuster, 1976.

Steig, William. *The Amazing Bone.* Farrar, 1983.

The Golden Touch
A Greek Myth

Characters: Midas (left hand)
Marigold (right hand)
Wizard (right hand)

If you don't have a wizard puppet, put a sorcerer's hat on any puppet. See the skit "Wanted: A Whiz of a Wiz" for making the hat and for making a crown that will turn any puppet you have into a king.

If you have a boy puppet but no girl, Midas could have a son named Marty.

Midas could be a queen if you have a woman puppet but no man puppet.

Props: pot
gold coins
garden with flowers and bird
small pillow with gold or yellow paper pinned to one side
bowl with grapes
yellow pompoms
silhouette of girl cut from gold or yellow paper and attached to
a stick

The pot can be any bowl, even a plastic margarine tub.

You can cut the coins from gold or yellow paper. You could also use rocks, bottle caps, or poker chips. You might want to spray these with gold paint, but it's not necessary.

One way to make the garden is to cover one long side, both short sides, and half of the bottom of a shoe box with green paper. Cover the remaining side and the other half of the bottom with gold or yellow paper. Cut three flowers and a bird out of colored paper. Then trace around them on gold or yellow paper. Cut these out. Draw an eye on the birds. Glue the colored bird to the gold or yellow bird with a plastic drinking straw between them. Repeat this with each of the three flowers.

Turn the shoe box upside down. Poke five holes in the bottom. Put a flower into three of the holes. Stick the bird into the fourth. The fifth will be where you'll put the silhouette of Marigold in Scene 5.

Cut a picture of grapes from a magazine or newspaper ad or out of green or purple paper. Cut a bowl from colored paper. Glue the grapes in the bowl. Tape this to a small wooden block or box to make it stand. If you don't have gold or yellow pompoms to serve as grapes, you could cut some circles out of gold paper or paint a few small rocks gold or yellow.

Note: This skit may sound more complicated than it really is. One day, I moved from classroom to classroom and performed it eleven times in six hours without a stage.

Preparation: Put pot at stage left.

SCENE 1: COUNTING ROOM

(Midas stands to the right of the pot, bends over it, picks up gold, and drops it back into the pot.)

Midas: Gold! Gold! Gold! Magnificent, marvelous gold!

Marigold: *(enters stage right, crosses to Midas, and kisses his cheek)* Good morning, Daddy. Would you like to come out to the garden with me?

Midas: No, because I have to count my gold.

Marigold: Why? You counted it just last night.

Midas: I know. I count it all the time because that's my favorite thing to do. Gold is the most important, valuable, and beautiful thing in the world!

Marigold: I don't think so. It's not as pretty as the flowers in the garden. *(crosses to pot, bends over it, sniffs, straightens up, and then stands back)* And it certainly doesn't smell as nice.

Midas: You're just too young to appreciate gold now, but you will when you're older.

Marigold: I think I'll always like flowers better. Good-bye, Daddy. *(kisses him and exits stage right)*

(Take off Marigold. Put on Wizard.)

Midas: *(turns back to pot, picks up some gold, and drops it back into the pot)* Gold! Gold! Gold! Magnificent, marvelous gold!

Wizard: *(pops up behind Midas)* Hello.

Midas: *(turns around fast and shows surprise)* Who are you?

Wizard: Someone who knows all about you. *(holds out an arm)* I've come to grant you one wish.

Midas: One wish is all I need, because there's only one thing I want: More gold!

Wizard: *(crosses to pot, looks in, and then steps back)* It looks to me as if you already have enough gold.

Midas: No one ever has enough because gold is the most important, valuable, and beautiful thing in the world.

Wizard: I can think of other things more important, valuable, and beautiful.

Midas: I can't. I wish everything I had were made of gold. *(raises an arm)* That's it! Can you do it?

Wizard: Do what?

Midas: Can you fix it so that everything I touch turns into gold?

Wizard: Yes . . . but I don't think you'll like that very much.

Midas: Of course, I will. *(hugs self)* I'll love it!

Wizard: Very well. Your wish for the Golden Touch will come true at sunrise tomorrow. *(drops down out of sight)*

(Take off Wizard.)

Midas: *(looks around)* Where did he go? *(straightens up and addresses audience)* Oh, well. It doesn't matter. What's important is that by this time tomorrow, I'll have more gold, gold, gold! *(turns to pot, picks up some gold, and throws it up so that it falls back into the pot; carries the pot off stage left.)*

SCENE 2: THE BEDROOM

Setup: Put the small pillow at stage left with the yellow or gold side on the bottom. Put Midas lying down with head on the pillow and face turned away from the audience.

Midas: *(stands up, stretches, and addresses audience)* It's morning again. *(turns and starts off stage right)* Time to count my gold. *(addresses audience and raises arm)* Gold! Today's the day that everything I touch turns into gold! *(crosses to pillow, touches it, holds it up so audience can see the gold or yellow side, and dances around with it)* It works! Hooray! I'll run out to the garden and change the flowers to gold before Marigold wakes up. Then she'll love them more than ever. *(runs off stage right)*

SCENE 3: THE GARDEN

Setup: Take down pillow. Put flowers and birds at center stage.

(Midas runs in stage right, crosses to flowers, touches each one as well as the bird, and turns them all around so the audience can see their gold or yellow sides.)

Midas: *(shows excitement)* Splendid! Marigold will be thrilled when she sees them. While I'm waiting for her to wake up, I think I'll go inside and find something to eat. *(pats stomach)* I'm hungry. *(exits stage right)*

SCENE 4: DINING ROOM

Midas: *(enters stage right, crosses to grapes)* Mmmmm, these grapes look delicious. *(picks up pompom, puts it to mouth, drops it, and puts hand to cheek)* Ouch! I think I broke my tooth. *(He picks up another pompom and repeats procedure. Midas picks up several pompoms but drops each one after trying to eat it. Finally, he gets angry and throws the bowl offstage.)* Phooey! The Golden Touch has made it impossible to eat. I might as well go out to the garden and wait for Marigold. *(exits stage right)*

(Put on Marigold.)

Setup: Take down flowers and bird. Put bowl of grapes at center stage and put pompoms behind it.

SCENE 5: THE GARDEN

Setup: Put flowers and bird at stage left.

Midas: *(enters stage right, crosses to flowers, and looks at them)* These are the most beautiful flowers I've ever seen, but the garden is awfully quiet this morning. Last time I was here, I heard birds singing. *(bends over, puts ear next to bird, and then straightens up)* I guess golden birds don't sing.

Marigold: *(skips in stage right)* Good morning, Daddy. I looked for you in the counting room, but you weren't there.

Midas: No, I've been waiting here for you, so I could show you my surprise.

Marigold: *(eagerly)* What surprise?

Midas: I turned all your flowers into gold. See? *(steps back and points to flowers)*

Marigold: *(leans forward to look at flowers and then looks at Midas)* You ruined them, Daddy!

Midas: No, I didn't. I made them even more beautiful and valuable.

Marigold: You made them ugly. *(goes over and sniffs one)* And they don't smell pretty anymore. *(puts ear next to bird and then straightens up)* The bird isn't singing either. You've spoiled everything! *(cries)*

Midas: There, there, dear, don't cry. *(comforts her)*

(Take off Marigold. Put silhouette into Midas's hands. Put on Wizard.)

Midas: *(horrified)* Oh, no! I've turned my precious little girl into a lifeless metal lump. *(puts silhouette next to flowers and cries)*

Wizard: *(pops up next to Midas)* Why are you crying?

Midas: *(looks up)* I've lost what is dearest and most important to me.

Wizard: *(leans over and looks at flowers)* What do you mean? I see you have more gold now than you've ever had.

Midas: *(bitterly)* Gold? What good is glittery metal without the love of my darling daughter?

Wizard: Ah . . . you seem to have learned something from your wish.

Midas: That was a stupid wish. I wish I'd never made it.

Wizard: Do you want to get rid of the Golden Touch?

Midas: Yes! Tell me how.

Wizard: Take a bath in the river. Fill a cup with that water and pour it over everything you want to change back.

Midas: I will. Thank you. *(runs off stage right)*

(Drop down Wizard and take him off. Put on Marigold.)

(Midas runs in stage right, carrying cup; crosses to garden; and pretends to pour water over silhouette. He puts down the cup, picks up silhouette, and drops it offstage. Pop up Marigold.)

Midas: *(hugs Marigold)* Thank heavens, you're you again! *(kisses her)*

Marigold: Of course, I'm me, Daddy. Who else would I be?

Midas: Would you like to help me turn the flowers back?

Marigold: Oh, yes!

(Midas picks up the cup and pretends to pour water over the flowers and bird. Marigold turns them around so their colored sides show.)

Marigold: *(claps hands)* Hooray! They're pretty again. *(bends over and sniffs)* And they smell nice again, too.

Midas: *(looks at them, bends down to sniff each one, straightens up, and spreads arms wide)* Ahhhhh! They certainly do.

Marigold: Don't you like them better this way, Daddy?

Midas: Yes indeed. From now on, I'm going to spend more time here enjoying them with you. The only gold I want to see is the gold of your beautiful hair. *(strokes her hair and hugs her)*

Note: If your girl puppet has brown hair, omit the last dialogue line.

Variations of "The Golden Touch"

Balian, Lorna. *The Sweet Touch*. Humbug, 1994.

Catling, Patrick. *The Chocolate Touch*. Morrow, 1979.

Newby, Robert. *King Midas: With Selected Sentences in American Sign Language*. Gallaudet Univ. Pr., 1990.

Storr, Catherine. *King Midas*. Raintree-Steck Vaughn, 1993.

Wells, Rosemary. *Max and Ruby's Midas: Another Greek Myth.* Dial, 1995.

Books about Wishes Gone Wrong or Getting Too Much of a Good Thing

Bailey, Carolyn. *The Little Rabbit Who Wanted Red Wings.* Putnam, 1988.

Bush, John. *The Fish Who Could Wish.* Kane/Miller, 1991.

Craig, M. Jean. *The Three Wishes.* Scholastic, 1986.

Gliori, Dobi. *Willie Dear and the Wish Fish.* Macmillan, 1991.

Rayner, Mary. *Mrs. Pig's Bulk Buy.* Macmillan, 1981.

Robertson, Janet. *Oscar's Spots.* BridgeWater, 1993.

Steig, William. *Sylvester and the Magic Pebble.* Simon & Schuster, 1987.

Watson, Pauline. *Wriggles, the Little Wishing Pig.* Harper, 1978.

Books about Gold

Nixon, Joan Lowery. *Fat Chance, Claude.* Puffin, 1989.

Rumpelstiltskin. (any version)

Shute, Linda. *Clever Tom and the Leprechaun.* Lothrop, 1988.

Wildsmith, Brian, and Jean de LaFontaine. *The Rich Man and the Shoe-Maker.* Oxford Univ. Pr., 1980.

Picture Books with Greek Myths

Hutton, Warwick. *Perseus.* Simon & Schuster, 1993. (Hutton has also written about the Minotaur, Odysseus, Persephone, and the Trojan Horse.)

Rockwell, Anne. *The Robber Baby: Stories from the Greek Myths.* Greenwillow, 1994.

Wells, Rosemary. *Max and Ruby's First Greek Myth.* Dial, 1993. (Pandora's Box)

PART FOUR

Skits about Books, Reading, and Libraries

Books for This Section's Skits

▼▲▼▲▼▲▼▲▼▲▼▲▼▲▼▲▼▲▼

These titles could go with any of the skits in this section.

Alexander, Martha. *How My Library Grew, by Dinah.* Wilson, 1983.

Bonsall, Crosby. *Tell Me Some More.* Harper-Collins, 1961.

Brillhart, Julie. *Story Hour—Starring Megan!* Albert Whitman, 1992.

Bunting, Eve. *The Wednesday Surprise.* Houghton, 1990.

Caseley, Judith. *Sophie and Sammy's Library Sleepover.* Greenwillow, 1993.

Deedy, Carmen A. *Library Dragon.* Peachtree, 1994.

Freeman, Don. *Quiet! There's a Canary in the Library.* Children's Pr., 1969.

Gibbons, Gail. *Check It Out! The Book about Libraries.* Harcourt, 1985.

Greene, Carol. *I Can Be a Librarian.* Children's Pr., 1988.

Hautzig, Deborah. *A Visit to the Sesame Street Library.* Random, 1986.

Hutchins, Hazel. *Nicholas at the Library.* Firefly, 1990.

Hutchins, Pat. *The Tale of Thomas Meade.* Morrow, 1988.

Johnson, Jean. *Librarians A to Z.* Walker, 1989.

Kimmel, Eric A. *I Took My Frog to the Library.* Viking, 1990.

McPhail, David. *Fix-It.* Dutton, 1984.

Marshall, Rita. *I Hate to Read.* Creative Education, 1992.

Matthews, Liz. *Teeny Witch Goes to the Library.* Troll, 1991.

Paige, David. *A Day in the Life of a Librarian.* Troll, 1985.

Pinkwater, Daniel. *Aunt Lulu.* Simon & Schuster, 1991.

Poulet, Virginia. *Blue Bug Goes to the Library.* Children's Pr., 1979.

Radlauer, Ruth S. *Molly at the Library.* Simon & Schuster, 1991.

Sadler, Marilyn. *Alistair in Outer Space.* Simon & Schuster, 1984.

Thaler, Mike. *Cannon the Librarian.* Avon, 1993.

Weil, Lisl. *Let's Go to the Library.* Holiday, 1990.

Any Book in the World
A Miggs and Jiggs Skit about Interlibrary Loan

Characters: Miggs (left hand)
Jiggs (right hand)

Prop: any book

Note: There really is a book called *Pickle-Chiffon Pie* by Jolly Roger Bradfield and published by Rand McNally in 1967. It went out of print years ago, but you might like to borrow it on interlibrary loan and read it for yourself. The brightly colored cartoons and funny text tell children that "the most wonderful thing of all" is "kindness, love, and consideration for others."

Preparation: Open book so it lies flat on the stage or in your lap. Miggs is reading at beginning of skit.

Jiggs: *(enters stage right)* Rats!

Miggs: *(looks at Jiggs)* What's wrong?

Jiggs: The library doesn't have the book I want to read.

Miggs: What book is that?

Jiggs: *Pickle-Chiffon Pie.*

Miggs: What a weird name! I don't believe there really is such a book.

Jiggs: But there is. The new girl in my class told me about it. She said the teacher at her old school read it out loud, and it was really funny.

Miggs: Then I want to read it, too. I like funny books.

Jiggs: But we can't. I already told you, the library doesn't have a copy.

Miggs: That's O.K. We can still get the book.

Jiggs: How? Should we write a letter to the author and ask for a copy?

Miggs: No.

Jiggs: Should we write to the publisher and ask for a copy?

Miggs: No.

Jiggs: Should we write to Santa Claus and ask for a copy?

Miggs: No. Just go back to the library.

Jiggs: I've already told you twice: The library doesn't have *Pickle-Chiffon Pie.* I looked in the computer, but it wasn't listed under either the author or the title.

Alternative Dialogue: . . . in the card catalog . . .

Miggs: The library can still get *Pickle-Chiffon Pie* for you. In fact, it can get almost any book in the world for you.

Jiggs: How?

Miggs: The staff can try to borrow whatever you want from other libraries. That's called "interlibrary loan."

Jiggs: Does interlibrary loan cost a lot? I spent all my allowance on bubble gum and video games.

Miggs: Interlibrary loan is free, just like all the other services of the _____.

Note: Say your library's name.

Jiggs: Cool! I'm going to run right back to the library and ask the librarian to borrow *Pickle-Chiffon Pie* for me.

Miggs: While you're there, check out some cookbooks. Maybe we can find a recipe for pickle-chiffon pie.

Jiggs: I think I'd rather read about it than eat it. Pickle-chiffon pie sounds awful. *(exits stage right, gagging)*

Tell-ephone Me a Story

A Miggs and Jiggs Skit to Promote Your Dial-a-Story Service

Characters: Miggs (left hand)
Jiggs (right hand)

Props: spelling book

Preparation: Open book so it lies flat on the stage or in your lap. At beginning of skit, Miggs is reading it.

Jiggs: *(enters stage right)* Tell me a story, please, Miggs.

Miggs: Not now. I'm studying for a spelling test.

Jiggs: That sounds boring. Wouldn't you rather tell me a story?

Miggs: No, because I want to do well on the spelling test tomorrow. Why don't you listen to those stories on tape you borrowed from the library last week?

Jiggs: The batteries in my tape recorder are dead.

Miggs: You could buy some new ones.

Jiggs: I don't have any money.

Miggs: Then do something else.

Jiggs: I don't want to do anything else. I want to hear a story.

Miggs: Then find somebody to tell you one—**SOMEBODY WHO ISN'T ME!**

Jiggs: There's nobody here but you and me.

Miggs: Then I guess you won't be able to hear a story, will you?

Jiggs: Rats!

Miggs: *(raises arm)* Hey, I just thought of something.

Jiggs: What?

Miggs: The telephone.

Jiggs: I hate to tell you this, Miggs, but Alexander Graham Bell already thought of the telephone over a hundred years ago.

Alternative Action: If Miggs is a movable mouth puppet, cock its head to one side.

Miggs: I didn't mean I **INVENTED** the telephone. I was just thinking that the telephone could tell you a story.

Jiggs: Wow! A telephone that talks by itself! You really **HAVE** thought of something new!

Miggs: The phone won't talk by itself, Jiggs.

Jiggs: Then how can it tell me a story?

Miggs: _____ has a service called Dial-a-Story. If you dial _____, you'll hear a story.

Notes: Say your library's name. Say your phone number.

Jiggs: You mean the librarian will read to me?

Miggs: No, the stories are all on tape. You can hear a different recorded story every week.

Note: Specify the interval appropriate for your situation.

Jiggs: What story will I hear this week?

Miggs: Why don't you dial _____ and find out?

Note: Say your phone number.

Jiggs: I'll do that right now. *(exits stage right)*

Miggs: *(addresses audience)* I'm going to hurry and finish my homework. Then I can hear a story, too.

Look It Up

A Miggs and Jiggs Skit
to Teach about the Card Catalog

Characters: Miggs (left hand)
Jiggs (right hand)

Prop: Copy of *TV Guide*

Note: For all catalog drawer letters in the skit, substitute the guide letters on your card catalog drawers. You may want to jot them down in the right column beside the asterisks.

Preparation: Open *TV Guide* so it stands center stage with its cover facing the audience. You might need to slip a metal bookend between the pages to help it stand.

(Miggs stands to left of magazine, looking into it as if reading.)

Jiggs: *(enters stage right)* What are you reading?

Miggs: *TV Guide.* I want to see if there's anything good on television tonight.

Jiggs: Are there going to be any shows about pioneers?

Miggs: No.

Jiggs: Rats! The teacher talked about pioneers at school today, and I'd like to know more about what it was like to live back then.

Miggs: Then why don't you read the Little House books?

Jiggs: Are they about pioneers?

Miggs: You bet. The author was a pioneer herself, and she wrote all about how her family traveled in covered wagons and lived in log cabins.

Jiggs: Cool! Do you think I could get those books at the library?

Miggs: Sure. Why don't you go there right now and check out *Little House in the Big Woods?* That's the first book in the series.

Jiggs: I will. *(turns to go, but then turns back)* Uh, Miggs?

Miggs: Yes?

Jiggs: The library has lots and lots of books. How am I going to find the one I want?

Miggs: Look in the card catalog.

Jiggs: Oh, I don't need to go to the library to do that. I got one of those in the mail the other day.

Miggs: You got a card catalog in the mail?

Jiggs: Yes. And I think I'll order some of the Christmas cards in it. They're really cute.

Miggs: That may be, but the library has a different kind of card catalog. It definitely wouldn't fit into your mailbox because it's a big box with drawers full of cards.

Jiggs: You mean, we can play games like "Go Fish" at the library?

Miggs: No, Jiggs, the cards in the card catalog aren't for playing games. They're for giving you information.

Jiggs: What kind of information?

Miggs: The kind of information you need to find a book. . . . Do you know how to use *TV Guide?*

Jiggs: Sure. I read it all the time, because it tells me what I need to know to watch any show on television.

Miggs: Right! And the card catalog tells you what you need to know to find any book in the library.

Jiggs: Do the cards give you the name of the book, Miggs?

Miggs: Yes. The name of the book is called the *title.* Every book in the library has a title card in the card catalog.

Jiggs: Does the title card tell you anything besides the name of the book?

Miggs: Yes, it also tells you the author's name and the call number.

Jiggs: *(addresses audience and calls the way a parent calls a child home to dinner)* "Number! Number!"

Miggs: Why are you yelling that way?

Jiggs: You told me to call "Number," so I did. Who is Number anyway, and why does she have such a funny name?

Miggs: I wasn't asking you to call anyone named Number. I was telling you that every catalog card has a call number in the top left-hand corner. This call number tells you where to find the book on the shelf.

Jiggs: The card catalog talks? Cool!

Miggs: No, Jiggs, the card catalog doesn't talk.

Jiggs: Then how does it tell you where to find the book?

Miggs: I think you'd understand what I'm saying better if you could see a real catalog card. Why don't you go down to the library and look up the card you want under the author?

Jiggs: Why is Arthur sitting on all the cards? Is he the librarian?

Miggs: Not Ar-thur, Jiggs, au-thor. *Author* is what you call the person who wrote the book. Since Laura Ingalls Wilder wrote *Little House in the Big Woods,* you look for her name in the card catalog. That's called looking up the book under the author's name.

Jiggs: How do I find her name among all those cards in all those drawers?

Miggs: The cards are filed alphabetically in the drawers. That means all the cards with names, titles, and words beginning with the letter *A* are in the first drawers. All the cards that have names, titles, and words beginning with the letter *M* are in the middle drawers. The cards with names, titles, and words starting with the letter *Z* are in the last drawer. The drawers are marked on the outside with guide letters—like the guide words at the top of each page in the dictionary. If a drawer is marked "*B-R-O-W* to *C-L*," then names, titles, and words beginning with letters in between *B-R-O-W* and *C-L* are in that drawer.　＊

Jiggs: Is that where you'd find the title card for *Charlotte's Web?*

Miggs: Yes. Because the first three letters, *C-H-A,* come between *B-R-O-W* and *C-L.*　＊

Jiggs: Would the title card for *Digging Up Dinosaurs* be in this drawer?

Miggs: Do the first three letters, *D-I-G,* come between *B-R-O-W* and *C-L?*　＊

Jiggs: *(sings alphabet song)* "A, B, C, D. . . ." No.

Miggs: That's right. The title cards for *Digging Up Dinosaurs* would be in the next drawer, *C-O* to *D.*　＊

Jiggs: Then I'd find the author card for Laura Ingalls Wilder in the drawer with all the *L* cards, right?

Miggs: No. Author's names are written with the last name first, the way they are in the telephone book. Laura's name would be written Wilder, comma, Laura Ingalls.

Jiggs: Then her author card would be in the drawer with all the *W* cards, right?

Miggs: Now you're catching on! What drawer would you look in to find the title card for *Little House in the Big Woods?*

Jiggs: The *W* drawer.

Miggs: The *W* drawer?

Jiggs: Sure. If you look up the author by her last name, you look up the title by its last word. *Woods* is the last word, and *woods* starts with *W.* You'd look up Woods, comma, Little House in the Big.

Miggs: *Woods* starts with *W,* all right, but you look up the title by its first word. Unless the first word is *a, an,* or *the.* Then you look up the second word. For example, the title card for *A Light in the Attic* would be in the *L* drawer for *light,* not the *A* drawer for *a.*

Jiggs: Oh, I get it! You'd look in the *L* drawer for *Little House in the Big Woods* because *little* is the first word, and *little* starts with *L.*

Miggs: Right! Now let's go to the library and look up some catalog cards. Then you can see the call numbers and how they help you find the book on the shelf. In fact, this is a very good day for you to learn about the card catalog, because the librarian is explaining it to _____ class today.

Note: Say the teacher's name.

Jiggs: Oh, boy! Let's go!

(Miggs and Jiggs exit stage right.)

Get Lost in a Book

Characters: Child (right hand)
Monster (left hand)

> If you don't have a monster, perhaps a bear, lion, crocodile, or similar creature could try to frighten Child, who can be either male or female.
> If you don't have any humans, a little animal like a mouse or a rabbit could be reading. (In this case, a cat could play Monster's part.)

Props: two of your favorite adventure books

Preparation: Open the first book so it stands at center stage with both front and back covers facing the audience. Put the second book so it stands at the extreme right of the stage with only the front cover facing the audience.

(Child stands in front of second book and looks into its pages as if reading it.)

Monster: *(enters stage left, looks at Child, laughs, and then addresses audience)* Get ready to hear some screams, because *(points)* I'm going to scare that kid silly.

(Monster tiptoes toward Child. Child sits absorbed in book. Monster stands right behind Child and growls. Child turns page. Monster puts its mouth next to Child's left ear and growls. Child turns page and leans closer into book. Monster puts its mouth next to Child's right ear and growls. Child just reads.)

Monster: *(pokes Child in back or taps Child on shoulder)* Hey, you!

Child: Ouch! *(turns around and asks grumpily)* What do you want?

Monster: *(incredulously)* Don't you know?

Child: How could I? You haven't told me.

Monster: But you know what I am, don't you?

Child: Sure, you're a big, ugly monster.

Monster: If you know I'm a monster, you must know what I want.

Child: Well, I don't, so why don't you just tell me?

Monster: I want to do what monsters always do: **SCARE YOU!**
(leans forward and growls loudly right in Child's face)

Child: Get lost.

Monster: *(sounds offended)* What did you say?

Child: Get lost . . . in a book!

Monster: Are you trying to insult me?

Child: No, I'm giving you good advice. It's fun to get lost in a book.

Monster: How can I do that?

Child: Go to the _____, check out some good books, and start reading. Pretty soon you'll find yourself doing new things and going new places.

Note: Say your library's name.

Monster: I hope I don't get carsick.

Child: Don't worry. You won't be going by car.

Monster: You mean, I have to go in a plane? *(shakes)* Oh, dear, flying makes me nervous.

Child: No, you won't be going by plane. You go in your imagination.

Monster: I don't think I have an imagination. Is that some sort of helicopter or submarine?

Child: No. Imagination means pretending. When you read, you pretend to be the characters in the book. You go where they go and share their adventures with them. When you read *Swamp Angel* by Anne Isaacs, you get to travel in your mind to Tennessee and wrestle a giant bear. When you read *Henry the Sailor Cat* by Mary Calhoun, you can sail on the ocean, see dolphins and whales, and even save a man from drowning.

Alternative Dialogue: Briefly describe books you'd recommend to children.

Monster: Wow! Reading sounds very exciting!

Child: It is. Your imagination gets lost in the story until you're so wrapped up in the book, you're not aware of anything else. You can't hear your mother calling you for dinner or your baby brother or sister bawling, and . . .

Monster: A ferocious monster can sneak up behind you without your even knowing. Right?

Child: Right!

Monster: You must have been wrapped up in a good book when I tried to scare you.

Child: I was. I was riding in a hot-air balloon headed for power lines and had to save myself from sizzling on the wires.

Alternative Dialogue: Describe briefly a highlight in the book you selected, or use the dialog supplied if you picked Mary Calhoun's *Hot-Air Henry.*

Monster: How thrilling! I want to get lost in a book, too.

Child: Then why don't you try that one over there? *(Child points to book at center stage.)* Creatures from another planet will pick you up in their spaceship and take you into outer space.

Alternative Dialogue: Briefly describe the book you selected. If you picked *Alistair in Outer Space* by Marilyn Sadler, use the dialogue supplied.

Monster: Oh, boy! I can't wait to get there. Good-bye. *(runs behind book)*

(Take off Monster.)

Child: *(turns back to own book and reads for awhile, then turns around and calls)* Isn't that good? *(no answer)* How do you like the book? *(no answer)* Don't you know it's polite to answer people when they talk to you?

(Child crosses to book and puts it down on the stage.)

Child: *(addresses audience)* He must like the book, all right, because he really **DID** get lost. I hope you'll get lost in a book soon, too. Good-bye. *(exits behind the book at stage right)*

Adventure Books

Calhoun, Mary. *Henry the Sailor Cat.* Morrow, 1994.

———. *Hot-Air Henry.* Morrow, 1981.

Isaacs, Anne. *Swamp Angel.* Dutton, 1994.

Sadler, Marilyn. *Alistair in Outer Space.* Simon & Schuster, 1984.

Don't Monkey Around with Library Books
A Skit about Taking Care of Books

Characters: Book (left hand)
Monkey (right hand)

If you don't own a monkey, substitute any other puppet with movable arms.

The easiest way to make a talking book is to open a Little Golden Book to the middle. Slip a large rubber band over the left-hand pages and another large rubber band over the right-hand side. Move the rubber bands over until they're about two inches from the book's spine. Slide your thumb under the rubber band on the front cover and your fingers under the rubber band on the back cover. (Keep some extra rubber bands handy just in case one breaks.)

Props: bookmark cut from the corner of an envelope
pencil

Preparation: Book is lying face up on the stage or in your lap.

Monkey: *(enters stage right, rubbing hands)* Making all those mud-pies sure was fun, but now I'd like to do something else. *(looks down at book)* Hey! I can read this book I got at the library yesterday. *(leans over to pick up book)*

Book: *(jumps away)* Keep your hands off me! They're filthy.

Monkey: That's because I was playing in the mud.

Book: Well, wash your hands if you want to read me. I don't want muddy fingerprints messing up my pages.

Monkey: *(exits stage right, returns stage right, crosses to book, and shows it both sides of his hands)* See? They're clean. **NOW** may I read you?

Book: **IF** you promise you'll always have clean hands when you read.

Monkey: *(raises one arm)* I promise. *(pulls book up and pretends to read for awhile)* I wonder what happens next. I'd better turn the page and find out. *(reaches for bottom of page)*

Book: *(jumps back)* Not that way!

Monkey: What do you mean *(mimics)*, "Not that way"?

Book: You were going to turn my page from the bottom.

Monkey: Isn't that all right?

Book: No, because you might tear it that way. It's better to turn pages carefully from their top right corners.

Monkey: Reading you is too much work, so I'll just put you down. *(puts book down with pages open and cover on top)*

(Book screams.)

Monkey: *(holds hands over ears and cringes)* Stop! You're hurting my ears!

Book: Well, you're breaking my back! *(screams)*

Monkey: I'm not even touching you.

Book: But you put me down with my pages open. That hurts. *(screams)*

Monkey: What do you want me to do?

Book: Put me down with my pages closed.

(Monkey puts book down with pages closed.)

Book: Ahhhhh! That's better.

Monkey: Now you've made me lose my place.

Book: There are better ways of keeping your place than putting me down with my pages open.

Monkey: Oh yeah. I could bend down a corner of the page. *(reaches for top right corner of book)*

Book: *(jumps back)* No! Folding them down makes the corners tear off.

Monkey: Well, what if I stick an old banana peeling inside you?

Book: Yuck! Keep me away from food, drinks, and other messy stuff that could make me sticky.

Monkey: Then how can I keep my place?

Book: Use a bookmark. You can get one at the library or make your own by cutting off the corner of an old envelope.

Monkey: *(picks up bookmark and holds it out)* Like this?

Book: Perfect!

Monkey: *(slips bookmark over upper right-hand corner of book page)* I think I'll draw now. Here's a pencil. *(picks up pencil)* Now, where's some paper? *(looks around)* Since I can't find any paper, I guess I'll draw in you. *(moves toward book)*

Book: *(jumps back)* Oh no, you won't! You should draw only on drawing or writing pieces of paper, never in books.

Monkey: *(throws pencil offstage)* Then I won't draw. I'll build some-thing with blocks in the playroom. Good-bye. *(turns to go)*

Book: Wait! Don't leave me here!

Monkey: *(turns back)* Do you want to play with blocks, too?

Book: No, but I want you to put me away on your bookshelf now that you're finished reading me.

Monkey: *(whines)* I don't want to go all the way upstairs. Why can't I just leave you there on the floor?

Book: I could get lost or hurt if I stay here.

Monkey: How?

Book: Lots of bad things could happen. Somebody could acciden-tally kick me under the couch, your dog could chew me into little pieces, or your baby brother could scribble on me or tear my pages.

Monkey: That would mess you up, all right.

Book: That's why you should keep all of us books on bookshelves. Then we won't get lost, and we'll be safe from pets and little children who don't know how to take care of us.

Monkey: I don't want to keep you at all. You're so bossy, I'm going to take you back to the library.

Book: I hope you **WILL** return me on time, because other people are waiting to read me. But today is not a good day for you to take me to the library.

Monkey: Why not?

Book: Because all the rain will get me wet, and then my pages will wrinkle.

Monkey: How about if I put you in a plastic bag? Will **THAT** make you happy?

Book: Make that **TWO** plastic bags. It's really pouring out.

Monkey: Boy, are you fussy!

Book: No, I'm not. I'm just asking you to take good care of me because I belong to everybody. If you're rough, I'll fall apart and no one can ever read me again.

Monkey: *(hangs head and wipes tear from eye)* That would be sad.

Book: **NOW** do you understand why I've asked you to treat me carefully?

Monkey: I sure do. Now I know you shouldn't monkey around with library books.

Alternative Dialogue and Action: If you don't use a monkey puppet, say, "From now on, I'll always treat library books with TLC." *(puppet pats or hugs the book)*

Little Red Riding Hood's Goodies

Characters: Mother (left hand)
Little Red Riding Hood (right hand)
Honey Bear (left hand)

If your puppet collection has a man instead of a woman, Little Red Riding Hood can talk to her father.

If you don't have a bear puppet, you might want to substitute some other animal and change the type of food it wants. For example, a rabbit might be interested in carrots, and a mouse might crave cheese.

Props: basket
bed
cookbook

If you don't have a small basket, you can make one by cutting off the bottom of a small box, such as the kind gelatin, baking soda, and bars of bath soap come in. Cover this with brown paper and attach a strip of brown paper for a handle.

A little pillow or baby blanket folded in a rectangle can serve as the bed.

(Mother stands at stage left, facing stage right, with basket at her feet or in your lap.)

SCENE 1: LITTLE RED RIDING HOOD'S HOUSE

Mother: *(calls)* Little Red Riding Hood. Little Red Riding Hood.

Little Red Riding Hood: *(enters stage right)* Yes, Mother?

Mother: *(picks up basket and holds it out)* Please take this basket of goodies to your grandmother, dear. She's sick in bed, and these will cheer her up.

Little Red Riding Hood: Sure, Mom. *(takes basket)*

Mother: *(admonishes)* Now be careful when you go through the forest. Don't talk to any strangers, and don't dawdle.

Little Red Riding Hood: I won't. I want to hurry home so I can finish my library book before supper. *(skips off stage right and sings)* "A tisket, a tasket. I've goodies in my basket."

Mother: *(addresses audience)* I think I'll read a few pages of my own book before I start supper. *(exits stage left)*

(Take off Mother. Put on Honey Bear.)

SCENE 2: IN THE FOREST

Little Red Riding Hood: *(enters stage right, skipping and singing)* "A tisket, a tasket. I've goodies in my basket."

Honey Bear: *(jumps out stage left)* Good afternoon, little girl. I'm Honey Bear. What's your name?

Little Red Riding Hood: Little Red Riding Hood.

Honey Bear: *(looks at basket)* That's a very pretty basket, Little Red Riding Hood. Did you say you have goodies in it?

Little Red Riding Hood: Uh-huh. I'm taking them to my grandma who lives in the cottage on the other side of the woods. *(points offstage)* She's sick in bed, and these will cheer her up.

Honey Bear: That's a long walk for a little girl. Wouldn't you like me to deliver the goodies for you? *(leans toward basket)*

Little Red Riding Hood: *(jumps back)* No, thank you. And I'd best be on my way.

Honey Bear: Don't rush off. I'd like to get to know you—*(looks at basket)* and your basket of goodies, too.

Little Red Riding Hood: Well, I can't stay any longer. My mom wants me to come straight home. 'Bye. *(skips off stage right and sings)* "A tisket, a tasket. I've goodies in my basket."

Honey Bear: *(watches her go and then addresses audience)* Those goodies in her basket might be honey cakes so . . . *(sings)* "She'll take the high road *(Honey Bear moves up in the air.)*, and I'll take the low road *(moves down in air)*, and I'll get to Grandma's before her. *(pretends to push)* I'll shove the old lady in the closet. *(jumps to one side)* And I'll jump into her bed. And when Red Riding Hood comes, I will eat the goodies." *(runs off stage left, shouting)* Yum!

Note: Raise and lower arm to move puppet up and down.

SCENE 3: GRANDMA'S HOUSE

Little Red Riding Hood: *(calls from offstage)* Knock, knock.

Honey Bear: *(stands up, faces stage right, and calls)* Who's there?

Little Red Riding Hood: *(still offstage)* Owl.

Honey Bear: Owl who?

Little Red Riding Hood: *(still offstage)* Owl you know unless you open the door?

Honey Bear: Cut out the knock-knock jokes and tell me who's really there.

Little Red Riding Hood: *(still offstage)* Your granddaughter.

Setup: Put bed at stage left with Honey Bear on it.

Honey Bear: Oh, yeah, the little kid with the funny name. What was it now . . . ? Crimson Cloak?

Little Red Riding Hood: *(still offstage)* No, it's Little Red Riding Hood!

Honey Bear: Oh, that's right. Come on in. *(beckons)* Bring that basket of goodies right over here by me.

Little Red Riding Hood: *(enters stage right, crosses to Honey Bear, and sets basket down; looks at Honey Bear, shakes, and gasps)* Grandma, what big eyes you have!

Honey Bear: All the better to see that basket of goodies you have, my dear. *(looks at basket)*

Little Red Riding Hood: *(looks at Honey Bear's paws, shakes, and gasps)* Grandma, what big paws you have!

Note: Omit this and the following line of dialogue if Honey Bear puppet lacks paws.

Honey Bear: All the better to take that basket of goodies **I** have, my dear. *(slides basket over to the left of him)*

Little Red Riding Hood: *(looks at Honey Bear's mouth, shakes, and gasps)* Grandma, what a big mouth you have!

Honey Bear: All the better to **EAT** the goodies, my dear. *(pounces on basket and looks inside)* Hmph! There's nothing but library books in here! *(throws basket away in disgust)* Where are the goodies you said you had?

Little Red Riding Hood: The library books are the goodies.

Honey Bear: What's so good about library books? They don't have honey or peanut butter in them, do they?

Little Red Riding Hood: No.

Honey Bear: Oatmeal or raisins?

Little Red Riding Hood: No.

Honey Bear: Chocolate chips or coconut?

Little Red Riding Hood: No.

Honey Bear: Sugar or molasses?

Little Red Riding Hood: No.

Honey Bear: Then what **DO** library books have in them anyway?

Little Red Riding Hood: Words and pictures.

Honey Bear: *(incredulously)* Words and pictures?

Little Red Riding Hood: Uh-huh, words and pictures.

Honey Bear: You can't make honey cakes with words and pictures.

Little Red Riding Hood: No, but you can tell stories with them. The _____ has lots of books that use words and pictures to tell stories.

Note: Say your library's name.

Honey Bear: What kind of stories?

Little Red Riding Hood: **ALL** kinds of stories. Scary stories, adventure stories, animal stories, funny stories, make-believe stories, and stories about real people.

Honey Bear: Can you do anything with words and pictures **BESIDES** tell stories?

Little Red Riding Hood: Yes. You can explain things and give information.

Honey Bear: I don't understand what you're saying. *Explain* and *information* are big words.

Little Red Riding Hood: Well . . . let's say you wanted to learn about snakes. You could go to the library and read books that give information about them and explain how they live. The books would tell you whatever you wanted to know about these reptiles.

Honey Bear: *(shivers)* Do I have to read about snakes? They're scary!

Little Red Riding Hood: Of course not. I just used reptiles as an example, but you can learn about lots of other things at the library, too.

Honey Bear: Like what?

Little Red Riding Hood: Pets. Sports. Monsters. Whales. Weather. Volcanoes. Magic. The solar system. Origami. Crafts. Drawing. . . .

Honey Bear: Stop! Stop!

Little Red Riding Hood: But I'm just getting started.

Honey Bear: I get the idea.

Little Red Riding Hood: That's good, because it would take a long, long time to tell you about everything you can learn from the words and pictures in books at the library.

Honey Bear: That's all very nice, I suppose, but I don't need to read a book to learn that I'm hungry. Since you can't make honey cakes with words and pictures, I don't think your library has anything for me.

Little Red Riding Hood: You can't **EAT** library books, but you **CAN** read them and learn how to make honey cakes.

Honey Bear: You **CAN?**

Little Red Riding Hood: Sure. Wait here. *(exits stage right, returns with cookbook, and pushes it into Honey Bear's face)* You see this book?

Honey Bear: How can I help but see it? You shoved it right in my face.

Little Red Riding Hood: This book *(pushes it at Honey Bear)* is full of recipes that use honey.

Honey Bear: Do the recipes taste good?

Little Red Riding Hood: Why don't you look at the book and find out for yourself?

Honey Bear: I think I will. *(He hums while looking at the book from top to bottom and from left to right. He sniffs the edges of the book loudly, pretends to bite off the upper left corner, chews it, and swallows loudly.)* You know what, little girl? Library books **ARE** goodies. They don't taste bad, after all. *(noisily eats book and burps)* "Ahhhhh!"

Versions of "Little Red Riding Hood"

See the books listed for the skit "Little Blue Riding Hood."

Space Creatures Meet Mother Goose

Characters: Eep (left hand)
Opp (right hand)

Props: spaceship
sign with your library's name on it
any Mother Goose book

> You could eliminate the spaceship, if you prefer, but it adds a nice visual element to the skit. It doesn't have to be elaborate. You could simply cut a paper plate in half and cover it with aluminum foil. You might want to draw several small circles near the base for portholes. Attach it to a stick of some sort or a strip of cardboard. You can hold onto this handle as you fly the spaceship across the stage.

Note: The wording and punctuation for the verses come from *The Random House Book of Mother Goose,* selected and illustrated by Arnold Lobel (Random House, 1986). If you prefer other versions of the rhymes, feel free to substitute those.

Preparation: Set sign near stage right or in your lap at an angle that allows both puppets and audience to read it.

SCENE 1: OUTSIDE THE LIBRARY

(Hold the spaceship with your right hand. Raise your right arm as high as you can and fly the spaceship from stage right to stage left. Bring your arm down in an arc, so it will look as if the spaceship is landing just offstage. You might like to make an eerie noise as you fly the UFO.)

(Aliens enter from stage left and look around.)

Opp: So this is what Earth looks like.

Eep: I think it is rather pretty.

Opp: So do I. I think I will like living here once we have taken over the planet.

Eep: I think I will, too. But do you think Earth people will give us much trouble?

Opp: That is what we are supposed to find out. The High Command has sent us here to learn all about Earth culture.

Eep: How can we do that?

Opp: We could try to find a library. I always go to one back home whenever I want to learn something new.

Eep: Do you think Earthlings are smart enough to have a library?

Opp: I do not know. But we can look for one anyway.

Eep: *(grabs Opp's arm and points to sign)* Look! That sign says, "_____."

Note: Say your library's name.

Opp: Then let us go inside and read about life here on Earth.
(Aliens exit stage right.)

SCENE 2: INSIDE THE LIBRARY

(Aliens enter stage left and look around.)

Setup: Remove library sign. Put Mother Goose book face up at center stage or in your lap.

Eep: This looks like a library all right. It has plenty of books.

Opp: Which one shall we read first?

Eep: *(looks down, sees book, and picks it up)* How about this one? It must be especially important to be sitting out like this.

Alternative Action: If your alien lacks arms, make it just look at the book.

Opp: *(looks cover over from top to bottom and from left to right)* "Mother Goose Rhymes."

Eep: Earth geese make up verses! They must be more advanced than the animals living on our planet.

Opp: I'll say! None of the creatures there are smart enough to write.

Eep: Let us read what this fabulous fowl has written.

(Aliens lay book on the stage or in your lap and open it. They pretend to read.)

Opp: "Pussycat, pussycat, where have you been? I've been to London to visit the queen."

Eep: We were right! Their animal life is very advanced. Not only do geese here write, but cats travel about on their own.

Opp: **AND** a reigning monarch receives them! That is indeed impressive.

Eep: Now that we know about their animals, we should try to learn about Earth people. That is really our mission.

Opp: You are right. *(turns page and points)* Here is something about a person. *(reads)* "Jack be nimble, Jack be quick, Jack jump over the candlestick." *(looks at Eep)* Earth people play with fire. They must be very stupid.

Note: Because it is hard to turn pages with puppets on, you might want to turn a number of pages at once.

Eep: Yes. *(points to page)* Let us read about this person with the funny name.

Opp: *(reads)* "Little Boy Blue, come blow your horn. The sheep's in the meadow, the cow's in the corn. But where is the little boy tending the sheep? He's under a haystack fast asleep."

Eep: Earth people fall asleep on the job. They must be lazy as well as stupid.

Opp: We will not have any trouble taking over this planet.

Eep: But it says, "The sheep's in the meadow, the cow's in the corn." That sounds as if animals have already taken over the Earth.

Opp: You are right. We had better read on. *(reads)* "Ding, dong, bell, Pussy's in the well. Who put her in? Little Johnny Green."

Eep: No wonder the animals rebelled. People treat them badly.

Opp: Since humans mistreat them, the animals will probably want to cooperate with us.

Eep: Maybe not. They might want the planet all to themselves instead of having to share it with us.

Opp: We need to learn more about the animals. Let us keep reading.

Eep: *(turns page)* Here is information about them. *(reads)* "Hey diddle, diddle, the cat and the fiddle, the cow jumped over the moon; the little dog laughed to see such sport, and the dish ran away with the spoon." *(looks straight at Opp)* Uh-oh!

Opp: Are you thinking what I am thinking?

Eep: I do not know what you are thinking, but I am thinking that cows are invading outer space.

Opp: That is what I am thinking as well.

Eep: I am also thinking that maybe the cows are planning to take over our planet.

Opp: I am thinking that, too.

Eep: We had better hurry home and warn the High Command to prepare a counterattack. *(runs off stage left)*

Opp: Wait for me! *(runs off stage left)*

SCENE 3: OUTSIDE THE LIBRARY

(Hold spaceship in your right hand. Raise your right arm as high as you can and move it straight across from left to right.)

Puppeteer: You don't have to be an alien from outer space to go to the library and learn something new. But don't just pick up a Mother Goose book. Look in the computer to find what you want or ask the librarian to help.

Setup: Remove Mother Goose book. Put up sign.

Alternative Dialogue: Look in the card catalog. . . .

Books about Aliens

See the books listed for the skit "Moon Rock Soup."

Never Be Bored Again!

A Miggs and Jiggs Skit
to Introduce the Library's Services

Characters: Jiggs (right hand)
Miggs (left hand)
Elephant (left hand)

> If you have a mouse but no elephant, you might try putting a trunk (a gray sock or strip of material) over its nose. Or you could substitute some other puppet that is bigger than Jiggs.

Props: dust cloth
tote bag
items from the library's circulating collection

> For props, select a picture book, a book with chapters, and at least one nonfiction book as well as one item to represent each type of material children can borrow from your library. For example, pick a magazine, an audiocassette, a record, and a kit containing a book and audiotape, etc. If all this won't fit in a bag or would make it too heavy to carry, cut replicas out of cardboard or glue pictures from suppliers' catalogs onto cardboard. If your library has special bags, use those. Otherwise, use any tote bag you have or a grocery bag.

Preparation: Put library materials inside bag and set the bag near your left foot.

SCENE 1: MIGGS'S LIVING ROOM

Jiggs: *(stands at center stage and sighs loudly)* I'm **BORED.**

(Miggs enters stage left, dusting. Miggs dusts all around stage and then dusts Jiggs's head.)

Jiggs: *(jumps back)* Hey! Cut it out!

Miggs: Oh, sorry, Jiggs. But you were sitting so still, I thought you were part of the furniture.

Jiggs: *(sarcastically)* Ha. Ha. Very funny.

Miggs: I thought so. Why are you just sitting in here on such a beautiful day? Why don't you go outside and play?

Jiggs: There's nobody to play with. *(sighs loudly)* There's nothing to do.

Miggs: You could help me clean. *(tries to give dust cloth to Jiggs)*

Jiggs: *(turns away from dust cloth)* I think I'll go out after all. Doing nothing outside beats cleaning up inside. *(exits stage right)*

Miggs: And I'll go dust the bedroom. *(exits stage left, dusting the stage along the way)*

(Take off Miggs. Put on Elephant.)

SCENE 2: OUTSIDE

Jiggs: *(enters stage right and looks around)* Rats! There's nobody around to play with and nothing going on. *(sighs loudly)* I'm so bored. *(stands facing stage right)*

(Elephant enters stage left with tote bag, crosses toward stage right, and bumps into Jiggs.)

Jiggs: *(turns around)* Hey, watch it!

Elephant: *(puts bag down)* I'm sorry, but you really shouldn't be sitting in the middle of the sidewalk.

Jiggs: I know, but *(sighs loudly)* I don't have anything better to do.

Elephant: Then why don't you go to the _____? You'll find lots to do there.

> **Note:** Say your library's name.

Jiggs: Like what?

Elephant: Well, for one thing, you can attend special programs. The library holds storytimes every Thursday and shows films on Saturday afternoons. Sometimes they bring in magicians, clowns, and dancers.

> **Note:** Briefly describe the types of programs your library offers or adapt the given dialogue.

Jiggs: That sounds like fun. But there isn't any program at the library right now, so *(sighs loudly)* I still don't have anything to do.

Elephant: Even when the library isn't holding programs, you can still have fun there. You can read books and magazines, put together puzzles, play with puppets, draw pictures, listen to tapes, and watch the gerbils.

> **Note:** Mention briefly activities children can do at your library or adapt the given dialogue.

Jiggs: I wish the library were open all the time. Then I could just move in and never be bored again.

Elephant: You can't **LIVE** at the library, but you **CAN** take some of its books and other things home to play with.

Jiggs: *(shows horror)* No, I couldn't! That would be stealing!

Elephant: It isn't stealing because you wouldn't keep them. You'd just borrow them for awhile and then return them.

Jiggs: And that would be O.K.?

Elephant: Of course, because that's what the library is for. It has all kinds of wonderful books and other things people can borrow for _____ and enjoy at home.

> **Note:** Specify your loan period.

Jiggs: What kinds of things?

Elephant: Let me show you. I was just at the library and checked out a bunch of cool stuff. *(pulls books out of bag)* See the books I got? The library has lots of great books.

Jiggs: I knew that.

Elephant: But did you know how many different kinds of books it has? It has all types of stories to read for fun plus loads of information books that tell you about lots of different things. There are books about holidays, dinosaurs, sports, cars, outer space, animals, airplanes, ghosts, monsters, and firefighters.

Jiggs: Cool!

Elephant: You said it. The library also has books to help you write reports for school, plan a party, and explore other countries. There are books that teach you how to make things, do magic tricks, learn a new sport, and take care of your pet. I couldn't possibly tell you about all the books at the library, so you'll have to go there and see them for yourself.

Jiggs: I'll go right now.

Elephant: While you're at the library, look for all the other things you can borrow, like . . . *(pulls items out of tote bag one at a time, sets them down, and talks briefly about each one)*

Jiggs: Wow! You sure got a lot of cool stuff from the library. I wish I could get some for myself, but *(hangs head)* I don't have any money.

Elephant: You don't **NEED** money. All you need is a library card.

Jiggs: I don't have one of those either.

Elephant: That's O.K. It's easy to get one.

Note: Explain your library's procedure for obtaining a library card.

Jiggs: I can't wait to get a library card of my own. Then I'll never be bored again because I'll be able to take home all this great stuff *(waves arms over pile of library materials)* for myself.

Elephant: You'll be able to take home many good things, all right, but probably not as much as I can.

Jiggs: Why not?

Elephant: You're not as strong as I am, so you won't be able to carry as much.

Alternative Action: If Jiggs lacks movable arms, move it back and forth behind the materials.

Storybook Characters Look for Work

Characters: Personnel Director (left hand)
Rabbit
Wolf
Troll
Pig
Dog
Bear

All except the first are right-hand puppets.

Personnel Director can be any puppet. If you lack some of the other characters, shorten the skit by eliminating those parts or substitute other job applicants. For example, a rooster, donkey, or cat could fill in for the dog because those animals also belonged to the Bremen-town Musicians. A girl could play Sleeping Beauty, who might seek work as a seamstress. The witch from "Hansel and Gretel" might want a position as a nanny. You can use any monster puppet for Troll.

Props: any book
a card on which you've written your library's name and
address

Note: This skit will go more smoothly if you arrange the puppets beforehand in the order in which they appear. I put the personnel director on my left side and stack the others in three piles on my right. I put Rabbit on top of Wolf in the pile closest to me, Troll on top of Pig in the middle pile, and Dog on top of Bear in the pile farthest from me. If your puppets are fairly flat, you might want to make only two stacks of three characters each.

Preparation: Open the book so it lies flat on the stage or in your lap. Lay the card faceup next to book.

(Personnel Director reads.)

Puppeteer: Bong. Bong. Bong. Bong. Bong. Bong. Bong. Bong. Bong.

Personnel Director: *(addresses audience)* This book is so good, I hate to stop reading. But it's nine o'clock, and that means clients will start coming any minute. I like my work here at the Jobs R Us Employment Agency because I get to meet many different people. *(looks off to right)* Here comes my first client now.

Rabbit: *(hops in stage right)* Hello.

Personnel Director: Hello. What is your name?

Rabbit: Peter.

Personnel Director: *(shakes Peter's paw)* Nice to meet you, Peter. What kind of job do you want?

Rabbit: I want to be a vegetable gardener.

Personnel Director: Have you ever worked in a vegetable garden before?

Rabbit: No, but I've spent a lot of time visiting my neighbor's garden.

Personnel Director: Then I'll need your neighbor's name as a reference.

Rabbit: It's Mr. McGregor.

Personnel Director: *(thinks)* Hmmmm, Mr. McGregor, Peter Rabbit. . . . Oh, no! You don't want to grow vegetables; you just want to eat them!

Rabbit: Yes, because they're yummy to my tummy. *(rubs tummy)* Mmmmmm.

Personnel Director: I don't think gardening is the right occupation for you, Peter. Gardeners are supposed to raise and sell vegetables, not eat them.

Rabbit: Rats!

Personnel Director: Go out into the waiting room, Peter, and I'll try to find you another job.

(Rabbit hops off stage right.)

(Take off Rabbit. Put on Wolf.)

Personnel Director: *(addresses audience)* I don't think any gardener would want Peter's kind of "help." I wonder who'll come in next.

Wolf: *(enters stage right)* Good morning, madam.

Personnel Director: Good morning. What is your name?

Wolf: B. B. Wolf.

Personnel Director: I can't use initials in our records, Mr. Wolf. Please tell me your full name.

Wolf: *(mumbles unintelligibly)* Big Bad Wolf.

Personnel Director: *(puts hand to ear)* What was that?

Wolf: *(mumbles unintelligibly)* Big Bad Wolf.

Personnel Director: Really now! Stop mumbling and speak up.

Wolf: *(puts mouth next to director's ear and yells)* **BIG BAD WOLF!**

Personnel Director: *(jumps back, shaking)* My heavens, what kind of name is that?

Wolf: I was named after my grandfathers. My father's father was Big, and my mother's father was Bad. But, hey, that's no reflection on **MY** character. I'm a real sweetheart of a guy who delivers meals to shut-ins and reads to the blind.

Personnel Director: *(congratulates Wolf)* That's very commendable of you. Are you looking for a job in social services?

Wolf: No, I want to be a pig farmer.

Personnel Director: Have you ever worked with pigs before?

Wolf: No, but I've known some, and that's given me a taste for the little porkers. . . . I mean, it's given me a taste of what it would be like to work with pigs.

Personnel Director: Did you decide you like pigs?

Wolf: Yes. *(smacks lips)* Especially with relish.

Personnel Director: What?

Wolf: I mean, I'd relish the opportunity to work with pigs.

Personnel Director: I see. How many pigs have you known?

Wolf: Three.

Personnel Director: *(thinks)* Hmmmm, three pigs, Big Bad Wolf. . . . Oh, no! You were going to eat them!

Wolf: *(dreamily)* Yes, pork chops *(smacks lips)*, bacon *(smacks lips)*, sausages *(smacks lips)*, ham *(smacks lips)*.

Personnel Director: I don't know any farmers who'd want you around their pigs. Go out to the waiting room, and I'll try to find you another job. *(pushes Wolf off stage right)*

(Take off Wolf. Put on Troll.)

Personnel Director: *(addresses audience)* The **NERVE** of some people. Imagine, a wolf applying for a job as a pig farmer!

Troll: *(enters stage right)* Good morning.

Personnel Director: Hello. *(looks at Troll from head to toe and from front to back)* I hope you won't take offense, but I must say I've never seen anyone quite like you before.

Troll: You mean, you've never seen a troll before?

Personnel Director: *(brightly)* Oh, you're a troll! Pleased to meet you, Mr. Troll. *(shakes hands with Troll)*

Troll: Just call me Harvey.

Personnel Director: All right, Harvey. What kind of job do you want?

Troll: I'd like to collect tolls on the bridge.

Personnel Director: Have you ever collected tolls on a bridge before?

Troll: No, but I used to live under a bridge. Whenever anyone crossed over it, I'd jump up to meet them.

Personnel Director: How very friendly of you. Was there much traffic on your bridge?

Troll: No. Just three brothers.

Personnel Director: Did they cross the bridge while commuting to work?

Troll: No. They crossed it to eat the grass on the other side.

Personnel Director: *(shows surprise)* Eat grass? How strange!

Troll: Not really. You see, these brothers were goats.

Personnel Director: *(thinks)* Hmmmm, three goats, a troll. . . . Oh, no! You wanted to eat them!

Troll: At least I wasn't charging them a toll.

Personnel Director: Nobody wants you taking money on the bridge. You'd better wait in the other room while I try finding you another job. *(pushes Troll off stage right)*

(Take off Troll. Put on Pig.)

Personnel Director: *(addresses audience)* This is turning out to be a very strange day.

Pig: *(enters stage right)* Howdy.

Personnel Director: Hello. What's your name?

Pig: First Little Pig.

Personnel Director: *(shakes Pig's foot)* Pleased to meet you, First Little Pig. What kind of work did you have in mind?

Pig: I want to go into the construction business.

Personnel Director: Do you have any building experience?

Pig: Yes indeed. I've built my own house—a hundred times!

Personnel Director: *(shows surprise)* A hundred times? Why so many?

Pig: I made it out of straw. Any time the wind blows—or someone breathes on it—it falls down. *(collapses)*

Personnel Director: *(pulls Pig up)* Straw is a very flimsy building material.

Pig: I'll say! Because any time the wind blows—or someone breathes on it—it falls down. *(collapses)*

Personnel Director: *(pulls Pig up)* Then why don't you use bricks?

Pig: Hey! Bricks are heavy. Didn't you know that?

Personnel Director: I'm aware of that.

Pig: Well, lifting heavy bricks is hard work. Did you know that?

Personnel Director: Yes.

Pig: Well, I don't like working hard.

Personnel Director: If you don't like hard work, you don't belong in the construction business. You'd better go out in the waiting room, and I'll try to find you another job.

Pig: *(looks around)* Is there someplace else I could wait? *(points offstage right)* There's a big, bad wolf out there, and every time he looks at me, he smacks his lips, like this. *(smacks lips)* It makes me **REALLY** nervous. *(shakes)*

Personnel Director: *(looks around)* I suppose you could hide in the bathroom. *(points offstage left)*

Pig: Thanks. *(exits stage left)*

(Take off Pig. Put on Dog.)

Personnel Director: *(addresses audience)* Pigs in the bathroom! **WHAT** will happen next?

Dog: *(enters stage right)* Good afternoon.

Personnel Director: Well, hello there. What is your name?

Dog: Bingo.

Personnel Director: Could you spell that, please?

Dog: B-I-N-G-O.

Personnel Director: **YOU** must be the farmer's dog.

Dog: I was, but I'm getting too old for farm work. I'm looking for something less strenuous now.

Personnel Director: Did you have anything in mind?

Dog: Well, I've always had this dream of becoming a singer.

Personnel Director: Do you have any performing experience?

Dog: I once belonged to a group called the Brementown Musicians. Ever heard of us?

Personnel Director: The name **DOES** sound familiar. Could you sing something for me, please?

Dog: *(sings terribly off key)* "Oh, where, oh, where has my little dog gone? Oh, where, oh, where can he be?"

Personnel Director: *(has been holding hands to ears and cringing throughout the song and now holds out an arm)* That's enough. Singing doesn't seem to be the right occupation for you. Why don't you go out in the waiting room while I try to come up with something else?

Dog: *(exits stage right, singing)* "How much is that doggie in the window?"

(Take off Dog puppet. Put on Bear.)

Personnel Director: *(addresses audience)* I wish someone would come in who's actually qualified for the type of job he wants.

Bear: *(enters stage right)* Good afternoon. I'm Papa Bear.

Personnel Director: *(shakes Bear's hand)* Pleased to meet you, Papa Bear. What type of job do you want?

Bear: I'd like to be a bank guard.

Personnel Director: Security work can be dangerous. Do you have a family to consider?

Bear: Yes, there's Mama and our baby.

Personnel Director: You must be one of the three bears.

Bear: *(thinks)* Let's see. . . . Mama's one, Baby's two, and I'm three. We're bears. . . . Yes, I guess you could say I'm one of the three bears.

Personnel Director: I've read about you. Didn't a little girl walk into your cottage one morning?

Bear: Yeah, that Goldilocks brat really trashed the place. She slopped porridge all over, broke a chair, and messed up all the beds. It took us a whole day to clean up after her.

Personnel Director: If the security at your house is so lax that a little girl can just walk right in, I don't think any bank would trust you with its money and valuables.

Bear: Does that mean I don't get the job?

Personnel Director: Not as a bank guard. But I **DO** have something for you and everyone else in the waiting room. *(picks up card and holds it out)* Report to this address.

Bear: *(looks at card and reads)* The _____. What are we supposed to do there?

Personnel Director: They hold storytimes and other special programs, so I think you'd all fit right in.

Bear: Sounds like fun! *(takes card and exits stage right calling)* Hey, gang, let's go down to the library for storytime.

Offstage voices: Story time? Oh, boy! Let's go! Wait for me!

Note: Say your library's name.

Note: If your puppet lacks movable arms, have it call out offstage.

Personnel Director: *(addresses audience and wipes brow)* Whew! It's been a very strange day at the Jobs R Us Employment Agency, but I managed to find work for everyone who came in. *(opens book)* Now I can get back to my book. You might want to go to the library and get a good book. When you read, you never know whom you'll meet or what will happen. 'Bye. *(looks down into book)*

Books about Looking for Jobs

Buehner, Caralyn. *A Job for Wittilda*. Dial, 1993.

Parish, Peggy. *Come Back, Amelia Bedelia.* HarperCollins, 1971.

Pellowski, Michael. *Clara Joins the Circus.* Parents, 1981.

Versions of Classic Tales

See the books listed for the skits "The Three Little Pigs" and "Little Blue Riding Hood."

Wanted: A Whiz of a Wiz

Characters: Queen (left hand)
Wizard
Dragon
Alien
Monster
Rabbit

All except the first are right-hand puppets.

Any woman or girl puppet can become a queen by wearing a crown. (If you prefer, any man or boy puppet can become a king.)

Any puppet can play Wizard if you give it the appropriate hat.

If you don't have a dragon, you can turn a crocodile into one by pinning or taping paper or felt flames in its mouth. You can also make a mythical monster—as well as an alien—out of socks. If you don't want to create new puppets, rewrite the skit a little to allow characters you already have to play the parts of what Wizard turns into.

Props: copy of *Peter Rabbit*
crowns for queen and rabbit puppets

To make a crown, cut V shapes from the top of a strip of yellow or gold paper that is long enough to fit around your puppet's head. Join the ends together with staples, tape, or glue to make a headband. Make another crown for your rabbit. Make sure both fit securely on the puppets' heads, so they won't fall off during the skit.

To make a tall pointed sorcerer's cap, cut a half circle out of purple paper. Make a cone out of it by stapling, gluing, or taping the ends together. Draw a moon and some stars on it with a marker or cut these out of foil and glue them in place. Make sure the hat fits snugly so it won't fall off. If necessary, make an elastic chinstrap by cutting a rubber band across the middle and stapling the ends to each side of the hat.

Feel free to choose your own favorite book for the queen and have her turn into its title character. You could use any puppet that would match up or a storybook doll (like Ramona or Paddington Bear), if you have one. You could also make a stick puppet by enlarging an illustration of your favorite book character, adding a crown, and attaching it to a stick of some sort.

Note: Changing puppets quickly can be tricky. Before performing this skit, you might want to ask an adult to sit at your right side and help you.

Preparation: Put the crowns on Queen and Rabbit before skit.

Queen: *(addresses audience)* Ever since the castle wizard retired last month, things around the palace have been all messed up. We need a new sorcerer desperately, but finding one who's a whiz of a wiz is really hard.

Wizard: *(enters stage right, crosses to Queen, and bows)* Good afternoon, Your Majesty. I'm Waldo the Wizard. I hope you'll forgive me for not knocking, but the guard told me to just walk right in.

Queen: I imagine you've come to apply for the job of castle wizard.

Wizard: Yes. I saw your ad for a whiz of a wiz in the classified section of *Wizard's Weekly.*

Queen: Are you a whiz of a wiz?

Wizard: I most certainly am. I graduated first in my class at the Academy of Wizard Arts and Sciences. Would you like to see my diploma?

Queen: No, thank you. Paper doesn't impress me. **DO** something that will impress me.

Wizard: Very well, Your Majesty. I shall demonstrate my amazing ability to turn myself into anything I want to be. *(spreads arms out and moves body in small circles)* Alakazam and alakazagon. Powers, transform me into a dragon. *(drops down)*

(Take off Wizard. Put on Dragon.)

(Dragon pops up.)

Queen: *(yawns)* **BIG DEAL.** A hundred wizards have applied for this job, and all of them turned into dragons. Do they teach you that trick in wizard kindergarten?

Dragon: Preschool, actually. But it impresses most people—especially when we breathe fire.

Queen: Well, it doesn't impress me. Besides, I'm fresh out of wienies to roast, so you can extinguish your flames.

Dragon: *(moves body in small circles)* Alakazam and alakazace. Behold, I'm a creature from 'way out in space. *(drops down)*

(Take off Dragon. Put on Alien.)

(Alien pops up.)

Alien: I'll bet those other wizards didn't do this, did they?

Queen: No, they didn't.

Alien: Then do I get the job? I just proved I can do something really different.

Queen: That's not a good enough reason for me to hire you. After all, I have no use for a creature from outer space.

Alien: (*moves body in small circles*) Alakazam and alakazonster. If it's useful you want, I'll turn into a monster. (*drops down*)

(Take off Alien. Put on Monster.)

(*Monster pops up.*)

Queen: (*jumps back and screams*) A monster! Help!

Monster: Don't be alarmed, Your Majesty. I'm really Waldo the Wizard. I used my amazing powers to turn into a monster.

Queen: Why?

Monster: You said you wanted something useful, and a monster is definitely useful. If enemies ever attack your castle, I can scare them away.

Queen: That **WOULD** be helpful, but I wish you'd look like yourself again. I don't want to see this ugly face anymore.

Monster: Your wish is my command. (*moves body in small circles*) Alakazam and alakazizard. My switching is done. Once again I'm a wizard. (*drops down*)

(Take off Monster. Put on Wizard.)

(*Wizard pops up.*)

Wizard: Now that I've shown you I can be anything I want to be, you must realize what a whiz of a wiz I am.

Queen: Not really. I can be anything I want to be, too.

Wizard: How can that be, Your Majesty? You're no wizard.

Queen: I don't need to be because I have book magic.

Wizard: What kind of magic is that?

Queen: It's a very powerful magic that happens every time I open a book. Whenever I read, I become the character in the story. Sometimes I'm a pirate sailing the seven seas. Sometimes I'm a detective solving baffling mysteries. Once I was a cat traveling in a hot-air balloon. (*flies through the air, then lands*) There's no end to the magic of what I can be and the adventures I can have when I read.

Wizard: Book magic sounds wonderful—and less tiring than my magic. (*wipes brow*) Whew! I'm worn out from all these switches. (*collapses*) I'm also a little confused. Who am I now? (*stands up and looks down at himself*) Oh, yes. I'm my old self again. (*thinks*) I'm . . . I'm . . . I'm . . . uh . . .

Queen: Waldo the Wizard.

Wizard: That's right.

Queen: (*scornfully*) Some whiz of a wiz. You can't even remember your own name.

Wizard: I may be a little absent-minded at times, but I still have great powers. Why, I can even read minds.

Queen: I find that hard to believe.

Wizard: But it's true. Shall I tell you what you're thinking about this very minute?

Queen: If you can.

Wizard: Of course, I can. I can even show you because my amazing powers enable me to conjure things out of thin air. *(spreads arms out and moves body in small circles)* Alakazam and alakazappy. Give the queen what she wants, and please make it snappy. *(pops down, picks up copy of Peter Rabbit, and pops back up)* You were wishing you could curl up with your favorite book, *The Tale of Peter Rabbit.*

Queen: *(congratulates Wizard)* You really **ARE** a whiz of a wiz!

Wizard: Does this mean I get the job?

Queen: It's yours for life. Can you start tomorrow?

Wizard: I'll be here at nine. See you then. *(puts down book, waves, and exits stage right)*

(Take off Wizard. Put on Rabbit wearing crown.)

Queen: *(addresses audience)* Now that the wizard problem is solved, I can relax and enjoy myself. *(opens book and reads a bit)*

(Take down Queen.)

(Rabbit pops up.)

Queen: See? I **TOLD** you I could be anyone when I read. Visit your library soon, so you can make book magic, too. Good-bye. *(picks up book and exits stage left)*

Stories about Wizards

See the books listed for the skit "The Wizard's Sneeze."

PART FIVE

Additional Skits

▼▲▼▲▼▲▼▲▼▲▼▲▼▲▼▲▼

A Ghost in the House
A Halloween Skit

Characters: Child (right hand)
Mr. (or Mrs.) Shudders (left hand)
Ghost (left hand)

The child can be either male or female, as can the person whose house is haunted. If you don't have people puppets, you could substitute animals.

Note: You could actually perform this skit at any time. Just omit the words "for Halloween" (indicated with an asterisk (✱) in the right-hand column).

If the Shudders character is female, change the character's name and pronoun references in the lines marked with a circle (●) in the right-hand column.

SCENE 1: CHILD'S HOUSE

Child: *(addresses audience)* It's been two whole weeks since I stuck fliers into doors all over town, but nobody's given me an odd job yet. I hope somebody hires me soon so I can earn money for a new bike.

Puppeteer: Ding dong.

Child: *(faces stage left and calls)* Come in.

Mr. Shudders: *(enters stage left, shaking)* Are y-you th-the p-person wh-who p-put th-the fl-flier in m-my d-door?

Child: I sure am. Do you have an odd job for me?

Mr. Shudders: *(still shaking)* Y-yes. I-I n-need y-you t-to g-get r-rid of a g-ghost f-for m-me.

Child: That's odd, all right. You're kidding, aren't you?

Mr. Shudders: *(still shaking)* I-I w-wish I w-were. I-I'm M-Mr. Sh-Shudders, and th-there's a g-ghost h-haunting m-my h-house. It m-makes m-me s-so n-nervous, I-I c-can't st-stop sh-shaking.   ●

Child: *(comforts Mr. Shudders)* Don't worry. I'll get rid of it for you if you tell me where you live.

Mr. Shudders: *(still shaking)* F-five S-sixty Sp-spectral St-street. B-but I-I'm st-staying at th-the H-Holiday Inn un-t-til th-the g-ghost is g-gone.

Child: I'll call you there as soon as I've gotten rid of it.

Mr. Shudders: *(hugs Child)* Th-thank y-you. *(exits stage left, still shaking)*

Child: *(addresses audience)* I don't believe in ghosts. Some neighbor kids are probably playing a trick for Halloween. I'd better go to Spectral Street and ask them to stop. *(exits stage left)*

SCENE 2: THE SHUDDERS HOUSE

Child: *(enters stage right and acts as if looking at house)* Here's Five Sixty Spectral Street. I'd better go inside and ask those kids to stop scaring Mr. Shudders. *(crosses to center stage, looks around, faces stage right, and calls)* Anybody home?

Ghost: *(flies in stage left)* Just me.

Child: *(turns around, screams, and jumps back)* It really **IS** a ghost!

Ghost: In the spirit!

Child: But what are you doing in a nice house like this? I thought haunted houses always had broken windows, loose shutters, and lots of dust and cobwebs.

Ghost: I lived in a place like that, but I didn't like it. The broken windows made it cold and drafty. *(shivers)* Brrrrr! The loose shutters bang-bang-banging against the house *(extends one arm and twists body back and forth)* gave me a headache. And the dust made it hard to keep clean since I wear white all the time. I decided to haunt a decent house for a change, so here I am.

Child: But you can't stay. Mr. Shudders doesn't want you here.

Ghost: That's **HIS** tough luck. **I'M** staying.

Child: If I don't get rid of you, Mr. Shudders won't pay me the money I need to buy a new bike.

Ghost: That's **YOUR** tough luck. **I'M** staying.

Child: That's what **YOU** think. *(taps or cocks head)* But I'll come up with a plan for getting rid of you. *(thinks)*

Ghost: I doubt it. *(glides back and forth in air)* Ooooooooooo.

Child: I know. I'll tackle you and drag you out. *(tackles Ghost and both fall on stage or in your lap)*

Ghost: *(flies out of Child's arms and then back and forth in the air)* You can't hang on to a ghost, silly. Oooooooooo.

Child: Rats! *(thinks)*

Ghost: *(flies back and forth in air)* Oooooooooo.

Child: I know. I'll tickle you until you leave. *(tickles Ghost)*

Ghost: *(stands still)* Ghosts aren't ticklish.

Child: Rats!

Ghost: I'll bet **YOU** are. *(tickles Child)*

Child: *(rolls around giggling)* Stop! Stop!

Ghost: *(flies back and forth in air)* Oooooooooo.

Child: *(stands up)* Rats! *(thinks)*

Ghost: *(flies back and forth in air)* Oooooooooo.

Child: I know. I'll fix it so you won't want to live here anymore.

Ghost: How could you do that?

Child: I'll smash the windows to make it cold and drafty. I'll loosen the shutters, so they bang-bang-bang *(extends arm and twists body back and forth)* against the house. And I'll bring in lots of dust and cobwebs to make the place absolutely filthy.

Ghost: Mr. Shudders wouldn't like that.

Child: Rats! You're right. *(thinks)*

Ghost: *(flies back and forth in air and chants mockingly)* I am here to stay. Nyaah, nyaah, nyaah, nyaah, nyaah, nyaah.

Child: I know. I'll pay you to leave. I'll give you fifty cents.

Ghost: *(very scornfully)* Fifty cents? Ha! *(turns away)*

Child: A dollar?

Ghost: Ha! *(turns away)*

Child: Two dollars?

Ghost: Ha! *(turns away)*

Child: All right then, **FIVE** dollars!

Ghost: Not for a million billion dollars. Ghosts have no use for money.

Child: Rats!

Ghost: You might as well give up, kid. *(laughs)*

Child: Never! But I **WILL** take a break. Sometimes singing helps me solve my problems, so that's what I'll do right now. *(clears throat and sings loudly and off key)* "This old man, he played one,"

Ghost: *(holds hands to ears and cringes)* Stop, please! You're hurting my ears.

Child: *(sings)* "He played knick knack on my thumb,"

Ghost: *(holds ears and cringes)* I beg you, cease!

Child: *(sings)* "Knick knack, paddy whack, give a dog a bone."

Ghost: *(holds ears and cringes)* No more, I implore!

Child: *(sings)* "This old man went rolling home." *(Ghost screams and flies off stage left.)*

Child: *(watches Ghost leave and then addresses audience)* I've just made a scientific discovery. Ghosts don't appreciate good music.

Books about Ghosts

Bright, Robert. *Georgie.* Scholastic, n.d.

Khdir, Kate, and Sue Nash. *Little Ghost.* Barron, 1991.

Halloween Stories

Asch, Frank. *Popcorn.* Parents, 1979.

Bauer, Caroline Feller, ed. *Halloween: Stories and Poems.* HarperCollins, 1989.

Carlson, Nancy. *Harriet's Halloween Candy.* Lerner, 1994.

Friskey, Margaret. *Perky Little Pumpkin.* Children's Pr., 1990.

Kraus, Robert. *How Spider Saved Halloween.* Simon & Schuster, 1988.

Mangas, Brian. *You Don't Get a Carrot Unless You're a Bunny.* Simon & Schuster, 1989.

Silverman, Erica. *Big Pumpkin.* Simon & Schuster, 1992.

Williams, Linda. *The Little Old Lady Who Was Not Afraid of Anything.* HarperCollins, 1986.

Wiseman, Bernard. *Halloween with Morris and Boris.* Scholastic, 1986.

Do Not Disturb

A Skit about Endangered Animals

Characters: Woodcutter (left hand)
Raccoon (right hand)

> If you don't have a raccoon, use some other tree-dwelling animal. I use a male puppet for Woodcutter, but any puppet could play this part.

Props: ax
(cardboard) tree
sign reading "Do Not Disturb"

> The sign can be just a large piece of cardboard.
> You could cut the ax out of cardboard and cover the blade with aluminum foil.

Preparation: Put tree at stage right. Put sign behind the tree so audience can't see the sign.

Woodcutter: *(enters stage left, carrying ax, and crosses to tree)* I'd better get busy. *(starts to swing ax)*

Raccoon: *(runs out from behind tree, waving arms)* Stop! You can't chop this tree down!

Woodcutter: Of course I can. I have my trusty ax right here. *(waves ax)*

Raccoon: I know you **CAN.** I mean, you **SHOULDN'T.** *(grabs ax)*

Woodcutter: I **HAVE** to. *(pulls ax out of Raccoon's hands)* Some people are going to build a mall here, and this tree is in the way.

Raccoon: They shouldn't put a mall here.

Woodcutter: Of course, they should. What could be more important than a place for people to eat junk food, play video games, and buy lots of stuff?

Raccoon: The lives of animals, that's what! Some animals are endangered and just may become extinct.

Woodcutter: Who cares?

Alternative Action: If Raccoon is a movable mouth puppet, make it jump up and down.

Raccoon: **YOU** should. When any kind of animal dies, the world loses something it can never replace. Besides, when you upset the life of one animal, you upset the lives of many other animals—and people, too!

Woodcutter: O.K., O.K., you've convinced me: The lives of animals are important. *(pushes Raccoon back)* Now step aside, so I can get to work.

Raccoon: *(forces self between Woodcutter and tree)* Why are you still planning to cut down this tree? You agreed the lives of animals are important.

Woodcutter: This tree doesn't have anything to do with the lives of animals. *(pushes Raccoon aside)* Now get out of my way.

Raccoon: *(forces self between Woodcutter and tree)* This tree has **PLENTY** to do with the lives of animals. Don't you know how animals become endangered?

Woodcutter: No.

Raccoon: Then I'll tell you.

Woodcutter: *(wryly)* I had a feeling you would.

Raccoon: Some of the ways animals become endangered are natural. Usually, however, animals become endangered because of things people do.

Woodcutter: Can you give me an example?

Raccoon: Sure. When people use poisons to kill insects and rodents, they also kill the animals that eat bugs and mice. Many bats and weasels, for example, have died from eating poisoned animals. *(gags and collapses)*

Woodcutter: *(shows horror)* That's awful!

Raccoon: *(stands up)* Yes, and it gets even worse. When people poison rivers and oceans by spilling oil and dumping garbage in them, they kill lots of fish plus all the eagles and other animals that eat the contaminated fish. *(gags and collapses)*

Woodcutter: Water pollution is bad for people, too. We can't drink dirty water or swim in it either.

Raccoon: *(stands up)* Pollution is bad for everyone.

Woodcutter: If people stopped polluting and using poisons, we wouldn't have any endangered animals, would we?

Raccoon: I'm afraid we would, because people hurt animals in many other ways as well. For example, they've caused parrots and some monkeys to become endangered by capturing and selling them.

Woodcutter: That's mean!

Raccoon: I know. It's also mean to kill animals just for fun or to get decorations, but some people do. They hunt creatures like leopards so they can make coats out of their lovely furs. They hunt egrets and swans to get their feathers, rhinos to get their horns, and elephants to get their ivory tusks.

Woodcutter: *(admonishes and says indignantly)* There ought to be a law against that!

Raccoon: There is. Many places have made it illegal to kill endangered animals.

Woodcutter: *(nods)* Good! That will fix everything!

Raccoon: I'm afraid not, because a lack of space is the greatest threat of all.

Woodcutter: What does space have to do with the survival of animals?

Raccoon: EVERYTHING! Animals like tigers, eagles, and elephants need large territories for hunting or grazing. They often don't have this space, however, because people keep taking over their land.

Woodcutter: *(indignantly)* That's awful! I wouldn't want anyone pushing me out of my home!

Raccoon: Then why are you pushing **ME** out of **MINE?**

Woodcutter: I'm not. I'm just going to chop a tree down. *(pushes Raccoon back)* Now step aside.

Raccoon: *(forces self between Woodcutter and tree)* This tree **IS** my home! Many of us animals and birds need trees to live in. We need them for food as well.

Woodcutter: I can see now that trees are very important to you animals.

Raccoon: Trees are very important to people, too!

Woodcutter: How can that be? We don't eat trees.

Raccoon: Do you like eating apples?

Woodcutter: Mmmmm, yes.

Raccoon: Oranges?

Woodcutter: Mmmmm, yes.

Raccoon: Bananas?

Woodcutter: Mmmmm, yes.

Raccoon: And **WHERE** do all those yummy fruits grow?

Woodcutter: On trees.

Raccoon: Right! So do lots of other foods. Even chewing gum and chocolate come from trees.

Woodcutter: I didn't know that! People really **DO** need trees for food.

Raccoon: They also need trees to keep soil from washing away in the rain and blowing away in the wind. They need trees to clean the air, shelter them from wind, and cool them in summer.

Woodcutter: I've always thought trees were pretty to look at and fun to climb, but I never realized they were so useful.

Raccoon: *(nods)* Now you know: Trees are terrific!

Woodcutter: They're so terrific, I'll never chop one down again. *(throws ax offstage)*

Raccoon: *(hugs and kisses Woodcutter)* Thank you.

Woodcutter: *(pats Raccoon's back)* You're very welcome. I'm going to City Hall now and ask the mayor to forget about that mall. Then I'll plant a tree or two in my backyard. 'Bye. *(turns and exits stage left)*

Raccoon: *(wipes brow and addresses audience)* Whew! That was close! Now how can I protect this tree in case another woodcutter wants to chop it down while I'm out looking for food? *(thinks)* I know. I'll make a sign. *(ducks behind tree as if going into home and then pops out from behind tree, carrying sign; props sign against tree so audience can read it and then looks at it and nods)* There! That ought to do it . . . I hope. *(addresses audience)* If you'd like to protect wildlife, please

Don't keep wild animals as pets.

Leave birds' nests and animals' homes alone.

Don't make lots of noise in the woods.

Don't trample bushes or pick wildflowers.

If you make a campfire, put it out very carefully.

Save paper, because paper comes from trees. Thank you. Good-bye. *(exits stage right)*

Picture Books about Ecology

Bechtel, Beverly. *Lancelot the Ocelot.* Lerner, 1991.

Berenstain, Stan, and Jan Berenstain. *The Berenstain Bears Don't Pollute (Anymore).* Random, 1991.

Burningham, John. *Hey! Get Off Our Train.* Crown, 1990.

Cherry, Lynne. *The Great Kapok Tree: A Tale of the Amazon Rain Forest.* Harcourt, 1990.

Havill, Juanita. *Sato and the Elephants.* Lothrop, 1993.

Jeffers, Susan, ill. *Brother Eagle, Sister Sky: A Message from Chief Seattle.* Dial, 1991.

Leedy, Loreen. *The Great Trash Bash.* Holiday, 1991.

Levine, Arthur A. *Pearl Moscowitz's Last Stand.* Morrow, 1993.

Peet, Bill. *Farewell to Shady Glade.* Houghton, 1981.

————. *Wump World.* Houghton, 1974.

Pellowski, Michael J. *Messy Monster.* Troll, 1986.

Seuss, Dr. *The Lorax.* Random, 1971.

Van Allsburg, Chris. *Just a Dream.* Houghton, 1990.

Wildsmith, Brian. *Professor Noah's Spaceship.* Oxford Univ. Pr., 1980.

Nonfiction Books about Ecology

Brown, Laurene Krasny, and Marc Brown. *Dinosaurs to the Rescue: A Guide to Protecting Our Planet.* Little, Brown, 1992.

Earthworks Group Staff. *50 Simple Things Kids Can Do to Recycle.* Greenleaf, 1991.

Javna, John. *50 Simple Things Kids Can Do to Save the Earth.* Andrews & McMeel, 1990.

Showers, Paul. *Where Does the Garbage Go?* HarperCollins, 1994.

Cow Eats Out

Characters: Waiter (or Waitress) (right hand)
Cow (left hand)

> I use a person for the restaurant employee, but any puppet could wait on Cow.
>
> Horses, sheep, and goats graze, too, so you could substitute one of these animals for the cow.

Props:

table	knife
vase of flowers	fork
menu	spoon
small bowl	grass

> The table can be a small box. The kind catalog cards come in works well. Cover it with a handkerchief or piece of material for a tablecloth.
>
> Put a few small artificial or paper flowers into a pill bottle for the vase. If you don't have artificial flowers, cut a bouquet out of paper or a seed catalog and glue it onto a pipe cleaner or toothpick. Tape the toothpick inside the bottle so the flowers don't fall out.
>
> The menu can be a small rectangle of paper folded in half.
>
> If you use plastic utensils, the bowl won't be so heavy to carry.
>
> Fold a sheet of green construction paper in thirds lengthwise and tape the ends together to make a triangle. This will be the grass.

Preparation: Put knife, fork, and spoon in bowl and set offstage. Put vase in middle of table. Set menu next to it. Put table near stage right. Waiter stands at stage left.

SCENE 1: IN THE RESTAURANT

(Cow enters stage left.)

Waiter: Good afternoon, madam. *(bows slightly)*

Cow: Good afternoon. My friend suggested I eat lunch here today.

Waiter: Very good. Let me show you to a table.

Cow: Please don't. I came to eat, not to look at the furniture.

Waiter: I **MEANT,** I'll lead you to a place where you can eat. Are you a party of one?

Cow: No, no party. Today's not my birthday or anything special.

Waiter: I **MEANT,** will you be eating alone?

Cow: Yes.

Waiter: *(beckons)* Then please follow me. *(crosses to table with Cow following)* Here's a nice table. *(points)*

Cow: Those flowers look yummy. *(leans over and puts mouth next to them)*

Waiter: *(pulls her back)* You can't eat the flowers. They're not on the menu.

Cow: No, they're on the table. *(bends over them again)*

Waiter: *(pulls her back)* You may **NOT** eat the flowers!

Cow: Then what **CAN** I eat?

Waiter: *(picks up menu and holds it out)* I suggest you look at the menu.

(Cow puts face right up to menu, looks at it from top to bottom, and then steps back.)

Cow: You can put it down now. I've seen it enough.

Waiter: *(puts menu down on table)* Then you're ready to give me your order?

Cow: No, I don't want to order you around. Although farmers name cows Bossy, we aren't demanding at all.

Waiter: I **MEANT,** are you ready to tell me what you want to eat?

Cow: No. You haven't told me what kind of food you have yet.

Waiter: *(picks up menu and waves it in Cow's face)* I **TRIED** to give you the menu.

Cow: I don't want to eat that! *(takes menu and puts it on table)*

Waiter: You're not supposed to eat it. You're supposed to look at it so you'll know what you want. Everything you can eat is on this menu. *(points)*

Cow: *(puts her face right next to it and looks at it from top to bottom)* I don't see any food here.

Waiter: You're not supposed to. The menu just lists our dishes.

Cow: I don't care how many cups and saucers you have.

Waiter: I **MEANT,** the menu will tell you what we have to eat.

Cow: *(puts ear on menu)* I don't hear anything.

Waiter: It doesn't talk. You have to **READ** it. *(waves menu in front of her)*

Cow: Don't you know? Cows can't read.

(Waiter drops menu and groans.)

Cow: Why don't you just let me eat the flowers? *(bends over them)*

Waiter: *(pulls Cow back)* No! No flowers!

Cow: Then tell me what I **CAN** eat.

Waiter: Very well, I'll start with today's special.

Cow: No, today's not special. I already told you it's not my birthday.

Waiter: I **MEANT,** I'll tell you about the blue plate special.

Cow: I don't want to eat a plate! Yuck! *(gags)*

Waiter: You don't eat the plate. You eat what comes on the plate.

Cow: What's that?

Waiter: Roast beef.

Cow: *(shows horror)* I can't eat my relatives!

Waiter: Would you rather have chicken?

Cow: No. Some of my best friends are chickens.

Waiter: Then perhaps you'd like our pork chops.

Cow: No, I couldn't eat pork chops. Pigs are my favorite neighbors.

Waiter: You must be a vegetarian.

Cow: *(laughs)* Don't be silly. I'm a cow.

Waiter: I **MEANT,** you don't eat meat.

Cow: You're right. But I **DO** eat flowers! *(bends over flowers)*

Waiter: *(pulls Cow back)* No! No flowers.

Cow: Rats!

Waiter: I'm going to take the flowers away, so you can't eat them. Then I'll bring you some vegetable soup. *(grabs vase and exits stage left; returns carrying the bowl with the utensils in it; puts the bowl on the table, takes the utensils out, and puts them on the stage in front of Cow)* I hope you enjoy your meal.

(Cow sticks head into the bowl and makes slurping sounds.)

Waiter: *(pulls Cow out of bowl and sounds scandalized)* Madam! This is an elegant restaurant. How dare you stick your head in the bowl and slurp the soup? *(points)* Use the utensils.

(Cow picks up knife.)

Waiter: *(takes knife from her and throws it offstage)* You do not eat soup with a knife.

(Cow picks up fork.)

Waiter: *(takes fork from her and throws it offstage)* You do not eat soup with a fork.

(Cow picks spoon up by the bowl.)

Waiter: *(takes spoon from her, turns it around, and gives it back to her)* Yes, you eat soup with a spoon.

(Cow looks into the bowl and then at the waiter. She does this several times.)

Waiter: *(impatiently)* **IS** there a problem?

Cow: I don't know **HOW** to eat with a spoon!

(Waiter groans.)

Cow: *(throws spoon offstage)* I don't like your spoon. I don't like your attitude. And I don't like your restaurant. I don't know why my friend urged me to come here. Good-**BYE.** *(turns and stomps off stage left)*

Waiter: *(calls after her)* Well, good riddance! *(picks up bowl and exits stage right)*

SCENE 2: OUTSIDE THE RESTAURANT

Cow: *(enters stage left and crosses to grass)* Mmmmm, their grass looks delicious. *(puts head next to grass and makes noisy eating sounds; straightens up and addresses audience)* Now I know why my friend recommended this restaurant. I'll have to go thank her for telling me where to find the best-tasting lawn I've ever grazed on.

Setup: Take down table. Put grass at center stage.

Books about Restaurants

Barbour, Karen. *Little Nino's Pizzeria.* Harcourt, 1990.

Christelow, Eileen. *Robbery at the Diamond Dog Diner.* Houghton, 1988.

Day, Alexandra. *Frank and Ernest.* Scholastic, 1988.

Kovalski, Maryann. *Pizza for Breakfast.* Morrow, 1991.

Stadler, John. *Animal Cafe.* Simon & Schuster, 1986.

Books about Cows

Allen, Pamela. *Belinda.* Viking, 1993.

Cole, Babette. *Supermoo!* Putnam, 1993.

Dubanevich, Arlene. *Calico Cows.* Viking, 1993.

Ernst, Lisa Campbell. *When Bluebell Sang.* Simon & Schuster, 1989.

Harrison, David L. *When Cows Come Home.* Boyds Mills Pr., 1994.

Johnston, Paul B. *The Cow Who Wouldn't Come Down.* Orchard, 1993.

Obligado, Lilian. *The Chocolate Cow.* Simon & Schuster, 1993.

Pellowski, Michael. *Clara Joins the Circus.* Parents, 1981.

Happy the Clown's New Job

Characters: Happy the Clown (left hand)
Ringmaster
Child
Lion

All but Clown are right-hand puppets.

If you don't have a clown or want to make one, put a mask on one of your people puppets. Cut a circle large enough to cover your puppet's face out of light cardboard. Draw a face and hair on it. Tape or staple a rubber band securely to the back of the mask and then slip it over the puppet's head. You might also want to use small safety pins or loops of tape to attach pompoms down the front of your puppet.

Child can be either male or female, so the character has a name that works for either.

The Ringmaster could be male or female as well. You could substitute some other wild animal, such as a tiger, for the lion. If you have a cat puppet, perhaps you could use that. You might want to give it a mane made out of paper or yarn.

If the child or ringmaster puppet is female, change the pronoun references accordingly for the lines marked with an asterisk (✶) in the right-hand column.

Prop: stick

SCENE 1: BACKSTAGE

(Ringmaster enters stage right at the same time Happy enters stage left.)

Ringmaster: Happy, you're just the person I wanted to see.

Happy: Why is that, Boss?

Ringmaster: I wanted to tell you our lion tamer quit this morning. Until I can hire a new one, **YOU** get the job.

Happy: Why me?

Ringmaster: I know how much you like cats. You have three of them in your dressing room, don't you?

Happy: Well, yes . . . *(bends down and holds out arm to show height)* but they're itty-bitty little pussycats. *(straightens up and raises arm)* They're not great, big lions!

Ringmaster: Just think of Leo, our lion, as a great, big pussycat.

Happy: Will **LEO** think of himself that way?

Ringmaster: *(pats Happy's back)* Don't worry about it. You'll do just fine.

(Happy holds both hands to throat and gags.)

Ringmaster: What's wrong, Happy?

Happy: I'm sick, terribly sick. *(collapses)* I have to go to bed for a week . . . or however long it takes to hire a new lion tamer.

Ringmaster: You're faking. Now get up. *(grabs Happy's hand and pulls up)*

Happy: No, I'm not. *(sticks face in front of Ringmaster's)* See how pale I am? That means I'm really sick. *(collapses)*

Ringmaster: It means you're wearing your clown makeup. Now get up. *(pulls Happy up)*

Happy: I really **AM** sick. I have a fever that's burning me up. *(puts hand to forehead and collapses)*

Ringmaster: *(bends over and feels Happy's forehead)* You're not even warm. Now get up. *(pulls Happy up)*

Happy: But . . . but . . . but . . .

Ringmaster: *(admonishes)* No excuses! I expect to see you in the center ring tomorrow—**WITH THE LION!**

Happy: But . . . but . . . but . . .

Ringmaster: **BE THERE!** *(turns and stomps off stage right)*

Happy: *(addresses audience)* Oh, dear. I'd better run away and never come back.

(Child enters from stage right. Happy runs off stage right and collides with Child. Child falls onto stage or in your lap with Happy on top.)

Child: Ouch!

Happy: *(jumps up)* I'm sorry, Pat. Let me help you up. *(grabs Child's hand and pulls Child up)*

Child: Where are you going in such a hurry?

Happy: I'm running away from the circus, so I don't have to be a lion tamer.

Child: I don't understand. You're not a lion tamer.

Happy: I'm supposed to be one now. The circus's lion tamer quit this morning, and the boss wants me to fill in until someone else can be hired for the job.

Child: I guess the idea of facing a lion scares you a little, huh?

Happy: *(shakes)* I'm so scared, I can't stop shaking!

Child: I can understand why you're afraid, but running away never solves anything. Let's think of something else you can do.

Happy: *(still shaking)* I'm too nervous to think.

Child: Then **I'LL** think. *(thinks)* I know. Remember how we dressed up to go trick-or-treating last Halloween?

Happy: Pat! How can you think about candy at a time like this?

Child: I'm not. I'm thinking about the cool costume my mom made for me.

Happy: Your mother **DOES** make really super costumes. She's promised to make a vampire costume for me this Halloween, but this isn't the time to be thinking about vampire costumes.

Child: I wasn't. I was thinking about a lion suit.

Happy: I don't want to be a lion for Halloween!

Child: The costume wouldn't be for you. It would be for me to wear in your act tomorrow.

Happy: You don't want to be in my act tomorrow. You don't want to get into the ring with a lion.

Child: The lion won't be there. He'll be locked up in his cage.

Happy: He **HAS** to be there. The boss insists on seeing a lion in the ring with me.

Child: He will. He'll see me—**IN THE LION SUIT.**   *

Happy: Do you think that will fool him?   *

Child: Sure, because Mom will make a really lifelike costume. And I'll act really fierce, too. *(approaches Happy while growling)*

Happy: Back, Pat. I mean, back, Leo.

Child: *(moves back)* Grrrrr.

Happy: Lie down. *(points down)*

(Child lies down.)

Happy: Roll over.

(Child rolls over.)

Happy: Good girl! I mean, good kitty. *(leans over and pats Child on head)*

Child: *(jumps up)* See how easy it is to be a lion tamer?

Happy: *(hugs Child)* Thanks, Pat. You've saved my life!

Child: You're welcome. I'm going home now to help Mom make the costume. Good-bye.

Note: Roll one of Happy's arms while rolling your own wrist to make the appropriate gesture.

Alternative Dialogue: Good boy!

Happy: 'Bye, Leo. *(puts hand to mouth)* I mean, good-bye, Pat. See you tomorrow. *(Happy exits stage left. Child exits stage right.)*

(Take off Child. Put on Ringmaster.)

SCENE 2: THE NEXT DAY

Setup: Put stick at stage left. Happy stands at stage left.

Ringmaster: *(enters stage right and crosses to Happy)* Ready to do your act?

Happy: You bet!

Ringmaster: Not nervous?

Happy: Not at all.

Ringmaster: Did you decide to take my advice and think of the lion as a great, big pussycat?

Happy: I'm going to think of the lion as my friend.

Ringmaster: Whatever works. I'll go introduce you. *(crosses to right of stage and addresses audience)* Ladies and gentlemen, it is my pride, my pleasure, and my privilege to introduce to you our own, our brave, our fearless . . . *(points)* **HAPPY THE CLOWN!** *(Ringmaster cheers and claps while Happy crosses to center stage and bows.)* And from Kenya, the fiercest and most ferocious lion ever to prowl the African plains . . . *(points off stage right)* **LEO!** *(exits stage right)*

(Take off Ringmaster. Put on Lion.)

Happy: *(addresses audience and claps)* Let's hear it for the lion!

Lion: *(enters stage right and approaches Happy)* Grrrrr.

Happy: Wow! That's a really great costume, Pat!

Lion: Grrrrr.

Happy: Where **DID** your mom get that material? It looks real.

Lion: Grrrrr.

Happy: *(strokes Lion)* It even **FEELS** real.

Lion: Grrrrr.

Happy: *(looks at lion from head to toe and from front to back)* I don't see any snaps or zippers or anything.

Lion: Grrrrr.

Happy: You must have been practicing all night. You even **SOUND** real.

Lion: Grrrrr. *(starts biting Happy's costume)*

Happy: *(taps Lion's nose)* Don't get carried away. You're tearing my best costume.

Alternative Action: If the puppet doesn't have a movable mouth, move its head up and down over Happy.

Lion: Grrrrr.

Happy: Lie down. *(points to floor of stage or your lap)*

Lion: Grrrrr.

Happy: Lie down! *(pushes Lion down onto the stage or in your lap)*

Lion: Grrrrr.

Happy: Roll over.

Lion: *(from stage or your lap)* Grrrrr.

Happy: Roll over! *(pushes Lion over)*

Lion: Grrrrr.

Happy: Jump over the stick. *(bends over, picks up stick, and holds it out)*

Lion: *(grabs stick and pokes Happy in the stomach with it)* Grrrrr.

Happy: You want **ME** to jump over the stick?

Lion: *(nods and pokes Happy again)* Grrrrr.

Happy: O.K. That's a good idea for the act. *(jumps over stick)*

Lion: *(drops stick and pushes Happy down on the stage or in your lap)* Grrrrr.

Happy: You want **ME** to roll over?

Lion: *(nods and nudges Happy with his nose)* Grrrrr.

Happy: What a clever idea! *(rolls back and forth several times and then jumps up and listens)* Hear that applause, Pat? The audience loves us, so let's take a bow. *(bows)*

Lion: Grrrrr.

Happy: Take a bow! *(puts arm around Lion and together they bow)*

Lion: Grrrrr.

Happy: Come on, I'll walk you back to the cages. *(Happy puts an arm around Lion, and they exit stage right. Lion growls all the way.)*

(Take off Lion. Put on Ringmaster.)

SCENE 3: AFTER THE SHOW

(Happy stands at stage left.)

Ringmaster: *(enters stage right, crosses to Happy, and congratulates him)* That was sensational, Happy! You really have a way with cats!

Happy: That's because I think of them as my friends.

Note: Roll one of Happy's arms while rolling your own wrist to make him gesture appropriately.

Ringmaster: *(puts hand to head)* That reminds me. Your friend, Pat called just before your act. She told me to tell you she was really sorry, but she has a terrible cold and couldn't come today.

*
*

Happy: Pat wasn't here today?

Ringmaster: No, and she can't come tomorrow either. Her mother is making her stay in bed for a week.

*
*

Happy: Uh, if Pat wasn't here today, who was that in the ring with me just now?

Ringmaster: *(slaps Happy playfully on the back)* Quit kidding around. You know very well it was Leo, our lion.

Happy: L-l-l-lion? I was in the ring with a real l-l-l-lion?

Ringmaster: Yes! And the two of you were so fantastic together, I won't even bother hiring a new lion tamer. The job is yours forever. *(Happy faints.)*

Ringmaster: *(looks down at Happy and then addresses audience)* Some people get so emotional when they hear good news.

Books about the Circus

Chwast, Seymour. *Twelve Circus Rings.* Harcourt, 1993.

Daugherty, James. *Andy and the Lion.* Viking, 1938.

Ernst, Lisa Campbell. *Ginger Jumps.* Simon & Schuster, 1990.

Freeman, Don. *Bearymore.* Viking, 1976.

Gaskin, Carol. *A Day in the Life of a Circus Clown.* Troll, 1988.

Giannini, Enzo. *Zorina Ballerina.* Simon & Schuster, 1993.

Peet, Bill. *Ella.* Houghton, 1978.

———. *Randy's Dandy Lions.* Houghton, 1979.

Pellowski, Michael. *Clara Joins the Circus.* Parents, 1981.

Prelutsky, Jack. *Circus!* Simon & Schuster, 1989.

Seuss, Dr. *If I Ran the Circus.* Random, 1956.

Soloff-Levy, Barbara. *How to Draw Clowns.* Troll, 1991.

Vincent, Gabrielle. *Ernest & Celestine at the Circus.* Greenwillow, 1989.

Books about Wearing Costumes

See the books listed for the skit, "The Mysterious Visitors."

Books about Lions

Brenner, Barbara, and William Hooks. Lion and Lamb series. Bantam.

Hadithi, Mwenye. *Lazy Lion.* Little, Brown, 1990.

McKean, Thomas. *Hooray for Grandma Jo!* Crown, 1994.

Honey Bear's Hat Shop

Characters: Honey Bear (right hand)
Customer (left hand)

> If you don't have a bear puppet, you could substitute another animal and change the type of store the customer expects.
>
> Customer can be any puppet you want to use. If the puppet is male, change pronoun references accordingly for the line marked with an asterisk (✱) in the right-hand column.

Props: dust cloth
small mirror (either a hand mirror or
   a stand-up mirror)
any hat
Santa hat

space helmet
party hat
firefighter's helmet
chef's hat
crown

> You can make a Santa hat by cutting a half circle out of red paper. Make a cone by taping, gluing or stapling the edges together. Glue cotton balls around the base and one at the top.
>
> Make a space helmet by cutting down a small paper bag or box and cutting an opening for the face.
>
> Make the party hat the way you did the Santa hat, but draw big polka dots on it with markers instead of adding cotton.
>
> To make a firefighter's helmet, cut a rectangle out of red construction paper and round all the corners. Draw an inverted *U* near one of the short sides and cut around it. Fold it forward so it stands up. You might also want to draw a little shield with a number on it.
>
> Cut the traditional mushroom-shaped chef's hat out of white paper and glue it to a headband made by joining the ends of a strip of white paper.
>
> Make the crown by cutting V shapes out of the top of a strip of yellow or gold paper and taping or gluing the ends together to make a band.
>
> Customer can wear any hat you have or want to make or buy. Make sure all the hats are big enough to slide easily on and off Customer's head.
>
> If you don't have a small mirror or compact, you can make one by gluing aluminum foil to a small cardboard square. If you have a mirror that stands up, such as the kind used for applying makeup, you could set that at stage left. You could also make one by cutting two frames out of cardboard and gluing them together with a sheet of aluminum foil between them. Tape this to a metal bookend or wooden block so it will stand.

Preparation: Put the hand mirror down at stage right. (If you're using a stand-up mirror, put it at stage left so the customer can look into it and ignore the directions for picking it up and putting it down.) Put any hat on Customer.

Honey Bear: *(dusts, throws cloth offstage, and addresses audience)* Now, I'm ready for business.

Customer: *(enters stage left, wearing any hat)* Hello, Honey Bear. Is this your new hat shop? I heard you were opening one.

Honey Bear: This is it.

Customer: I'm surprised you aren't running a honey store.

Honey Bear: I was going to, but I ate all the honey myself.

Customer: You can't make any money that way.

Honey Bear: That's why I'm selling hats instead. Would you like to buy one?

Customer: Yes indeed. I've had the one I'm wearing for a long time, so now I'd like something different.

Honey Bear: You've come to the right place. *(takes hat off Customer's head and puts it down)* I'll go into the back room and pick out something you'll like. *(exits stage right, returns with Santa hat, and puts it on Customer)* How do you like this one? *(holds up mirror)*

Customer: *(looks in mirror)* I look like—ho! ho! ho!—Santa Claus.

Honey Bear: *(puts down mirror)* Don't you like—ho! ho! ho!—Santa Claus?

Customer: Of course, but I don't want to look like him.

Honey Bear: He probably wouldn't want to look like you either. *(takes Santa hat off Customer and sets it down)* I will find another hat for you. *(exits stage right, returns with space helmet, and puts it on Customer)* Do you like this one? *(holds up mirror)*

Customer: *(looks in mirror)* I look like an astronaut. 10, 9, 8, 7, 6, 5, 4, 3, 2, 1, blast off! *(spreads arms wide, leaps up into the air and then back down to the stage)*

Honey Bear: *(puts down mirror)* Astronauts are brave people.

Customer: I know, but this isn't the look I had in mind.

Honey Bear: Very well. I will find you another hat. *(takes space helmet off Customer's head, puts it down, and exits stage right; returns stage right with party hat and puts it on Customer)* How about this one? *(holds up mirror)*

Customer: *(looks in mirror)* This looks like a birthday hat.

Honey Bear: *(puts down mirror)* Yes. *(starts to sing)* "Happy birthday . . ."

Customer: It isn't my birthday, so I don't want this hat.

Honey Bear: Picky, picky, picky. *(takes party hat off Customer and puts it down)* But I have another great hat for you. *(exits stage right, returns with firefighter's helmet, and puts it on Customer)* I bet you'll **LOVE** this one! *(holds up mirror)*

Customer: *(looks in mirror)* It makes me look like a *(makes the sound of a siren)* firefighter.

Honey Bear: *(puts down mirror)* Yes. Aren't *(makes the sound of a siren)* firefighters great?

Customer: They certainly are, but this is **NOT** the look I had in mind.

Honey Bear: Picky, picky, picky. *(takes firefighter's helmet off Customer and puts it down)* Let me see what else I can find for you. *(exits stage right, returns with chef's hat, and puts it on Customer)* This one's my personal favorite. *(holds up mirror)*

Customer: *(looks in mirror)* It makes me look like a cook.

Honey Bear: *(puts down mirror)* I know. Bake me some honey cakes.

Customer: I hate to cook, so I don't want this hat.

Honey Bear: Picky, picky, picky. *(takes chef's hat off Customer and puts it down)* But I'm sure I have something you'll like. *(exits stage right, returns with crown, and puts it on Customer)* How is this one? *(holds up mirror)*

Customer: *(looks in mirror, puts hand to head, and tilts head first to one side and then to the other as if admiring hat)* It's wonderful! It makes me look like a queen. *(jerks arm down and shouts)* **OFF WITH HIS HEAD!**

Alternative Dialogue: . . . look like a king.

Honey Bear: *(puts down mirror, quickly takes crown off Customer, and puts it down)* You'd better not take that one.

Customer: Then what else do you have?

Honey Bear: Nothing, picky person. You have seen and rejected them all.

Customer: *(crosses over to hats, looks them all over, and picks up original hat)* I didn't see **THIS** one.

Honey Bear: *(drops mouth open, stares at Customer's face, stares down at hat, stares back at Customer's face)* But . . . but . . .

Customer: Help me try it on. It's just what I've always wanted.

Honey Bear: But it's your **OWN** hat!

Customer: I know. It does seem to be made for me, doesn't it? Help me try it on.

Honey Bear: But . . . but . . .

Customer: Please! Help me try it on! *(holds out hat)*

Honey Bear: Oh, very well. *(puts hat on Customer)*

Customer: Now hold up the mirror, so I can see how it looks.

(Honey Bear holds up mirror and Customer looks into it, patting head while tilting it first to one side and then to the other.)

Customer: I love it! *(takes mirror from Honey Bear, puts it down, and shakes his hand)* Thank you for helping me find the perfect hat.

Honey Bear: But . . . but . . .

Customer: Be sure to send me a bill. I'll include a generous tip with my payment. Good-bye. *(exits stage left)*

Honey Bear: *(drops mouth, watches Customer leave, and then addresses audience)* She bought her own hat! If that isn't the strangest thing I've ever seen, I'll eat my hats. *(looks down at hats and then back at audience)* Oh, well. I think I'll eat them anyway. *(eats hats noisily and burps)* Mmmmm, those were good. But now that I've eaten my merchandise, I have to close my store. Good-bye. *(exits stage right)*

*

Books about Hats

Berenstain, Stan, and Jan Berenstain. *Old Hat, New Hat.* Random, 1970.

Blos, Joan. *Martin's Hats.* Morrow, 1984.

Gelman, Rita Golden. *Hello, Cat, You Need a Hat.* Scholastic, 1993.

Geringer, Laura. *Three Hat Day.* HarperCollins, 1987.

Keats, Ezra Jack. *Jennie's Hat.* HarperCollins, 1966.

Lear, Edward. *The Quangle Wangle's Hat.* Harcourt, 1988.

Moncure, Jane Belk. *Word Bird's Hats.* Child's World, 1982.

Nodset, Joan. *Who Took the Farmer's Hat?* HarperCollins, 1963.

Seuss, Dr. *The 500 Hats of Bartholomew Cubbins.* Random, 1989.

Slobodkina, Esphyr. *Caps for Sale.* HarperCollins, 1947.

Smath, Jerry. *A Hat So Simple.* BridgeWater, 1993.

Smith, William. *Ho for a Hat!* Little, Brown, 1989.

Stoeke, Janet Morgan. *A Hat for Minerva Louise.* Dutton, 1994.

The Wizard's Sneeze

Characters: Queen (left hand)
                  Wizard
                  Spider
                  Bear
                  Pig
                  Duck

> All except the Queen are right-hand puppets.
> The queen puppet needs to have movable arms.

Props: broom
          magic wand
          book of magic

> You can make a broom by gluing a small rectangle of yellow paper to a Popsicle stick, pencil, or plastic drinking straw. Round off the upper corners of the rectangle.
> You can make a magic wand by cutting a star out of foil and gluing it onto a Popsicle stick, pencil, or plastic drinking straw.

Note: In many ways, this skit is similar to "Wanted: A Whiz of a Wiz," so please see the notes for that skit.

Preparation: Put broom at stage left.

Queen: *(addresses audience)* I'm tired of all the rain we've had this week. I hope the wizard can make it stop.

Wizard: *(enters stage right and talks through his nose as if he has a bad cold)* The guard said you wanted to see me, Your Majesty.

Queen: Yes. I'd like you to do something about the weather so we'll have a nice day for tomorrow's pig roast.

Wizard: I'll try, Your Majesty, but I'm not sure I can do anything.

Queen: Why not? You've worked weather spells before.

Wizard: But not when I was sick. My magic doesn't always work right when I'm sick.

Queen: What's the matter with you?

Wizard: I've caught the sneezix bug that's going around, so every time I sneeze . . . ah, ah, ah, **AH-CHOO!**

(Drop down Wizard and take him off. Put on Spider and pop it up.)

Queen: *(looks all around)* Where did he go? He didn't even finish his sentence! *(looks down, screams, grabs broom, and hits Spider)* Take **THAT,** you horrid spider, and **THAT,** and **THAT,** and **THAT!** *(hits Spider each time she says "that")*

Spider: I'm not **REALLY** a spider, Your Majesty.

Queen: You certainly **LOOK** like one. Yuck! *(hits Spider again)*

Spider: Please stop hitting me, Your Majesty. I'm really the wizard.

Queen: How can **THAT** be?

Spider: When I sneezed, I turned into a spider.

Queen: Why did you want to do that?

Spider: I didn't **WANT** to, but that's what happens when you get sneezix. You turn into an animal whenever you sneeze.

Queen: Can you use magic to change yourself back?

Spider: I can **TRY.** *(moves in small circles and waves legs)* Alakazam and alakazee. Change me back to look like me!

(Drop Spider down and take it off. Put Bear on and pop it up.)

Queen: *(looks around)* **NOW** where is he? *(turns around)* Oh, no! The bearskin rug has come to life! *(pokes Bear in stomach with broom and pushes it back)* Back, Bruno, back!

Bear: I won't hurt you, Your Majesty. Please put the broom down.

Queen: Is that you, Wizard?

Bear: Yes. When I sneezed, I turned into a bear.

Queen: I thought you were going to turn back to your regular self.

Bear: I **WANTED** to, but my magic doesn't always work right when I'm sick.

Queen: Maybe it would work better if you had your magic wand. I'll get it for you. *(exits stage left)*

Bear: *(addresses audience)* I hope this works. Switching hurts.

Queen: *(enters stage left, carrying wand)* Here it is. I'll wave it while you recite the appropriate spell.

Bear: Thank you. *(moves in small circles)* Abracadabra and abracadoo. Make me a wizard, instead of a zoo.

(Drop Bear down and take it off. Put on Pig and pop it up.)

Queen: *(drops wand and looks around)* Oh, dear, he's vanished **AGAIN.** *(turns around)* Aaugh! The pig for the roast got loose! You won't get away from me, Porky!

(Queen tackles Pig, and they fall on the stage or in your lap.)

Pig: *(squirms and struggles under Queen)* Please get off me, Your Majesty. Oof!

Queen: *(looks around and sounds confused)* I hear the wizard, but I don't see him.

Pig: I'm underneath you, Your Majesty. I have turned into a pig.

Queen: *(jumps up hastily)* If you don't change back to your regular self, someone might roast you tomorrow.

Pig: I think I need my book of magic.

Queen: I'll get it for you. *(exits stage left)*

Pig: *(addresses audience)* I hope the magic works this time. I'm getting awfully sore. *(groans)*

Queen: *(enters stage left, carrying book)* Here you go.

Pig: Will you please hold the book for me while I read?

(Queen opens book, and Pig reads. Then Pig closes book and turns to her.)

Pig: I'm ready to try again, Your Majesty. Please wave the wand.

(Queen picks up the wand and waves it. Both puppets move in small circles.)

Pig: Razzle, dazzle, frazzle, pop! Magic, make this switching stop!

(Drop Pig down and take it off. Put on Wizard and pop him up.)

Queen: *(drops wand and addresses audience)* Here we go again! *(turns around and hugs Wizard)* Thank heavens, you're back! *(steps back)* Will you please do something about the rain now?

Wizard: I'm very sorry, Your Majesty, but when I'm sick, I can cast only three spells a day.

Queen: Then why don't you go to bed and rest up for tomorrow?

Wizard: I will. You ought to lie down, too, Your Majesty; you're starting to look a little pale. *(exits stage right)*

(Take off Wizard. Put on Duck.)

Queen: *(addresses audience and puts hand to head)* I **AM** feeling a little strange. I hope I'm not getting sick, too. . . . Ah, ah, ah, **AH-CHOO!**

(Drop down Queen and hold up Duck.)

Duck: *(looks down at itself and then addresses audience)* Gadzooks! I caught the wizard's sneezix. . . . Oh, well, at least I'll enjoy the weather now. It's a great day for ducks. *(dances off stage left, quacking to the tune of "Singing in the Rain")*

Books about Sneezes

Brown, Ruth. *The Big Sneeze.* Lothrop, 1985.

Schechter, Ellen. *I Love to Sneeze.* Bantam, 1992.

Stone, Rosetta. *Because a Little Bug Went Ka-Choo!* Beginner Books, 1975.

Books about Wizards

Glassman, Peter. *Wizard Next Door.* Morrow, 1993.

Kent, Jack. *The Wizard.* Weston Woods Pr., 1989.

Slater, Teddy, retel. *Walt Disney's Sorcerer's Apprentice Storybook and Magic Tricks.* Disney, 1993.

Smith, Janice Lee. *Wizard and Wart.* Harper-Collins, 1994.

Books about Rain

Aardema, Verna. *Bringing the Rain to Kapiti Plain.* Dial, 1981.

Ginsburg, Mirra. *Mushroom in the Rain.* Simon & Schuster, 1987.

Stevenson, James. *We Hate Rain!* Greenwillow, 1988.

Yashima, Taro. *Umbrella.* Viking, 1958.

APPENDIX A

▼▲▼▲▼▲▼▲▼▲▼▲▼▲▼

Alphabetical List of Puppets and Their Skits

Any of these puppets can also play Miggs and Jiggs. Remember, too, that you can often substitute puppets you do have for those you don't. Notes following the list of characters for each script suggest a few alternatives, and you will probably think of others as well. Most of these puppets are standard characters in children's literature, so you can use them to act out many other published skits, picture books, and folk tales.

Notations indicate whether a puppet should have a movable mouth or movable arms if possible.

Skits are listed in the order in which they appear in the book.

Appendix B gives directions for creating the characters. Appendix D lists books with instructions for sewing or crocheting some of these puppets. Appendix E tells what companies sell some of the characters.

Alien: "Moon Rock Soup," "Space Creatures Meet Mother Goose," and "Wanted: A Whiz of a Wiz" (movable arms)

Alien: "Space Creatures Meet Mother Goose"

Bear: "Help! Help! Help!," "Detective Jiggs Takes the Case," "How the Bear Lost Its Tail," "Rabbit Makes Trouble," "Little Red Riding Hood's Goodies," "Storybook Characters Look for Work," "Honey Bear's Hat Shop," and "The Wizard's Sneeze" (movable mouth)

Bird with Long Beak: "The Fox and the Crane"

Child (can be boy or girl): "The Golden Touch" (a girl is preferable for this skit), "Get Lost in a Book," "Little Red Riding Hood's Goodies" (a girl is preferable for this skit), "A Ghost in the House," and "Happy the Clown's New Job" (The child puppet can also be Person in "Moon Rock Soup" and Customer in "Honey Bear's Hat Shop.") (movable arms)

Clown: "Happy the Clown's New Job" (movable arms)

Cow: "Something Good to Eat" and "Cow Eats Out"

Crocodile: "A Monkey for Lunch" (movable mouth)

Dog: "Brer Fox Eats the Wash" and "Storybook Characters Look for Work"

Dragon: "Wanted: A Whiz of a Wiz"

Duck: "Brer Fox Eats the Wash" and "The Wizard's Sneeze"

Elephant: "Who's Really Better?" and "Never Be Bored Again!" (movable arms)

Fox: "How the Bear Lost Its Tail," "Only Two Hops," "Brer Fox's (Not-So) Great Idea," "The Fox and the Crane," and "Brer Fox Eats the Wash"

Ghost: "A Ghost in the House"

Lion: "Happy the Clown's New Job"

Man: "Peter Rabbit," "The Golden Touch," and "Do Not Disturb" (With the appropriate hat, the man puppet could play all Wizard's parts. He can also be Person in "Moon Rock Soup," Personnel Director in "Storybook Characters Look for Work," Mr. Shudders in "A Ghost in the House," Waiter in "Cow Eats Out," Ringmaster in "Happy the Clown's New Job," and Customer in "Honey Bear's Hat Shop.") (movable arms)

Monkey: "A Monkey for Lunch," "The Urge to Scratch," "Who's Really Better?" and "Don't Monkey Around with Library Books" (movable arms)

Monster: "Get Lost in a Book," "Storybook Characters Look for Work," and "Wanted: A Whiz of a Wiz"

Pig: "Something Good to Eat," "The Three Little Pigs," "Storybook Characters Look for Work," and "The Wizard's Sneeze"

Pig: "The Three Little Pigs"

Rabbit: "The Urge to Scratch," "Only Two Hops," "Brer Wolf Plays House," "Brer Fox's (Not So) Great Idea," "Something Good to Eat," "Rabbit Makes Trouble," "Peter Rabbit," "Brer Fox Eats the Wash," "Storybook Characters Look for Work," and "Wanted: A Whiz of a Wiz"

Rabbit: "Peter Rabbit"

Raccoon: "Something Good to Eat," "Rabbit Makes Trouble," and "Do Not Disturb"

Spider: "The Wizard's Sneeze"

Wizard: "The Golden Touch," "Wanted: A Whiz of a Wiz," and "The Wizard's Sneeze" (With the appropriate hat, a man puppet can play these parts.) (movable arms)

Woman: "Who's Really Better?," "Little Red Riding Hood's Goodies," "Wanted: A Whiz of a Wiz," and "The Wizard's Sneeze" (In addition, she could be Person in "Moon Rock Soup," Personnel Director in "Storybook Characters Look for Work," Mrs. Shudders in "A Ghost in the House," Woodcutter in "Do Not Disturb," Waitress in "Cow Eats Out," Ringmaster in "Happy the Clown's New Job," and Customer in "Honey Bear's Hat Shop.") (movable arms)

Wolf: "Brer Wolf Plays House," "Brer Fox's (Not So) Great Idea," "The Three Little Pigs," and "Storybook Characters Look for Work" (movable mouth)

APPENDIX

▼▲▼▲▼▲▼▲▼▲▼▲▼▲▼▲▼

B How to Make Almost No-Sew, Inexpensive Puppets

The information on these pages might spark your imagination and help you get started making simple, inexpensive, no-sew puppets. Feel free to personalize your creations according to your ideas and the supplies you have available.

Before you begin, round up any materials you think will come in handy. You will definitely need mittens and socks or gloves. You can also use markers or fabric paint; scissors; glue; scraps of paper, felt, fake fur, or fabric; old cereal boxes; a needle and thread; and some type of stuffing. (You can buy the last item at craft stores, crumple scraps of paper or facial tissue, or use cotton balls.) Pompoms, buttons, wiggly eyes from craft stores, yarn, and pipe cleaners also come in handy.

If you don't already have these things, you might be able to obtain some without spending money. Family members, friends, and coworkers will probably give you their mateless socks, gloves, and mittens. (You can often find these lying along the road as well.) People you know who sew or do crafts might donate their leftovers to you. Whenever you run across something that may come in handy, store it with your supplies for making puppets.

Mitten Puppets with Movable Mouths

Any mitten can become a talking-mouth puppet when you sew or glue facial features and ears to the back of it. Your thumb forms the bottom jaw of the puppet, and your fingers form the face. By bending your wrist you can show the face, which is actually on the back of your hand.

In general, wiggly eyes, buttons, and paper or felt circles make good eyes. Attach these on the part of the mitten that covers the second joints of your fingers. Black buttons, pompoms, and paper or felt circles work well for noses. Attach these on the mitten at the tip of your middle finger. You can cut ears out of paper or felt and attach one on the mitten at the base of your little finger and one at the base of your index finger. You can also draw facial features on the mitten with markers or fabric paint.

Bird with Long Beak

Add eyes to a white mitten. To make the beak, cut two long triangles out of orange felt. The base of each will be as wide as the mitten. The apex of each will extend out about an inch or so past your fingertips. Glue the two triangles together with the lower part of the mitten (from the first joints of your fingers to the tips) between them. Fold a rectangle of orange felt in half around your thumb and glue the edges of the felt together. (You could also coat the thumb with orange fabric paint.)

Bear

Add eyes and half-circle ears to a brown or black mitten. Cut a small circle from tan felt or paper and glue this over the lower part of your mitten. Put a nose in the middle of it.

Cow

Start with a brown, black, or white mitten and add eyes as well as raindrop-shaped ears. Put a triangle-shaped horn next to each ear, and draw two nostrils near your fingertips.

Dog

Add eyes and nose to a brown, black, gray, or white mitten. Attach a floppy ear cut from paper, fake fur, or felt next to the base of your index finger and another ear next to the base of your little finger. (If you put them any closer to your fingertips, they'll tangle in the puppet's mouth when it talks.)

Duck

Add eyes to a white mitten. Cut orange felt to fit over the part of the mitten that covers your fingers from the first joints to the tips. Glue the beak in place. (You could also coat this part of the mitten with orange fabric paint.) Fold a rectangle of orange felt in half around your thumb and glue the edges of the felt together. (You could also coat the thumb with orange fabric paint.)

Fox

Add eyes, nose, and triangle-shaped ears to a red mitten.

Pig

Add eyes, a snout, and triangle-shaped ears to a pink mitten. The snout can be a small circle cut from pink paper with two black dots drawn in the center for nostrils.

Rabbit

Add eyes, nose, and two long ears to a white, brown, or gray mitten. You might want to add pipe-cleaner whiskers as well.

Raccoon

Cut a black mask out of paper or felt and glue it in place on a gray mitten. Add eyes, nose, and half-circle ears.

Wolf

Add eyes, nose, and triangle-shaped ears to a gray mitten.

Sock Puppets with Movable Mouths

Most of the ideas for the mitten puppets will also work with socks. In addition, stockings make good crocodiles and dragons.

In general, slide the sock over your arm with your fingers in the toe and your thumb in the heel. When you move your fingers away from your thumb, your puppet can talk, sing, yawn, bite, and eat. If you want your puppet's mouth to open wider, make a slit in the stocking while you're wearing it by cutting around your hand from the base of your index finger to the base of your little finger. (See figure 4.) Cut out one of the side panels on a cereal box. Fold it in half with the unprinted part on the inside. Round off the corners. (If it's too long, shorten it a little.) Lay this shape on a piece of red or pink felt or paper, trace around it, and cut it out. Put glue all along the borders of the plain side of the cardboard and tuck the edges of the sock around it so they stick to the glue. (You might want to trim off a little of the sock to make it lie flat when glued.) Then glue the red or pink paper or felt in place so it covers up the cardboard and excess sock.

FIGURE 4.   How to Make Sock Puppets with Movable Mouths

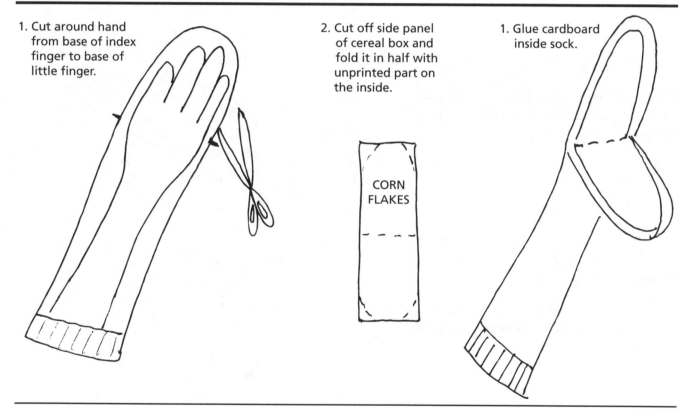

1. Cut around hand from base of index finger to base of little finger.

2. Cut off side panel of cereal box and fold it in half with unprinted part on the inside.

CORN FLAKES

1. Glue cardboard inside sock.

Bird with Long Beak

Fold the cardboard strip in half but don't round off the corners. Instead, measure the width at the bottom and make a mark in the middle. Draw a straight line from the right side of the fold to this mark and another straight line from the left side of the fold to this midpoint. Cut along these lines to make a long pointed beak and glue the edges of the sock around it. Cover the outside of the beak with orange felt or fabric paint. Add eyes.

Crocodile

Add eyes and a jagged row of teeth to a green sock. (The teeth can be V shapes cut out of a strip of felt about half an inch wide and long enough to go around your hand from the base of your index finger to the base of your little finger. Glue this fringe in place.)

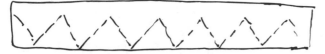

Cut teeth for crocodile.

Dragon

Pin or tape flames cut from red, orange, or yellow paper or felt to the lower jaw of your crocodile.

Add flames to turn crocodile into dragon.

Sock Puppets with Movable Arms

Sock puppets with movable arms would work for the aliens, clown, ghost, and people. To make every character, start out by loosely stuffing the toe of a stocking with cotton, crumpled paper, wadded facial tissues, or any other kind of stuffing. Slip a rubber band loosely over this head to hold the stuffing in. Insert your hand into the sock with your index finger pointing up into the head. Mark the places where your thumb and middle finger will stick out to become the puppet's arms. Remove the sock and cut out the armholes. If you don't want your fingers to show, don a glove before pulling these sock puppets on. Add facial features and, if necessary, hair, ears, antennae, or decorations.

FIGURE 5.
How to Make Sock Puppets with Movable Arms

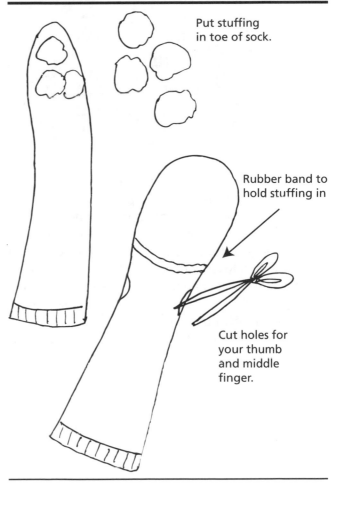

Put stuffing in toe of sock.

Rubber band to hold stuffing in

Cut holes for your thumb and middle finger.

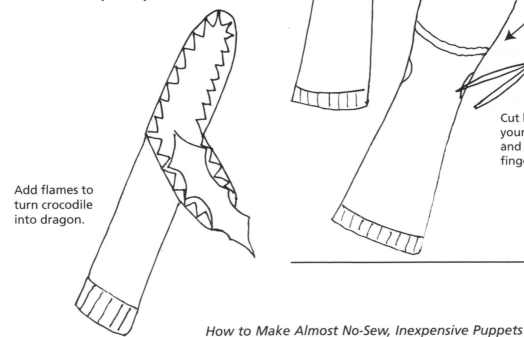

Alien

Try bending a pipe cleaner in half and sewing it to the top of the puppet's head for antennae. A pompom or the cap from a tube of toothpaste could be the nose. An extraterrestrial could have one big eye or maybe three little ones.

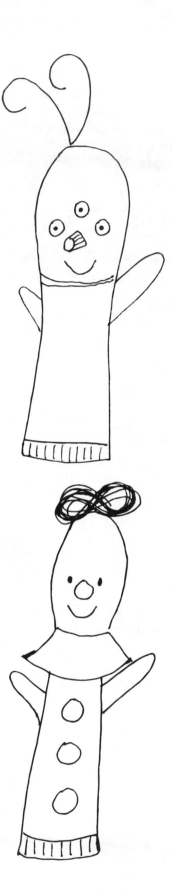

Clown

A red pompom, if you have one, makes a great nose. You could also glue pompoms like a row of buttons down the front of the sock and add a collar cut from colorful material. You can make a simple wig by bringing the ends of a very long piece of red yarn together. Keep folding your lengths of yarn in half until your wig is about four inches long. Tie a short piece of yarn around its middle and sew the wig on top of the puppet's head. If you don't feel the puppet has enough hair, make another wig with another piece of red yarn and sew this on behind the first.

Ghost

Draw three black circles to represent two eyes and an open mouth on the face part of the sock.

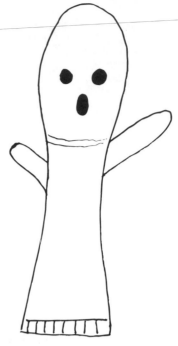

Woman (Girl) or Man (Boy)

Draw a face and attach hair made from paper, yarn, or string. (See the instructions for making the clown's hair.)

Glove Puppets with Movable Arms *(inspired by Kathy Manthey of East Moline, Illinois)*

Glove puppets could work for the lion, monkey, and people. Glue the middle three fingers together (except when making a spider). Cut a head out of paper or felt, add facial features (see the next section on felt puppets for patterns), and glue it over these fingers. The thumb and little finger become the puppet's arms. Remember that the larger the glove, the easier it will be to put on and take off the puppet. Worker's gloves from a hardware store will slide on and off your hand with little trouble.

Clown

Follow the general description for making the clothing of a sock-puppet clown. Use the face shown in the following section on felt puppets with interchangeable heads, or make your own.

Lion

Start with a light brown glove. Cut a mane from dark brown paper, felt, or fake fur and glue it over the middle three fingers. Cut a head, complete with half-circle ears, from light brown paper or felt and add facial features to it. Glue it in the middle of the mane.

Monkey

Start with a dark brown glove. On a tan piece of paper or felt, draw a pear shape with half circles for ears where the pear widens. Cut this out and draw a face on it. Glue it over the middle three fingers. Cut a half moon out of dark brown felt or paper and glue it upside down at the top of the monkey's head. Cut half circles out of tan felt or paper and glue them over the tips of the thumb and little finger to make hands.

People

Cut circles out of tan, pink, or brown felt or paper, add facial features, and glue them over the middle three fingers. You can either draw or paint hair on these heads or sew or glue lengths of yarn in place. Cut half-circles out of tan, pink, or brown paper or felt and glue them over the tips of the thumb and little finger to make hands.

Spider

Add eyes to a black glove about halfway between the wrist and the base of your fingers. Do *not* glue the fingers together. When you wear this puppet, arch your wrist so the audience can see its eyes. (You could also glue a large black pompom on the back of your hand and attach the eyes to this.)

Felt Puppets with Movable Arms and Interchangeable Heads

Create your own basic puppet pattern, use those in figure 6, or find one in a book. (Some of the titles in appendix D provide patterns.) For figure 6 patterns (pages 223–4), photocopy and enlarge them 200 percent. Trace around the basic shape on two thick-nesses of felt. Cut these shapes out and glue or sew them together around the edges, leaving the bottom open for inserting your hand. Make several bodies out of different colors of felt. Attach Velcro in the face area of each one. Cut a variety of heads, complete with ears, out of these same colors of felt. Add facial features and attach Velcro to the back of each. By changing the heads, each puppet body can play many parts.

Any color: person (Cut face and half-circle hands out of tan, pink, or brown felt or paper.)

Brown: bear, cow, dog, lion, monkey, monster, and rabbit

Gray: elephant, monster, rabbit, raccoon, and wolf

Pink: alien, person, and pig

Yellow: alien, clown, and person

FIGURE 6.   Patterns for Felt Puppets with Interchangeable Heads

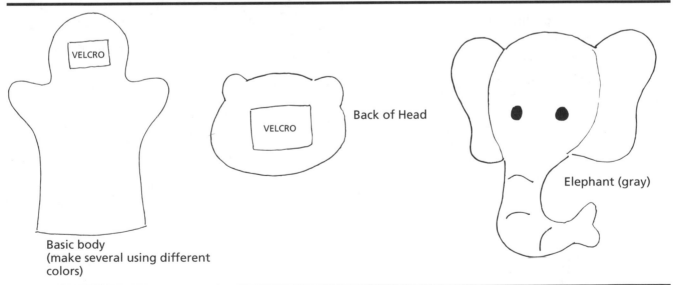

VELCRO

VELCRO

Back of Head

Elephant (gray)

Basic body
(make several using different colors)

FIGURE 6. (Continued)

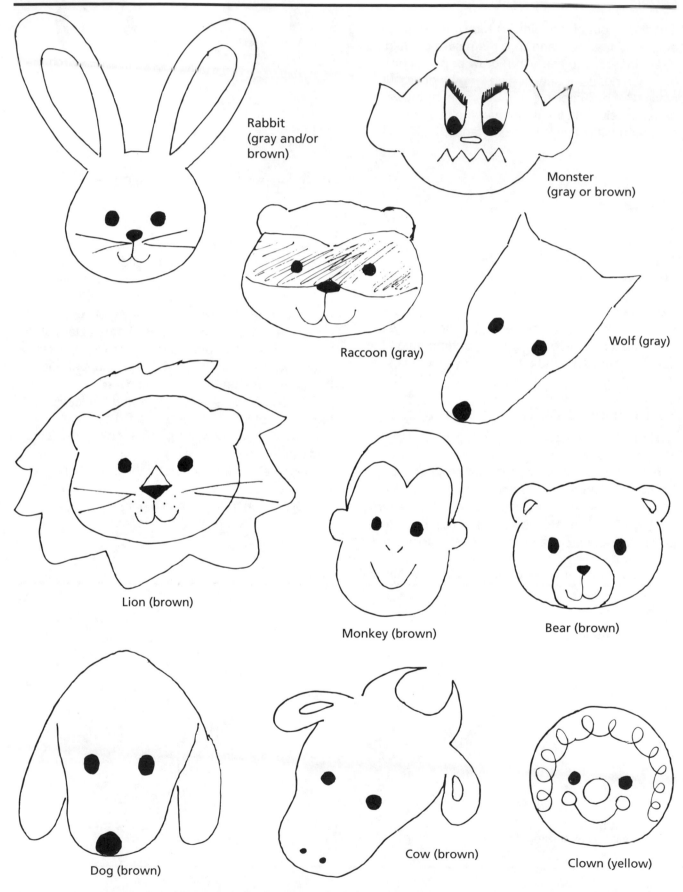

Rabbit
(gray and/or
brown)

Monster
(gray or brown)

Raccoon (gray)

Wolf (gray)

Lion (brown)

Monkey (brown)

Bear (brown)

Dog (brown)

Cow (brown)

Clown (yellow)

FIGURE 6. (Continued)

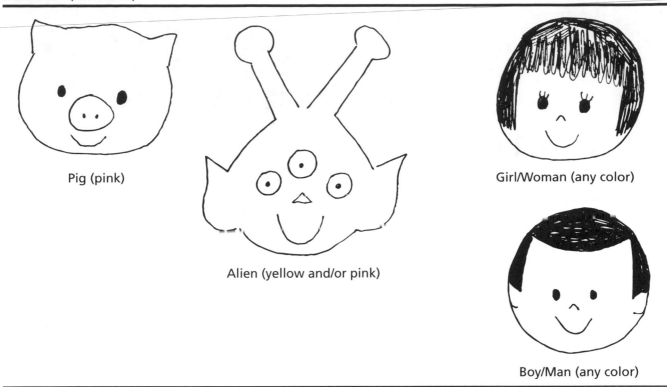

Pig (pink)

Alien (yellow and/or pink)

Girl/Woman (any color)

Boy/Man (any color)

FIGURE 7.   Patterns for Little Cricket Stick Puppet and Resting Cricket

Photocopy and enlarge both crickets 200 percent. Glue the copies to light cardboard, color them, and cut them out. Attach the standing cricket to the end of a stick. Attach the resting cricket to the middle of a strip of cardboard about half an inch wide and long enough to fit easily over the rabbit puppet's tail when you join the ends together to make a band. Tape or glue the ends together so they won't come apart.

C Picture Books to Present with Puppets

Children's picture books offer a wealth of wonderful stories, some of which you can adapt for use with puppets. Following is a list of titles I've presented with puppets.

Circles (●) denote books that the puppeteer will mostly tell while the characters on their hands speak a little dialogue and dramatize some of the narration.

Triangles (▲) indicate that the puppeteer can present the book as a skit by delivering most of the lines the way they're written in the book.

Squares (■) before the names of the required puppets mean you can easily substitute other characters if you lack the specified ones.

Before performing these skits, tell the children the titles and authors of the original books. This gives credit where credit is due, helps children associate books with good times, and might even motivate your audience to read.

This section includes only titles in print at the time of publication. Many other books that have gone out of print will also work well with puppets, so browse through your own collections. (Don't forget to check your collections of fables because many of those short tales have only two characters.)

●Brown, Margaret Wise. *The Golden Egg Book.* Western, 1976.

Puppets: ■Rabbit, ■Duck

Carlson, Nancy. *Harriet's Halloween Candy.* Lerner, 1994.

Puppets: ■two dogs

Eliminate the need for a third character by having Harriet give the treats for Walt to her mother instead of directly to her little brother. You could avoid the difficulty of showing the passage of time by having Harriet muse aloud about where to hide the candy before she goes to school. Once she rejects all the possible hiding places, she can crawl inside her trick-or-treat bag and move around while you make noisy eating sounds.

▲Christian, Mary Blount. "Spring Fever." In *Penrod Again*. Macmillan, 1987.

Puppets: Bear, ■Porcupine

You can cut the vacuum cleaner out of cardboard and drop an unbreakable container filled with paper clips to simulate the crash of the broken teacup.

●Daugherty, James. *Andy and the Lion*. Viking, 1938.

Puppets: Child, Lion

You can skip part one. A girl puppet can play Andy's part if you don't have a boy puppet.

▲Flack, Marjorie, *Ask Mr. Bear*. Simon & Schuster, 1968.

Puppets: Child, Hen, Cow, Sheep, Bear, Mother

▲Gackenbach, Dick. *Claude the Dog: A Christmas Story*. Houghton, 1979.

Puppets: two dogs, Child

●Janice. *Little Bear's Thanksgiving*. Lothrop, 1967.

Puppets: Bear, Child (hand puppets); ■Sparrow, ■Squirrel, ■Owl, and ■Mouse (finger puppets)

▲Kent, Jack. *The Wizard*. Weston Woods Pr., 1989.

Puppets: Wizard, Mouse

Enlarge the pictures of the mouse's imaginings and hold them up for the audience to see. (You can write the appropriate text on the back of each one to read during your presentations.) You might want to invent an opening scene in which someone asks the wizard if he has a particular spell. The wizard could say he has spells for everything from aardvarks to zebus, but he can't find the bottle he wants on the disorganized shelves. The customer can suggest he alphabetize his stock.

●Lester, Helen. *Tacky the Penguin*. Houghton, 1988.

Puppets: two penguins, ■Hunter

Have one puppet represent Neatly, Goodly, Perfect, Angel, and Lovely. Use only one hunter, which can be any person or an animal that eats penguins. You can make Tacky's Hawaiian shirt by cutting two armholes in a rectangle of loud material.

Lionni, Leo. *Alexander and the Wind-Up Mouse*. Knopf, 1969.

Puppets: two mice, Woman, Lizard

Open with a mouse puppet searching for crumbs. Then a maid comes in, screams, and hits it with a broom. Cut a wind-up key out of cardboard, cover it with aluminum foil, and tape it to the back of one mouse. Make a garbage can by covering a cylindrical container (like a coffee can) with gray paper or aluminum foil. After Annie's mother discards some old toys, hold the Willy puppet behind the can with only his head showing. Make the lizard out of an old sock.

▲Lobel, Arnold. "Cookies." In *Frog and Toad Together*. HarperCollins, 1971.

Puppets: ■Frog, ■Toad

Since it would be hard to show the characters carrying out their plans, have them only talk about what they could do with the cookies. At the end Frog can carry the cookies offstage and call to the birds.

▲————. "The Crickets." In *Mouse Soup*. HarperCollins, 1977.

Puppets: ■Mouse, Crickets

Make the crickets as stick puppets.

▲————. "The Letter." In *Frog and Toad Are Friends*. HarperCollins, 1979.

Puppets: ■Frog, ■Toad, Snail

You can make a snail stick puppet with a small loop of tape behind its head. Frog can stick the letter over the tape when he asks Snail to deliver his message to Toad. At the end of the skit, Frog can bring the snail onstage, and Toad can pull the letter off the tape.

▲————. "The List." In *Frog and Toad Together*. HarperCollins, 1971.

Puppets: ■Frog, ■Toad

Since it would be hard to show the list blowing away in the wind, you could have Toad accidentally leave it behind at Frog's house.

▲————. "Shivers." In *Days with Frog and Toad*. HarperCollins, 1979.

Puppets: ■Frog, ■Toad

▲————. "The Story." In *Frog and Toad Are Friends.* HarperCollins, 1979.

Puppets: ■Frog, ■Toad

Since it's hard for a puppet to pour water on itself, substitute jumping up and down for this action.

▲McGovern, Ann. *Stone Soup.* Scholastic, 1986.

Puppets: ■Man, ■Woman

▲McKissack, Patricia. *Flossie & the Fox.* Dial, 1986.

Puppets: Girl, Fox, Cat

Omit the narration. Use a stuffed cat instead of a puppet so you can have three characters onstage at one time. Preface its line with "Meow," so the audience will know it is talking. If you're using a stage, you could have Flossie jiggle the cat a little. If you're performing in the open, you could bounce the cat up and down with your leg.

●Mann, Pamela. *The Frog Princess?* Gareth Stevens, 1995.

Puppets: Frog, ■Horse, ■Chicken, ■Cat, Prince, Princess

If you need to make substitutes, rewrite the skit a little to include different books.

▲Mayer, Mercer. *You're the Scaredy Cat.* Rain Bird Prod., 1991.

Puppets: two children, Dog

▲Minarik, Else Holmelund. "Birthday Soup" In *Little Bear.* HarperCollins, 1957.

Puppets: ■two bears, ■Hen, ■Cat, ■Duck

To avoid having more than two characters onstage at any time, have each guest exit into the dining room. As Little Bear announces to the audience that he must serve the soup, his mothor can arrive with the cake, which can be a cardboard cutout.

▲————. "Little Bear Goes to the Moon" In *Little Bear.* HarperCollins, 1957.

Puppets: ■ two bears

You can omit the space helmet or create one by making a facial opening in a cut-down paper bag or small box.

▲————. "Little Bear's Wish." In *Little Bear.* Harper-Collins, 1957.

Puppets: ■ two bears

▲Pfister, Marcus. *Hopper Hunts for Spring.* North-South, 1993.

Puppets: ■ two rabbits, ■Mole, and Bear

●Shannon, George. *Lizard's Song.* Greenwillow, 1981.

Puppets: ■Lizard, ■Bear

If you don't have a lizard, you could substitute any tree-dwelling animal and have it sing, "Tree is my home." If you use a finger puppet for the singing animal, it will be easier for Bear to carry it in a little bag.

▲Van Leeuwen, Jean. "Bedtime." In *More Tales of Oliver Pig.* Dial, 1981.

Puppets: ■ two pigs

▲————. "Sleeping Time." In *Tales of Amanda Pig.* Dial, 1983.

Puppets: ■ two pigs

●Walsh, Ellen Stoll. *Brunus & the New Bear.* Harcourt, 1993.

Puppets: Child, Bear, small stuffed bear

▲Wolff, Patricia Rae. *The Toll-Bridge Troll.* Harcourt, 1995.

Puppets: Child, ■Troll

APPENDIX

▼▲▼▲▼▲▼▲▼▲▼▲▼▲▼▲▼▲▼▲▼

D

Books with Puppet Patterns and Scripts

Although books on puppetry abound, only a handful seem appropriate for the bibliography of a work advocating a simple approach for a single puppeteer. Those titles that require multiple puppeteers or a great deal of equipment, advanced skill, and preparation time do not appear on this list. With four exceptions, the bibliography includes only titles in print at the time of publication. The four marked *o.p.* are worth borrowing on interlibrary loan if your collection doesn't already own them. Two of the four have revisions forthcoming.

Books with Directions for Making Some of the Puppets Needed in the Skits

Beaton, Clare. *The Felt Book: Easy-to-Make Projects for All Ages.* Sterling, 1994.

A children's book, it tells how to sew a monster puppet with movable arms out of felt.

Champlin, Connie, and Nancy Renfro. *Storytelling with Puppets.* ALA, 1985. o.p., rev. forthcoming.

In the book you'll find patterns for sewing a bear, people, a raccoon, a monkey, an elephant, a clown, and a rabbit.

Dolan, Charlou Baker. *Charlou's Five-Finger Puppets and Stuffed Toys.* Macmillan, 1987.

Written by a puppetmaker who has taught her craft to many pupils, this book provides actual-sized patterns plus step-by-step directions and helpful hints for sewing a bear, lion, rabbit, dog, monkey, raccoon, fox, and dragon and an alligator that can serve as a crocodile.

Jenny, Gerri, and Sherrie Gould. *Toys and Games for Children to Make.* Murdoch, 1990.

In addition to explaining how to make toys and games, the book tells how to turn socks into dog, raccoon, and lion puppets.

MacLennan, Jennifer. *Simple Puppets You Can Make.* Sterling, 1988. o.p.

The author provides directions and complete patterns for a rabbit, bear, lion, troll, wizard, and monkey (all with movable arms) as well as a dog, a monster, a dragon, and an alligator that can serve as a crocodile (all with movable mouths). You will have to enlarge the patterns.

Peterson, Carolyn Sue, and Brenny Hall. *Story Programs: A Source Book of Materials*. Scarecrow, 1980.

The manual gives step-by-step directions and patterns for making a bear, lion, man, and woman with cloth bodies and Styrofoam heads. It also tells how to make a sock into a dog puppet.

Renfro, Nancy. *Puppet Shows Made Easy*. Nancy Renfro Studios, 1984.

The author gives patterns for movable mouth puppets that would work for the wolf, the fox, the dog, and the crocodile in the skits. You could use her directions for puppets with movable arms to make all your people, the aliens, and many of the animal characters. These puppets have cloth bodies and heads made from either paper bags, plastic bottles, or Pellon.

Rottman, Fran. *Easy-to-Make Puppets and How to Use Them: Early Childhood*. Regal, 1978.

Rottman provides basic patterns for making people puppets and information on creating heads, costumes, and wigs. The book also gives general directions for making animal and people puppets out of socks. The bird sock puppet would work well for the crane in "The Fox and the Crane."

Schramm, Toni A. *Puppet Plays: From Workshop to Performance*. Teacher Ideas Pr., 1993.

The author, a librarian, describes how she conducts puppetry workshops with children. Her patterns for cloth puppets can help you sew people and a rabbit, lion, bear, wolf, and dragon. Some puppets are made completely out of felt; others have Styrofoam heads and felt bodies.

Verkest, Susan. *Crocheting Storybook Hand Puppets: Complete Instructions for 21 Easy-to-Make Projects*. Dover, 1980.

By following the step-by-step directions in Verkest's book, you can crochet a wolf, a woman, a man, a girl, Little Red Riding Hood, a goose (if you leave the scarf off Mother Goose, you can use her for the duck in "Brer Fox Eats the Wash" and "The Wizard's Sneeze"), a pig, a rabbit (substitute gray or brown yarn for the pink and skip the basket), and a bear. Except for the wolf, all have hands that move. Using red yarn with the wolf pattern would allow you to create a fox from it as well.

Wallace, Mary. *I Can Make Puppets*. Firefly, 1994.

This children's book tells you how to make a dragon out of a sock, a pig out of a sponge, and a wizard with a cloth body and a cardboard tube for a head. You could create all your people puppets using the method described for making the wizard.

Wright, Denise Anton. *One-Person Puppet Plays*. Teacher Ideas Pr., 1990.

Using these patterns and directions, you could sew cloth versions of people and a crocodile, dog, dragon, fox, lion, monster, rabbit, and wolf.

Books with More Scripts

Bauer, Caroline Feller. "Puppetry." In *Caroline Feller Bauer's New Handbook for Storytellers*. ALA, 1993.

Bauer provides two simple puppet skits, a list of picture books you could act out with puppets, plus patterns for exchangeable animal-head puppets and simple people puppets with heads out of foam balls.

Boylan, Eleanor. *How to Be a Puppeteer*. Dutton, 1970. o.p.

Four scripts for solo puppeteers are included plus some basic directions on making simple puppets.

Champlin, Connie, and Nancy Renfro. *Storytelling with Puppets*. ALA, 1985. o.p., rev. forthcoming.

The authors offer many different ideas for incorporating puppets of all kinds (hand, finger, stick, overhead shadow, balloons, etc.) into your storytelling. Some involve audience participation. They give specific instructions for presenting some picture books with puppets as well as other information on manipulating puppets, building a puppet collection, and teaching children to work with puppets.

Hunt, Tamara, and Nancy Renfro. *Pocketful of Puppets: Mother Goose.* Nancy Renfro Studios, 1982.

If you want to use puppets but don't feel up to doing a whole skit, try presenting nursery rhymes with the simple paper puppets you can make using the patterns and directions in this book.

Hunt, Tamara, and Nancy Renfro. *Puppetry and Early Childhood Education.* Nancy Renfro Studios, 1982.

The authors tell how to use puppets in a variety of ways with young children and how to organize a puppetmaking workshop for volunteers. One chapter describes how to tell specific stories and act out picture books with puppets.

Schramm, Toni A. *Puppet Plays: From Workshop to Performance.* Teacher Ideas Pr., 1993.

Although most of the eight scripts in this book require multiple puppeteers, one person could present the Grimm fairy tale, "The Cat and Mouse in Partnership."

Schroeder, Joanne F. *Fun Puppet Skits for Schools and Libraries.* Teacher Ideas Pr., 1995.

Schroeder, a school librarian, offers many kinds of skits with various methods of presentation and types of puppets, including marionettes. Some skits require a good deal of preparation, but others do not. The author provides directions for making puppets and a stage. She also recommends several books to read with each skit.

Sierra, Judy. *Fantastic Theater: Puppets and Plays for Young Performers and Young Audiences.* Wilson, 1991.

The other twenty-nine plays in this book require a number of performers, but a single puppeteer could give "The Crocodile and the Hen," an African folk tale. Although the author provides patterns for presenting the play with rod and overhead shadow puppets, you could perform it with crocodile, hen, and lizard hand puppets.

VanSchuyver, Jan M. *Storytelling Made Easy with Puppets.* Oryx Pr., 1993.

One person can follow all of the author's suggestions without using a stage or having to spend much time planning and rehearsing. In addition to describing how to tell stories with puppets, VanSchuyver includes information on teaching children how to tell stories with puppets and offers solutions to ten common problems beginning puppeteers often have.

Wright, Denise Anton. *One-Person Puppet Plays.* Teacher Ideas Pr., 1990.

This book's approach to puppetry has much in common with the style found in *Amazingly Easy Puppet Plays.* Wright offers thirty simple scripts, patterns for puppets, and directions for making a portable tabletop stage. (You can, however, perform these plays without a theater.)

APPENDIX E

▼▲▼▲▼▲▼▲▼▲▼▲▼▲▼▲▼▲▼▲▼

Puppet Suppliers

Some of the companies (e.g., Applause, Dakin, and Russ) that manufacture puppets suitable for the skits in this book sell only through retailers. You might be able to find their products in the children's sections of department stores, children's specialty shops, card and gift shops (including those of museums and hospitals), and toy, school-supply, and novelty stores. Don't forget to shop at thrift stores and garage sales as well. I've found puppets so new they still have their store tags on them!

When preparing this manuscript, I obtained names of suppliers from puppetry books at the library and wrote to the companies asking for catalogs. Following are the companies that responded and that had puppets that would work for the skits in this book. If you are looking for other characters as well, you might want to contact these businesses and see what they offer.

Although the prices will change, they are listed to give you an idea of which companies charge the most.

ABC School Supply
3312 N. Berkeley Lake Rd.
P.O. Box 100019
Duluth, GA 30136–9419
(800) 669–4222

The ABC School Supply set of twelve fairy tale hand puppets costs $44.95 and includes a wolf, an old woman, a man, a king, a queen, and a girl. They also have a bear, a lion, and a dalmatian that sell for $9.95 each. For $44.95, you can get a set of six twelve-inch animals that includes a fox, a polar bear, a monkey, and a rabbit. You can get two sets of six eight-inch animal puppets for $34.95 each or $54.95 for both. The first set includes, among others, a dog, a lion, and a rabbit. The second includes a pig, a bear, a gorilla that could pass for the monkey, an elephant, and a crocodile whose mouth won't open. You can also get a set of family puppets (a mother, a father, a boy, and a girl) for $29.95. The family comes in your choice of ethnic group: Caucasian, African-American, Latino, or Asian.

Beckley-Cardy

1 E. First St.
Duluth, MN 55802
(800) 227–1178

This school supply company offers a monkey, a lion, a bear, and an elephant for $11.95 each. All are nine and one-half inches high and have arms that move. They also sell Latino, Asian, white, and black families (consisting of a mother, a father, a boy, and a girl) for $30; a monster for $30; and a raccoon for $12.

Childcraft

2920 Old Tree Dr.
Lancaster, PA 17603
(800) 631–5652

Childcraft offers a nice bunny and raccoon for $14.99 each.

Country Critters, Inc.

217 Neosho St.
Burlington, KS 66839

I highly recommend this company. Their customer service representative was very friendly on the phone, their puppets are suitable for the roles in these scripts, and the prices are lower than those of many other firms. The characters that fit into this book are a raccoon, fox, pig, dog, rabbit, bear, monkey, wolf, and spider. These are all full-bodied puppets (approximately 12″ to 14″) with arms that move. They are machine washable in cold water. With a $100 minimum order, any institution can order the puppets for $10.95 each. (The spider costs $13.49.)

Demco

P.O. Box 7488
Madison, WI 53707
(800) 356–1200

This library supply jobber sells a number of puppets from different companies. Those that would suit the roles in this book are the bear, long-beaked bird, elephant, fox, girl, monkey, pig, rabbit, rac-

coon, and spider. Call the bid department to see if you'd qualify for a quantity discount.

Happiness Express, Inc.

One Harbor Park Dr.
Port Washington, NY 11050
(516) 484–3700

Using the name, "Happiness Zoo," this company makes and sells puppets through Macy's, Sterns, FAO Schwarz, Toys-Я-Us, Filene's, and Dayton Hudson. The dog, monkey, cow, rabbit, and elephant would all work for the skits in this book. If stores in your area don't carry them, you can ask the buyer to order them for you by calling the sales director at the phone number listed.

HearthSong Processing Center

6519 N. Galena Rd.
P.O. Box 1773
Peoria, IL 61656–1773
(800) 325–2502; FAX: (800) 72–0331

HearthSong, a mail-order company, sells a boy, girl, king, princess that could be the queen, and wizard for $16.95 each or $14.95 each for two or more. They are 12″ to 13″ tall and have legs and feet.

Highsmith Co.

W5527 Highway 106
P.O. Box 800
Fort Atkinson, WI 53538–0800
(800) 558–2110

A library supply jobber, Highsmith sells the puppets of other companies. Those that fit the roles in these scripts are an alligator that could pass as a crocodile, and a cow, collie, monkey, pig, rabbit, raccoon, spider, and wolf whose mouth opens.

Mastercraft Puppets

P.O. Box 39
Branson, MO 65615–0039
(417) 561–8100

For $10.95 each you can get a bunny and a bear. For $13.95 each you can get a bunny and a puppy. They also sell many large puppets that would be good for interactive puppetry and storytelling, ventriloquist's figures, and books on puppetry, ventriloquism, and clowning. By request, you can get a catalog from this "creative resource center for the imagination."

Mister Anderson's Company
301 Nippersink Dr.
McHenry, IL 60050
(800) 442–6555

This business sells the puppets of various manufacturers. They ship only to schools and libraries. If you aren't a teacher or a librarian, ask someone who is to order for you. The company provides the following characters suitable for the roles in this book: bear, long-beaked bird (ask for the jayhawk), crocheted clown, cow, alligator that could be the crocodile, dog, baby dragon, duck, sitting elephant, fox, ghost (Caspar), lion, monkey, monster (one of the Wild Things from the Sendak book), pig, rabbit, raccoon, spider, and wolf. It also sells some books on puppetry.

Nancy Renfro Studios
P.O. Box 164226
Austin, TX 78716
(800) 933–5512

The studio makes more than 150 mitt puppets with movable mouths. Those that best fit the roles in this book are the elephant, dragon, and show people. The latter group includes a boy, girl, man, and woman for $18.95 each. (Specify whether you want pink, tan, or brown.) Be sure to order the show people to get characters with arms that move. The other puppets have movable mouths.

Puppet Safari Monkey Merchant, Inc.
326 W. 11th St.
National City, CA 91950–3221
(619) 477–1180

Puppet Safari sells some very large puppets that would be good for interactive puppetry and storytelling. The smaller ones suitable for the roles in this book are a bear, troll, pig, rabbit, and wolf. The prices for these range from $14 to $30.

National Organization

Amateur as well as professional puppeteers can join the Puppeteers of America, a national nonprofit organization. Members receive a quarterly journal, a membership directory, a discount for conferences and workshops sponsored by the group, and free advice on all aspects of puppetry. Write them at:

The Puppeteers of America, Inc.
c/o Membership Officer
#5 Cricklewood Path
Pasadena, CA 91107

You can order books, booklets, and pamphlets about all aspects of puppetry from the organization's store even if you don't belong to The Puppeteers of America. Contact them at:

The Puppetry Store
1525–24th St. SE
Auburn, WA 98002
(206) 833–8377

INDEX OF PLAY TITLES
▼▲▼▲▼▲▼▲▼▲▼▲▼▲▼▲▼▲▼▲▼

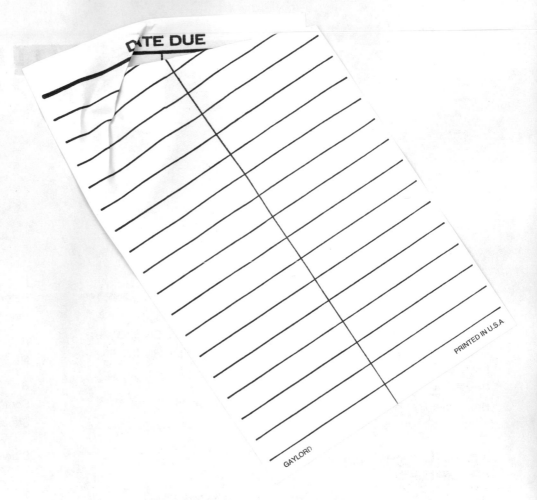

DATE DUE

PRINTED IN U.S.A

GAYLORD